Thin White Female in No Acute Distress

A Memoir

Nancy Anne Nicholson

PublishAmerica
Baltimore

ISBN: 1-4241-5885-0
PUBLISHED BY PUBLISHAMERICA, LLLP
www.publishamerica.com
Baltimore

Printed in the United States of America

Dedication

This book is dedicated to any woman who has ever loved effusively, deeply, painfully, untruthfully, or wrongly, and learned in the end it doesn't matter, because once you love someone—even for the wrong reasons—a part of them remains in your heart forever.

Acknowledgments

I would like to personally thank the following people who helped me *get real*: My mother, Lois Adamson, whose charity, wisdom, and courage are indefinable; my precious stepdaughter, Angela; my dear friend, Tricia Matteson, who started as my protégé and became my mentor; and all my siblings, but especially Patty and Bill. I also want to thank my fantastic husband, Dave, for being so uncomplicated and easy to love. Lastly, I am deeply thankful for having worked with a therapist named Patricia, without whom a happy ending to this story would not have been possible.

Prelude

When I was six years old, I had a boyfriend named Stevie. He was a year older, a head taller, and lived conveniently next door in the duplex attached to ours. He was always shirtless and probably had a promising future in baseball, though I didn't really put that much importance on athletics or sports when I was six. Sure, I liked the way he held his worn leather mitt and how he bravely caught a pitched ball bare-chested, but what I *most* liked about Stevie was that he was a bully.

Yes, my first boyfriend was a midget version of my father, the feisty kid on the block with a reputation for never losing, whom I would end up losing to my younger sister, Patty, who had batted her long lashes and wrapped her tiny hand around Stevie's arm, complimenting him on such big, big muscles right in front of me. (I should note this was the one and only time my sister stole one of my boyfriends, the reasons for which are disturbing and will soon become obvious).

Being the bully that he was, Stevie didn't feel obligated to tell me he was sorry for dumping me for my kid sister, but later in the alley behind our brick duplex, he told me I was cuter than Patty and kissed me on the cheek. He then spit on the ground and yelled for Patty—the tomboy of the family—to play ball.

I was heartbroken and humiliated over losing Stevie, and a lesson or two murked in the aftermath: I should never, ever trust a bad-boy bully no matter how talented and cute, and should trust a sister even less.

But all I learned that summer day in Muskegon, Michigan, was that I needed to try much, much harder if I was going to impress the bad boys.

Chapter One

In the winter of 1972, my parents got divorced. I was fourteen years old, and this should have been a dark, gloomy period like it had been for my friend, Aileen, who cried for weeks when her parents split and told me it was the worst thing that had ever happened to her. She said it was even worse than when her Grampa O'Malley died.

Aileen was never one for telling the truth (actually, neither was I), but *my* parents' divorce meant nothing more to me than Dad was gone and life would therefore be good. Especially good was the fact we were leaving Oklahoma and heading back to Washington State. Mom sold the house, called Bekins Van Line movers, and loaded my two sisters and me, along with our cat Little Bit, into an aged Ford Country Squire, and off we went. I waved goodbye to tall, scrawny, pathetic Aileen, who cried as she waved back.

For most of the trip, I was excited about a future without Dad, until we got to California. There, just as San Francisco's skyline loomed ahead, I couldn't stop thinking about my father, and the fact I'd probably never, ever see him again. I thought, maybe he'll change? Maybe he'll be nicer now that he and Mom were no longer married? Or, maybe he'd get that frontal lobotomy Mom was always wishing for and he'd become a passive, likeable weirdo.

Meanwhile, my mother had other thoughts, which she shared with my sisters and me at nearly every milepost.

"Your father is going to hell, you know, and I feel sorry for the devil!"

Mom had muttered this while not even out of our driveway in an upscale suburb of Oklahoma City three days before. A few hours later, on Interstate 40 heading west, Mom reiterated biliously, "May we never set eyes on that fool again!"

"Fool" was one of the less colorful descriptions my mom favored when describing my father, preferring "sonofabitch" by a huge margin. It was no secret I agreed, but my initial euphoria that we were finally leaving drab Oklahoma for emerald-green, lake-filled Washington State began to fade with each passing state, while my anxieties grew. Alarming thoughts unrelated to Dad raced through my mind:

What if nothing changed in Washington?

What if my nose remained crooked as a hawk's?

What if mother stayed grumpy forever?

What if Sue and Patty became best friends and I became a measly box on the bottom of the sister pyramid?

I choked back tears, especially when San Francisco was behind us. My good mood long gone, I whined to my mother, "I thought we were going to stop to sight-see in San Francisco? You promised, you know."

"Really? I *promised?*" she mocked, "Well, isn't that just too bad? Your father *promised* a lot of things, too, and look what happened? By now, you should have learned that promises are made to be broken. Come to think of it, that's the only thing your father taught any of you kids."

Patty, who had turned thirteen the prior December, looked at me sideways and shrugged. This was no time to remind our mother that she had said the exact same thing around San Antonio, when our youngest sister Susie wanted a cheeseburger because it had been promised.

Patty rubbed her stomach and groaned. "But, Mother, I'm starving!"

"And I'm so hungry I'm about ready to eat my shoes!" To prove it, I lifted my right foot to my mouth but it got nowhere near its target on account of having joints about as limber as a piece of driftwood, even at fourteen.

"Hold your horses."

"Sorry, Mother, I don't see any horses, just a lot of flat drab freeway." Such sarcasm usually would have gotten me grounded, but I knew my mother was currently busy with other more pressing matters, like breaking the speed limit and earning a spot in the Guinness Book of World Records.

Quelling hunger pangs, I slumped back into my seat and watched the landscape pass in a speckled yellow and brown blur. My mother was fast approaching Category V on the Grouch Scale, a rating my Father, whenever he was around, routinely garnered. I chewed my hair and gazed dejectedly out the window at scenery we had passed several years before on a car trip in which my precious Little Bit nearly met her end after being flung from the car window by good ole dad.

It was day four of our trip, and we would already be in Washington by now if Mom had taken the shortcut from Oklahoma to Washington. Instead, because it was winter, she wanted to avoid the potentially treacherous mountain passes and had chosen a southern course through Texas, Arizona, New Mexico, California, Oregon, and finally Washington via Vancouver. It would take longer, but sightseeing was supposed to be in the plan. What hadn't been in the plan was to leave Oklahoma in January because that meant spending another "Christmas in Hell."

Our family hadn't even gotten a tree during the holidays, but "Santa" still brought us gifts, mostly practical things like blankets, rain bonnets, sweaters, and so on. Patty and I also got lighted makeup mirrors and Yardley makeup kits. Naturally, Dad didn't even stop by or call during the holidays. He already was starting *his* new life with another woman and her four daughters, and—much to my dismay and shock—my younger brothers, Billy and Marky.

Chapter Two

It was a deary November afternoon in 1971, when Mom came home from court and announced *the boys*—my baby brothers were known as a single unit—would now be living with *their* father. Not *your* father, but *their* father.

Aghast, I asked, "What? You're kidding, right?" My mother kidded a lot, but never while smoking and crying.

She sniffled, "Do I look like I'm kidding, Nancy?"

"No, but…" I had been tidying the house to use up some pent-up energy when the news was delivered, and I remember bending to pick up a football that was on the kitchen floor but the football didn't move because it was covered in peanut butter and jelly, an unusual bonding agent in any household but ours. Upstairs I could hear *the boys*, who were supposed to be packing but it sounded like they were stampeding with wild horses and banshees.

"Why on earth are the boys going to live with Dad? Dad doesn't like them and they don't like him, right? Don't they want to go back to Washington with us? We can't leave them here! Why didn't you tell the judge that? Huh?" The questioning never ended with me. Many times it wasn't answers I was seeking, but gossip.

My mother slumped at the kitchen table and put out Lucky Strike. She then shook another from its carton and sighed, rubbing a temple. "It isn't that simple. I just can't handle five kids right now."

"But you handled five before. I don't understand."

Mother blew a smoke ring. Her voice was weary. "It all boils down to money, Nancy, and besides, it's just temporary until I get on my feet. What's important is that the divorce is final. That's all that matters."

"Amen to that." I slumped at the table, feeling relieved that my parents were getting divorced. They were just too different to get along, with backgrounds miles apart. Mom was a well-bred, God-fearing, pampered only daughter from Illinois, whose father was an attorney and her mother a socialite. Dad was a rebellious, uneducated ex-Marine from Mississippi with movie-star looks and wandering ways. Furthermore:

She was a Democrat, he a Republican.

She was practical, he was reckless.

She liked to dance, he liked to drink.

She sought the bright side, he created the dark side.

No one could believe it had lasted sixteen years but now Dad was someone else's problem and if his new wife Kay thought she was getting a deal stealing him, just wait another sixteen years! She'd be sorry, all right, and clamoring for ways to rid *herself* of an aging, balding, Southern-grown horndog with Mississippi tags!

Upon learning the news of Kay's existence, I hoped she was an ugly, mean, warty, bug-infested, knock-kneed, pigeon-toed "other woman." In reality, Kay Allison was a petite, quarter-Cherokee-version of Mom, who was by all accounts beautiful and often compared to Sophia Loren. Of course, I hadn't actually *met* Kay and had only seen Polaroid shots, right before Mom burned them in the backyard along with a pair of men's boxer shorts with a pink-heart and red-devil pattern, several fat plaid ties, a fishing pole, and a brand-new tackle box. When the fire was a pile of embers, Mom dumped the contents of a cardboard file box on top of the rebuilding flames and began cackling.

"Oh dear, Bill!" Mom's sarcasm stabbed the air like a knife, "I think I just accidentally burned all your important FAA records. Goodness, I am sooooooooo sorry!" Then she turned to us kids, who were watching with varying degrees of interest, gathered around the growing fire after being

13

handed a bag of marshmallows. While Mom uprooted what little landscaping we had in our Oklahoma yard to fuel the fire, the five Nash kids stuck marshmallows onto wire hangers and pretended all families toasted marshmallows over the ashes of their father's belongings.

Things could have been worse; we could have been out of marshmallows.

Chapter Three

"Aunt" Linda was actually a former coworker of Mom's back in 1968, when they both worked for the same dentist. We were living in Cougar Hills then, in a gorgeous rambler with a daylight basement, but we didn't stay there long. Like always, as soon as we were settled, my family was uprooted thanks to Dad, a restless air-traffic controller who was always getting transferred, sometimes at his request, sometimes because it was an alternative to losing his job. When he told us we were moving to Oklahoma, he might as well have said Siberia.

As soon as we were back in the State of Washington, Linda's house was our first stop, and she made quite an impression. Wrapped in an apple-green wool cape, with a heavy cascade of red hair that dropped past her bosom to nearly her waist, she looked like a Green Goddess standing on the stoop of her house in Lake Hills, a quiet suburb of Bellevue. Her voice boomed.

"Lois! You made it!" Linda was wearing bright pink lipstick that showed off a toothpaste-commercial smile. "Welcome home!"

I had only seen pictures of Linda and seeing her in person made me gasp in awe. I turned to Mother. "*That's* Linda?"

"Of course. Who else would it be?"

Patty's eyes widened, as well. "Mom, you said Linda was pretty, but you didn't say she looked like a movie star."

Susie popped her head up. "Are we there yet?" She had slept nearly the entire trip, and began rubbing sleepy hazel eyes. She peeked out the window and asked again through a wide yawn, "We're at Linda's house?"

"Yes, we're finally here." Mom unlatched the back of the station wagon and everyone began retrieving bags, including a trio of ivory-colored Samsonite luggage. These suitcases were of another era, hard as rock, and roomy enough to fit a three-year-old and his toys, a fact I proved regularly while my family was living in Michigan. She set them on the driveway at Linda's feet and the two women hugged.

"Oh, Linda, thanks so much for inviting us to stay."

"I wouldn't have it any other way, Lois."

I was blatantly staring at Linda, who was recently divorced herself, and blurted, "Wow, Linda, your ex-husband must be as crazy as my Dad."

Linda guffawed, "They're all crazy! Come up here, sweetie, and give your Aunt Linda a hug!"

Mom glanced around. "Where are your kids?"

"Getting presentable." Linda hugged each of us one by one before returning to my mother's frail shoulders. "Everything is going to be fine, trust me."

"I know." Mom's voice cracked but she didn't cry. She had done enough of that in Oklahoma to last a lifetime.

Linda beckoned, "Come on, girls, let's go into the Owl House."

The moniker fit. Inside Linda's brick rambler was a museum of fake owls of every imaginable shape and size: Owl clocks, figurines, and knick-knacks; paintings, drawings, framed photographs and posters of owls, plus a large and winsome collection of owl salt-and-pepper shakers.

In her yellow kitchen, under a large macramé owl that stood guard over a yellow melamine kitchen table, "Aunt" Linda set down a carafe of red wine and a pitcher of juice. She poured juice for us kids, and red wine into two glasses, handing one to her dear friend, Lois.

"Honey, I'm so sorry. What can I say? Bill's an idiot." She turned and said unapologetically to us, "Sorry, girls, but you might as well learn the truth now." Linda patted our mother's arm affectionately. "We'll have some wine and talk late into the night."

I sat at the table enthralled by Linda's bubbly and welcome presence.

She was a ray of sunshine on a stormy day. And I wanted to steal her smile.

"I've got an idea. Tomorrow, let's ask the girls to watch Troy and Kristina and go paint the town, Lois. We'll forget all about Bill!"

Mom's face brightened as she sipped red wine. "I already have."

"Aunt Linda?"

"Yes, Susie?"

"Um." Susie's long brown bangs hid most of her face and she pushed them away. "I was wondering...how come you like owls so much?"

"Owls are a symbol of wisdom. You live here and you become wiser by the day...or a wiseass." She winked at Mom just as a little boy and girl turned the corner followed in short order by a Cocker Spaniel, who bounded passed the little girl and almost knocked her over.

"Stinky, watch it!" She looked up and pointed first at herself. "Hi. I'm Kristina and over there," she pointed to the dog and the boy, "that's Stinky number one and Stinky number two."

"Very funny, Kris." The boy grinned. "I'm Troy, nice to meet you. And the dog's name really is Stinky."

We laughed as Stinky made the rounds sniffing crotches before turning and running out the back door with Troy in pursuit.

Patty pinched her nose, "Ooh, he does stink!"

Linda shrugged. "Like a dishrag. Troy is supposed to be good about bathing him, but you know how that goes." She turned to her daughter, "Kristina, honey, take Lois's girls on a tour of the house so I can visit with Lois."

Seven-year-old Kristina nodded and motioned us to follow. Dressed in denim overalls and pale-blue fringed cowboy boots, she lead us to the living room first, where she reached for a Barbie doll in a bikini that had been stuffed between the sofa cushions.

Patty asked sweetly, "Can we meet your dolly?"

"Sure. Her name is Francie and she's in trouble. She beat up Laurie, my other doll, and stole her bathing suit. I have to spank Francie a lot." She turned facing Susie, who had plopped into a recliner. "You have pretty hair."

Susie shrugged indifferently as another throaty chortle emanated from the kitchen. Glasses chinked in an obvious toast before we heard our mother's hoarse voice.

"I still can't believe this is happening, Linda. It's like a bad, bad dream."

I tried earnestly to block out the conversation between Mom and Aunt Linda. Sitting on the beige carpet Indian-style, I reached for another of Kristina's dolls in feigned interest but my ears couldn't help but be trained on the kitchen, where Linda's voice was a vibrant purr.

"Don't worry. You'll get through this divorce, just like I did. You have a job at the office waiting. Dr. Dubois is thrilled to have you back."

Mom asked, "I know, but what went wrong? What happened to us?"

"Jerks, that's what happened. We married world-class jerks."

Living with our "Aunt" Linda was like being on vacation. We attended school, of course, but weekends were filled with movies, shopping, or ice-skating at the indoor arena less than a mile away. We visited Downtown Seattle and finally saw the infamous Space Needle, but the elevator ride was so terrifying for me that I became dizzy and sick to my stomach, so was not the least bit hungry when we arrived at the revolving restaurant. There, I couldn't even bring myself to look out the window. Afterwards, we went to the Woodland Park Zoo, where I found balance and serenity marveling at elephants and monkeys on solid ground.

Of course, it was not Mom's intentions to live with Linda forever. One day at the end of March, she came home from work holding a set of keys, and told us she had rented a house not far from Linda's house or Dr. Dubois' office. My sisters and I were excited about a home of our own, as was our cat Little Bit, who didn't get along with Stinky, but moving meant changing schools, again. By that time, if you count moving in with Aunt Linda, my family had moved eleven times, and changing schools never got any easier.

The last semester was nearly over when I enrolled as a junior at Hazen High School. I weighed ninety-two pounds that year, which is why I ended up inside a number of lockers. One minute I was trading Pee-Chees and consulting my class schedule and the next I was prisoner of a steel locker, usually my own, though I once ended up in a cluttered locker that smelled like old gym socks and I barely was released before I barfed. Even so, Nancy Anne Nash of Illinois, Michigan, Louisiana, California, Oklahoma, and Washington (twice), did not report such incidents to the principal given the raw hard facts: I was a new, scrawny student with a southern twang and a nose shaped like a hawk's. Being a good sport and keeping quiet seemed in my own best interests.

I managed to make a handful of friends, all "smart" girls who weren't interested in being cool, including a tall, enviably pretty girl named Brenda, and another popular, earnest student named Vicky, who had enough energy and pep for the entire class of 1974. I didn't participate in sports or join any clubs, though I occasionally went to church socials and bible study classes with Vicky, and played a lead role in a school theatre production of "Bus Stop." Otherwise, my high school years were spent with my big nose to my books, earning nearly straight A's with aspirations to be a schoolteacher.

I was smart but would waste this gift for most of my young adulthood, and focus my energies on proving I wasn't.

Chapter Four

During our first summer back in Washington, I answered a newspaper ad to be a nanny, telling Mrs. Bright—the lady in need of the nanny—that I had no formal experience being a nanny but I was a very experienced babysitter, pointing out I had four younger brothers and sisters, and once helped a friend watch a set of three-year-old quadruplets (for two hours, but it seemed like two weeks). When I added I was available seven days a week during the summer months, Carol Bright, the 32-year-old mother of Amanda Margaret, hired me without reservation, and the only reference was my own mother.

Mr. Bright was an architect with a prominent Seattle firm and he designed the waterfront mansion they lived in. To me, the interior resembled one of those fancy lobbies of an upscale hotel I'd seen on T.V., with high beamed ceilings, huge plate-glass windows, textured walls, ornate mirrors and museum-quality artwork. There were enormous vases filled with fresh flowers in every room of the Brights' house, each of which had outstanding views of Lake Washington.

A kitchen meant for entertaining formed the focal point of the house, and my favorite features were the etched-glass cabinet doors, behind which were displayed an assortment of elegant dinnerware and crystal stemware, not a plastic item in sight. On my first day on the job, I peeked in search of a chipped coffee cup or mismatched place setting like we had at home. Mom had nice china but it was reserved for guests and sat gathering dust in her maple hutch. Everything in Carol's kitchen was unblemished.

My first day babysitting Mandy, while Carol and Adam Bright were in Downtown Seattle to attend a Republican fund-raiser, I was reluctant to dirty a dish in the spotless kitchen and eventually ended up using a paper towel to eat the sandwich Carol told me to make. Meanwhile, six-month-old Amanda Margaret, nicknamed Mandy, napped peacefully in a white bassinette. After lunch, I sat on a wicker chair with a glass of iced tea, and took in the spectacular view of Lake Washington a few yards away. I couldn't believe I was being paid for this!

Over the summer months, I accompanied Carol, with Mandy in tow, to Carol's hairdresser in Medina, the Bellevue Yacht & Tennis Club, Frederick & Nelson's, the auto repair shop, and once to another couple's mansion in Yarrow Point, a lakefront suburb of Bellevue. This house was built on a canal of Lake Washington and I spent the afternoon sunbathing and swimming while Mandy cooed in her playpen. Nearby on the same property, Carol and her friend Andrea played tennis in matching white skirts, their lacquered hairstyles scarcely getting out of place.

When I was dropped off at home that night, Carol handed me fifteen dollars in cash for the day's "work" with assurances that as soon as Andrea decided to have babies, I was first on her list to call.

Carol explained, "Andrea has a sister in California who is pregnant so now Andrea is thinking she won't wait till next year to start a family. I told her that was smart because she's not getting any younger. Children are a blessing but, well, they *are* exhausting. Plus, Andrea's had some…female troubles. Anyway, after she has her baby, she wants to hire you, but only if I don't need you first. I have first dibs."

"Oh, I see. That's nice."

"Yes, hopefully it will happen because Larry's very anxious to start a family. He's a probate attorney who travels a lot and is in Baltimore currently. Andrea and Larry used to live in Baltimore, but you'd have to pay me to live in Baltimore. That humidity would kill me." She glanced at her watch. "Better get going. Adam is grilling."

"Okay," I nodded politely. Carol liked to chat and around adults I preferred to listen, so it was a good arrangement.

She headed for her silver Cadillac but suddenly turned. "Oh, don't forgot about next Wednesday, Nancy. I'll be hosting a bridge party and afterwards Adam and I must dash off to the Bellevue Art Museum for a benefit dinner, so I'll need you all day, actually probably till nine or so." I nodded and she scurried down the driveway to her car, where in the front seat slept baby Mandy in a green jumper and leather sandals with multicolored beads. It was an outfit way off the cute charts.

Inside our house, I hid my earnings under my mattress and through the bedroom window, heard my sisters laughing and splashing. I took a peek and watched them run through the sprinkler in their tank tops and cutoffs, giving their boyfriends a show. It figured they would pass the summer slacking off. Money and hard work (if you count changing diapers on a dimpled baby who never cried in a half-million-dollar house hard work) meant nothing to Patty and Sue. No, they were too busy wallowing in testosterone, exuded most prolifically by Patty's rough-edged boyfriend, Dallas McMurtry.

Dallas was not from Texas but White Fish, Montana, and showed up for dates with Patty on a motorcycle he had rebuilt himself. On his right biceps was a tattoo of a serpent and on the other arm a tattoo of a heart with the word "Mom" inside it. There was a Sleaze Factor about him that couldn't be ignored, but then again, he also had long sideburns and a swagger. All things considered, most importantly that I was unattached, I briefly considered stealing Dallas from Patty. Then I got real.

First, even if I did manage to steal him, I would have no idea how to handle him because Dallas McMurtry *oozed* cool, right down to the name. And second, I wasn't even on the verge of cool like Patty, who smoked and didn't look funny doing it (the one time I tried a cigarette, I had to lie down from the headache). No, I was more in the good girl/bookworm category on account of straight A's and weak lungs, and sister Patty, who hated school, was definitely in the cool category.

Midway through the summer, Dallas gave Patty a ring, and she immediately showed it off. "Isn't it beautiful? This means we're going steady."

I glanced at the thin gold-like band with a small topaz gem and envy ripped through me. It wasn't fair! I was oldest and smartest, not to mention employed as a nanny by the richest couple I had ever known. It should be me going steady! I looked at Patty and sneered. "Bet you a week's allowance it's stolen."

"So, you're just jealous."

I rolled my eyes. "I have better things to do with my time than waste it on boys."

Patty shook her head, "You're not normal, you know."

"Carol Bright thinks I am. She said I'm the best sitter she's ever had."

"That's because your social life sucks and revolves around *her* baby. In fact, I'll bet Kenny Mason has a more interesting social life and he's a total geek." Patty pointed. "Look at him, drooling over Susie's every word."

I ventured a peek through the living-room window, where indeed lanky Kenny, who had a slight lisp, was straddling his bike and looking like a sap.

"He does not."

"Oh yes, he does. Kenny at least has a girlfriend, even if Susie doesn't know it." Patty was still admiring her ring, hand up in the air, when she grabbed her jean jacket and announced, "Well, I'm off to the drive-in with Dallas. Have fun tonight staying home alone."

I swore at my sister's back and slumped onto our orange and brown sofa. Life wasn't fair. In fact, according to my mother, it was a freak show carnival.

Chapter Five

My mother had a theory about why things fell apart in Oklahoma, excluding the obvious reasons that living in a dustbowl full of tarantulas, tornadoes, and tumbleweeds was not exactly conducive to clean living and was a place where red clay replaced lawns and ruined everything, including but not limited to washing machines and shag carpeting. Mom hated living in Oklahoma and admitted she frequently fantasized of waking up and finding all the red clay replaced with rubies. Of course, she fantasized far more often that my father would consent to a frontal lobotomy, one she'd offer to perform free of charge, and it would be so easy, too! Mom knew where the power drill was and how to operate it, two not-so-inconsequential things she had up on not-so-handy Dad, and she imagined just one itsy bitsy hole to his handsome forehead that would destroy the frontal lobe of the brain where all the impulsive, stupid decisions were made. If successful, she might be tempted to use the drill on another area of stupid thinking located further south and between his legs.

Even God would surely understand the need for such drastic action because He was a major player in my mother's theory: Not going to church in Oklahoma is why things went to hell in a hand basket.

She claimed the proof was in the pudding (whatever that meant) because her kids sassed, skipped school, snuck out of the house in the middle of the night, and once, her two oldest, most responsible daughters—who were supposed to set an example for the younger children—had actually got caught shoplifting!

I knew Mom prayed silently every night for His guidance (and a couple of do-over days) but it wasn't the same as true worship in His house. Alas, the problem was not *getting* us kids to church; the problem was *keeping* us there without causing a scene. Patty particularly had an unnatural aversion to the house of the Lord, or at least His pew. Two sessions of kneeling alternating with standing and singing and my poor little sis was out like a light, eyes closed, breathing shallowly, and responsive only to the words, "Let's go home."

Susie didn't fare much better, complaining of an upset stomach the minute the donation bowl was headed their way, and I whined the entire time about how tedious church services were, questioning the Lord's choice of communion beverages, as well as the pastor's sermon techniques.

But Mom had decided, now that we were back to civilization, that things were going to change. A new year was just around the corner—1973—and she was determined that God be part of her family's fresh start. She poured another cup of coffee and walked to our T.V. console and turned off *Josie and the Pussycats*.

From the floor, where I was seated two feet away from the screen, I screamed, "Mother! What are you doing?"

Mom blew the top of her coffee and said simply, "Saving you girls from disgrace." She sat down and announced, "Girls, we are going church every Sunday from now on, starting tomorrow. No arguing." Her beloved Saint Margaret's Church was less than five miles away and she couldn't wait to be welcomed back into its beautiful stained-glass folds. Her *girls*, however, had no such sentiment.

"What?" Patty barked in horror, forgetting about Josie. "You can't do that to me!" Her blue eyes grew big and round, similar to the glazed donut she was eating at the time the announcement was made, and her jaw dropped. Making *her* go to church was the most egregious of maternal offenses. It was an outrage! She demanded to know, "What about my see—" She gave me a sideways glance.

I answered dutifully for my sister, "Syncope." My face became solemn because syncope was serious business. Pronounced sin-*ko*-pee, it was an unfamiliar word only if you had not spent many nights reading your mother's medical dictionary with a bag of potato chips at your side. It was my favorite pastime.

"Syncope? Oh for heaven sakes!"

"Well, it's true, Mother." The term's definition was "to faint or become lightheaded" and that was exactly what happened to Patty while in church. I narrowed my eyes at my Mother. "You *do* remember Patty always faints in church, don't you? And what about Susie's fear of the collection plate? You don't really want to have to deal with *that* again, do you?"

My Mother was a very smart woman and while she had her stone face on, the one that meant business, inside I could tell she was wavering, probably because I was right and she was now dealing with teenagers, a breed particularly resistant to reason and long-lasting good behavior.

Mother glared; the teenagers glared.

"What happens if I puke again?" Susie asked with thin arms crossed and lips pursed. She was the youngest of the daughters but already an experienced puker.

I could see my Mother's mind race with multiple choices: *Should I make them go to church, or allow them to fall astray because they have no spiritual guidance? Do I ground them or make them clean the house if they don't go to church?*

Patty begged, "Please, mom, I hurt my back the last time I fainted in church. It still aches every morning. I'm sure I have arthritis or something."

Susie melodramatically clutched her stomach. "I feel sick already." She darted towards the bathroom, where seconds later the toilet flushed. It then flushed again and I was pretty sure it was an unnecessary flush and if she kept doing that, the only toilet we had would be useless.

Suddenly, I yelped, "Omigod, I just remembered! I'm watching Mandy tomorrow while Carol gets her nails done. I can't possibly cancel now! Carol would kill me!" This was astonishingly the truth.

"She's getting a manicure on a Sunday?"

"Well, the lady comes to her house. She's Chinese or something and doesn't speak English and the whole process takes a long time. Carol has to like soak her hands for an hour and then she doesn't get just polish, she gets a *treatment*. It costs like thirty dollars. Anyway, I'm glad I bite my nails because it looks like too much work, but Carol has to have perfect nails. You know how rich people are."

We were rich once, though the last professional manicure Mother had was before I was born.

"Nancy, if you keep biting your nails, you're going to permanently deform your fingers."

"It's better than smoking." I looked directly at Patty, who shrugged, still more concerned about the church issue.

"So, Mom, can we stay home from church, please?" Patty was hunched over and rubbing her back. Overacting was a Nash specialty.

Mother sighed with resignation. "I give up. I can't hogtie ya'll and drag you to Church. Besides, that might send the wrong message to God." She threw her hands up. "At least one of us is going to be in His good graces."

As a consolation, I offered (before even being asked) to clean our house, including dusting and vacuuming. That was my specialty and I was pretty sure God would appreciate the gesture, especially if I unclogged the toilet.

In the process of going to church alone, Mom unwittingly entered the post-divorce dating world, and Lucky Date Number #1 was a divorced man she met during a St. Margaret's church social, a professional photographer who lived on Mercer Island. We girls ended up loving Dick's in-ground pool but didn't think much of Dick, who wore gaudy gold jewelry and slicked his hair back. After just two months of dating, he asked Mom and us girls to move in with him. Mom said no and Dick ditched her.

Next, Mother dated Herb, whom she met during an actual Sunday service when his knee froze while they were kneeling and she had assisted in helping him up. Herb was heavy and balding, but very polite, and brought candy and flowers not just for Mom, but for us, as well. After a while, however, Herb's generosity was overshadowed by his growing girth. He didn't have a beer gut, he had a full keg under his shirt! At restaurants, Mom said Herb slathered butter on everything and licked his plate clean. Thirty pounds later (on top of the two-hundred give-or-take he started with), my health-conscious Mother bid Herb farewell.

What followed was a string of "too's": Gordy (too old and serious), Walter (too weird, especially his obsession with the movie *Clockwork Orange*), and Cliff, whom mom met at a Parents without Partners' event, who was too *everything*, but most notably cheap.

Mother didn't give up. She knew there were more fishes in God's sea. And one was Bob.

Chapter Six

As asked, I opened one of our double wall ovens and checked the glistening twenty-pound Butterball that had been baking at a low temperature for nearly eight hours. All morning long, Mom had been basting the bird with a mixture of olive oil and butter that had turned the skin to a deep golden color. I was tempted to cut a piece of breast to taste but Mom was right behind me, making sure everything was perfect. Usually my sisters and I did a good job with the setting the table but Mom was being extra picky and wanted everything exceptionally nice. It was our first Thanksgiving back in Washington and she had invited Bob Adamson, a widower she met at a St. Margaret's bazaar, plus his three children to join us. I hadn't been all that excited, given Mom's prior dates, and moaned in protest.

"He better not be anything like Cliff because if he is, he'll probably bill us for the honor of his company!" I shook my head, having overheard Mother's last conversation with Cliff the Tightwad, and it was all about the cost of everything: *Remember, Lois, a penny saved is still a penny saved! You aren't going to throw away the chicken box are you? I recycle paper products. Did you know I can make a paper plate last three meals?*

Jeez, what a loser!

"Yeah, Mom," Patty nodded, "please don't make us to go to anymore

Parents Without Partners' events. It's not *Kids* Without Partners, you know."

"Yes, I know, but it's a safe way to meet people. What do you want me to do? Go to bars like your father?"

"So, what's Bob like? Is he old and fat?"

Mom removed her oven mitt. "No, Susie, he's not old or fat. He's very handsome and has three kids."

"*Three*? Are they boys?" Susie's licked her lips and asked eagerly, "Like, are they cute?"

Opening a bottle of Loganberry wine, Mother replied, "Two boys and one girl, and yes, they're cute and well-mannered."

"What are their names?"

"Tom, John, and Jill." Mom poured a small bit of wine for a taste before replacing the cork and setting the bottle on the table. "Now everyone go get ready. I want y'all to look your best."

An hour later and seated at our maple table and sipping sweet wine because *this* year was special, Mother offered the blessing, including a brief message to God to forgive her daughters for being unrepentant, and to please watch over Marky and Billy. The room remained quiet until the blessing was over. We said our amens and Mom stood to carve the turkey.

Bob reached for the knife, standing tall. "Please sit, Lois, and let me cut the turkey. You deserve to relax after cooking this wonderful meal."

Mom smiled and picked up her wine glass. "Thank you, but I didn't do all the work myself. The girls helped."

"Yes, we sure did." I took a sip of the ultra-sweet wine and nodded. "I still don't understand why you have to get up so early to cook a turkey."

Bob's youngest son, John, asked, "Who're Marky and Billy?"

Patty answered, "My little brothers. They live in Oklahoma."

Bob sliced the turkey like an expert and created two plates: One full of dark meat, the other all white meat. I already liked Bob as I accepted a part of white breast meat, which I slathered in cranberry sauce and butter.

Bob chuckled politely. "Well, things could be worse: They could be living in Kansas."

Mom groaned. "The kids' father almost killed us in Kansas with his crazy driving. He thought speed limits were merely suggestions."

Tom, Bob's oldest son, hadn't said much during dinner but now spoke up. "He's not the only one. In driver's ed, we have a lead foot in our class named Lisa who clipped Mr. Stuckey, our instructor, and he needed a dozen stitches."

Patty's blue-gray eyes grew wide with concern. "That's awful! I hope you weren't hurt." Her eyelashes fluttered, and I instantly thought of Stevie.

"Nah, I was watching from the sidelines." Tom grinned, "Everybody in my class knows to stay out of Lisa's way."

"Oh, that's a relief." Patty put her fork down and stared starstruck across the table at Tom. He was wearing a brown pullover sweater and his thick brown hair hung across his forehead. He was way cuter than Dallas and I could practically see the wildly beating hearts floating above my sister's strawberry-blond head. What a nympho!

I turned to Tom and gave him my best smile. "I'm in driver's ed, too."

Patty rolled her eyes. "Big deal."

I pointed a finger at my sister. "Well, I could drive you places, if you were nice."

Patty replied, "I don't need you—"

Mom reached for the gravy. "Girls, watch your manners. We have company."

Jill, who was Susie's age, giggled. "Dad lets Tom drive all the time even though he only has a permit." She turned to her father, "Right, Dad?"

Bob nodded. "Yes, but only on the local roads. Besides, better Tom is a better taxi service than me."

Looking at Bob Adamson, I decided Mother was right. He was very handsome, with thick wavy brown hair, just like all three of his children. That day, he was wearing a Western-style suit with a leather and silver bolo tie and I would not have been surprised to learn he had arrived by horse.

Because of Bob and his children (who would have been easy to hate based on their dimples alone), that turned out to be the best Thanksgiving in my memory and when Christmas arrived, we spent it at the Adamson's house a few miles away. It was like discovering a holiday I had never truly celebrated, at least not in the normal way. Sure, Mom always dutifully decorated and put on a good holiday face, and there was never a shortage of gifts, but it was the mood in the house that damped the festivities, all because my Father hated Christmas. He made the Scrooge look like Mother Goose.

Leaving the Adamsons' house on Christmas Eve, I whispered to Patty. "Do you realize Bob and Mom didn't argue even once? And Bob likes to sing Christmas carols! Can you imagine Dad standing around the tree and singing Christmas carols? He'd rather jump off a bridge wearing brick shoes. You know, I think Mom hit the jackpot with Bob."

Patty nodded, "Yeah, this was nothing like most of our Christmases. Remember the year Dad held a gun to Mom's head and then he broke my ceramic lamb? I loved that lamb."

Experiencing an odd feeling of detachment despite the horror of that night, I shrugged. "How could we ever forget? That was the night Mom said angels were watching over us. Angels and God."

Chapter Seven

Lois Mae Nash was not a woman not to be taken lightly, so when the local bank declined her loan application for a mortgage, she demanded to talk to the branch manager and pretty soon was arguing her case to a room full of stuffy and quite old-fashioned male bankers. *Divorced women don't own houses*, they claimed, *and they don't have bank accounts or stock portfolios, they have piggy banks!*

Such things may have been true, but my mother was determined to support her children as best she could. She had already left Dr. Dubois' office and found a job as a radiology transcriptionist for Overlake Hospital in nearby Bellevue. The job was full-time with insurance and benefits, providing her with her own typewriter and a desk. It was a start, and a good one.

At the bank and waiting in the lobby, Mom was fuming at the indifference with which she had been treated but as soon as we were called into an office, she flashed a million-dollar smile and smoothed the front of her tangerine mini-skirt, which missed her knees by about four inches. Three men in dark suits stared unabashedly at the shapely legs, not bothering to hide their male chauvinism because there was no need. The year was 1972; men were in charge, or so these men thought, until Mom mentioned a lawsuit.

I watched quietly from a chair next to her, wondering if she was bluffing.

"A lawsuit? Are you crazy? You can't sue us! That's absurd!" The tallest one with long graying sideburns and a goatee went pale.

"But, of course I can, because you are denying me a loan simply because I am divorced and that, gentlemen, is flagrant discrimination."

My eyes widened, wondering if we were going to get kicked out of the bank because Mom just cussed out some important men.

One of the bankers asked, "It's a what?"

"Discrimination, and don't pretend you don't know what that is." Mom's late father, my beloved Grandpa Taylor, had been a real-estate attorney, and she continued confidently, "Gentlemen, let me point out the facts in this case: First, I do not want to throw my hard-earned money away on rent each month. Secondly, I am employed full-time at a major hospital and have enough money for a down payment sitting in my account." She pulled out a piece of paper from her purse. "The house has an asking price of $21,000. It's a three-bedroom rambler and it's in a nice neighborhood where my kids won't have to change schools."

I nodded vigorously, hoping to convey how important that was.

Mother pointed to the photo of the house. "It's got a garden and a garage and I want this house, so if you do not seriously consider my application on my own financial merits, the next place I go after this meeting is my lawyer's office, and I warn you, I will fight tooth and nail. Believe me, I've been up against far worse than this."

She meant Dad, of course.

The bankers were speechless but when their petite brunette client mentioned, as she turned to leave, that what she *really* wanted was a mansion on the lake, inferring anything was possible with the right jury, the loan was approved on the spot.

When Mom told Patty and Sue, who had declined a boring trip to the bank, they both asked the same thing.

"Do we have to change schools again?"

I answered with a jubilant NO!

A month later, the Nash sisters were sitting on the curb in front of their "new" house in their "new" neighborhood, when Patty pointed to a group of boys in the cul-de-sac and declared, "Drew is definitely the cutest. He's the one with the long brown hair and dimples."

Susie and I craned our necks and looked yonder at the boys, who were playing basketball. Next to us sat Jill, nicknamed Jilly-Bean, who was also staring greedily. She sighed, "Yeah, Drew's cute, Patty, but you already have a boyfriend."

"I know, but I can still window shop. Besides, Dallas looks at other girls all the time."

Susie barely glanced up, throwing pebbles and gutter debris into the street. "They're all dorks and besides, I already have a boyfriend and he's a lot cooler than Kenny was."

"Who?" I asked, "And what's his name?"

Susie tossed another pebble and shrugged. "His name is Brad but he doesn't go to our school."

Patty turned her head. "Brad Mills? Dallas knows him and said he's a troublemaker. Besides, what happened to Kenny?"

"Kenny's living with his dad now, in Portland or something."

"What school does Brad go to? How old is he? Where does he live?" As oldest I felt an obligation to grill for details. If I had had a notepad, I would be scribbling.

"Brad's seventeen and doesn't go to school at all."

"What? He's a dropout? And seventeen? Susie, you're only thirteen!"

Susie stood and brushed off the back of her pants. "So, I don't look thirteen. Brad thought I was sixteen. And call me Sue now, it's more mature."

Sue was mature all right, thanks to boobs no thirteen-year-old deserved.

I said, "It's still wrong. I'm telling Mom."

Sue rolled her eyes. "So what. You wanna be a narc, that's your problem."

Jilly-Bean, who still had her eyes on the boys, pointed. "Hey, Nancy. Which one of the boys do *you* like?" We could have been discussing pastry choices at a Dunkin Donut.

I forgot about Sue and took another salacious look towards the boys, already choosing the one called Stu, who lived right next door with his younger brother, Matt. Stuart McGuinn was freckled and lanky, and did dumb things meant to impress the girls, but what they usually did was gross them out. Nevertheless, Stu had made it clear from day one he had a crush on me.

"I guess Stu. He likes me." *Too bad he was fixated on toads and worms.*

Jill giggled, "I know. He told me he thought were cute for a fraidycat. Well, I like Jake. Did you see those arms? I'll bet he lifts weights or something. He looks like a bodybuilder, and that blond hair is to die for!" She swooned and giggled some more, falling backwards onto the lawn. "I LUV Jake Bauer!"

Two weeks later, Jill was madly *in luv* with Drew Andrews, Sue claimed she and Brad Mills were going steady though a Brad sighting had yet to occur, and I was eyeing Matt's best friend Tracy, despite him being two years younger. I justified the attraction for three reasons: First, Tracy was extremely mature for a thirteen-year-old and didn't pull stupid prank after prank, exhausting my patience as Stu had. Secondly, Tracy had the coolest bike in the neighborhood, one he had to lock up carefully lest it be stolen. Thirdly, I looked Tracy's age and could probably pass for three years younger, something that my Mother told me I might hate now but would greatly appreciate when I was thirty.

"Thirty?" I had asked in exasperation. "What is it about thirty that is so special you suddenly get really smart and understand everything you never understood until that age?"

Mother's answer had been simple: "You'll understand *that* when you're ninety."

My romance with Tracy ended up lasting a marvelous two weeks but the humiliation and teasing I got from the neighborhood gang (especially Matt), proved too much and reluctantly, I ended it. Tracy took the news poorly and stormed off on his brand-new blue Raleigh 20 bicycle. It was just another loss in a lifetime of losses. Sulking curbside, I gave Jilly-Bean the bad news.

Jill reached over and patted my knee. "Nancy? Sorry about Tracy, but he was too young, and I'm sure you can do better."

"I guess."

Jill asked, "Hey, don't you wish we knew who we were going to marry?"

I grimaced. "Huh?"

"See, I want to know who I am going to marry *now*, even though it might be a long ways away. Like if only God could just send me a vision in a cloud, or a sign, and then I would know, even though I'll probably have lots of boyfriends in between. That way I can prepare for what my kids are gonna look like."

"Jeez, Jilly-Bean. I've never thought about who I'm gonna marry. I have trouble enough just going steady."

Jill put her arm around me, her best friend. "Yeah, you aren't exactly a guy magnet."

"It's the nose." I rubbed my nasal bridge in an attempt to file the hump, which I was convinced was growing by the week.

"Well, look at the bright side: You have a nice personality and you're the funniest person I've ever met. You really crack me up!"

"Whoopee." I twirled my forefinger into the air. "Boys don't care about personality or being funny. In fact, *they* want to be the funny ones."

Jill nodded. "Well, I've never met a boy who could do the wachucka-chucka-chucka. That's the funniest thing I've ever seen!"

I looked at Jilly-Bean, who very likely might someday be my stepsister. "You really think acting like a spaz having a fit and talking gibberish is funny?"

"Oh yeah! It's hilarious, especially when you cross your eyes and start drooling and your arms flap up and down. Where did you ever *learn* that?"

"I made it up." I answered glibly.

Jilly-Bean yelped, "See! That's what I mean. You're funny enough to be on Laugh-In, just like that Goldie girl!"

Chapter Eight

The boys came to live with us a few months after we moved into our house. While it was in their best interests, it put a considerable financial strain on Mom because she now had five mouths to feed on a tight budget that included a mortgage, and no child support since this was a concept not enforced and one my father had yet to embrace. To help out, I offered to be in charge while she was at work, for free, and while Mom was appreciative, I knew she oftentimes questioned whether it was wise. All my life, I have had a tendency of taking being-in-charge a bit too seriously, and sometimes this caused more problems than it solved. In fact, by the time Mom pulled into the driveway after work, I was already holding my Steno-Pad with a detailed list of infractions my siblings had committed during the course of any day.

One such breach in etiquette occurred two days after Marky and Billy moved in. They were jumping on the sofa using baseball bats as makeshift swords, swinging the bats with murderous intent. I put my hands on my hips and barked, "Mom's home so you better knock it off!"

Marky's bat swung madly but missed Billy and smacked the wall. "He started it!"

"Liar!" Billy hurled his bat and lunged for Marky, who escaped under Billy's legs and ran from the room. In retaliation, and needing *something* to abuse, Billy kicked the antique stereo, on which had been sitting an heirloom brown lamp with a beribboned shade. The lamp went tumbling.

Mom walked in and threw her sweater and purse down. "What happened to Mother's lamp?"

I uprighted Grandma Taylor's lamp and explained irritably, "The boys were fighting. I tried to stop them."

Mom passed the kitchen, where a puppy was sleeping outside the sliding doors. "Whose dog is that?" Her voice was weary.

"Ours! I got him from Davy Dawson, free!"

"I don't think so, Billy. Call Davy Dawson, whoever that is, and tell him to come get the dog. I have enough mouths to feed."

I followed my Mother down the hall toward her bedroom. "Mother, you won't believe the day I had."

"I could say the same." She pulled off her blouse and I gasped.

"Have you lost weight, Mom?" My mother had always been petite, but pretty soon she'd be shopping in the young girls' department.

She stepped out of her skirt. "I haven't had much appetite lately. I'm going to the doctor next week, but I'm sure it's just the stress of living in a looney-bin." She reached for a housecoat and tied it around her small waist.

"Oh." I sat on her bed and glanced down at my notes. "Well, today Patty borrowed one of your shirts *again*, and also one of your necklaces, the opal one that was Grandma Taylor's. I told her not to but she didn't listen, like always. And Sue called Dad twice but not collect like she was supposed to."

No one needed to tell me I had turned into the Ultimate Bitch, the older sister everyone despised, who without asking had become the eyes and ears of their Mother. It was a role I seemed deftly suited for. No, *perfect* for. Pausing to give Mom time to digest the news and formulate suitable punishments, I asked, "Well?"

Mom reached into a wicker basket and handed over a pile of dirty clothes. "Put these in the washer and start a load."

I whined, "But Mother!"

"Honestly, if you kids can't get along, I'll get you all a babysitter, including for you." She shuffled to the kitchen in slippers, where she began molding ground beef into patties. I was on her heels.

"Mother," I began soothingly, eager to recapture her affections and attention, "I didn't want to tell you, but, well, it's for Patty's own good. I caught her smoking in the garage yesterday. With Dallas."

Patty suddenly charged in yelling, "Sue is right! You are such a narc!"

"Well, it's a disgusting habit." I looked to Mom for support. "Patty's grounded, right?"

"Nancy, stop being such a tattletale. You should mind your own business."

"What? I thought Patty wasn't allowed to hang around with Dallas anymore? He has tattoos and drinks beer, you know."

"Shut up, you liar! You're lucky you're moving to college next fall. Everyone hates you."

Mom placed five patties into a frying pan. When they were done, she flipped the burgers onto a platter, along with buns. "Nancy, call the boys to the table. It's time to eat."

"They're already at the table." In their underwear, but at least they remembered to sit at opposite ends of the table. Billy was now almost twelve and Marky nine years old. Apart, they were mischievous like most boys their age, but together they became homicidal midget-sized monsters. Just the week before, Billy chased Marky with a butcher knife and when he threatened to break down the bathroom door, behind which Marky was cussing, I called the police, who called Mom at work, who grounded all of us for life.

(Note: My mother sincerely meant it when she imposed the ultimate sentence but "grounded for life" only worked on paper and was immediately lifted when she remembered that this would mean having five children with attention deficit disorder moaning and groaning within earshot for the rest of *her* days. Thus, grounded for life translated, on average, to just under six hours in the Nash household.)

Mom turned towards the dining room table. "Oh. Why are you boys in your underwear at the table?"

"You need to do laundry, mom." Billy grinned and I noticed for the first time my brother had really big front teeth for such a small boy. I used my tongue to check on the size of my own dentition, fearing a big nose was just the beginning, but my teeth seemed normal size, at least to my tongue. When dinner was over, I'd verify this in the bathroom mirror but for now, I hoped my brother's mouth would grow to match the teeth.

Marky moaned, "Mom, why do we eat so many hamburgers?"

"Because ground chuck is cheap." Mom rubbed her temples. "But then again, so is liver and onions so I think I'll make that for the rest of the week, or maybe goulash? After that, who knows? I could make pimento spread sandwiches on rye, I suppose."

Mom had effectively listed the Worst Meals of All Time. And who ever thought that adding buttered onions to liver would mask the disgusting taste of an organ that processed cow bile? *Bile*, for godsakes!

Sue bit into her plain cheeseburger and looked up. "Mom? There's something I want to tell you."

I put my fork down and forgot all about liver and onions. "Is it about Brad?" I was sure he probably knocked my sister up or something, *if* he existed.

"I'm not talking to you."

Mom asked, "Is it bad news? Because if it is, save it for later."

"Well, not really. I want to live with Dad."

"Over my dead body." Mom downed her glass of wine. "Pass the pickles."

Sue glared. "Dad said I could live with him. Besides, I hate my school and I hate living in Washington." She pushed her plate away and stood, arms crossed in teenaged rebellion. "Why can't I live with him?"

Patty used her fork to scoop up a tiny portion of baked beans. She turned to Sue and asked, "Why do you want to live with Dad? In Oklahoma?"

"Because."

"Because *why* Susan Kay? Give me a good reason." Mom always called us by our given names when she was irritated. And if she added the middle name, she was way beyond irritated.

Susan Kay screamed, "Because if I can't go live with Dad, I'll kill myself, and this time I'll do it right!" With this, she ran from the dining room and slammed the bathroom door. I waited for the toilet to flush, but there was only silence.

Unfortunately, the threat was not something to be taken lightly. Sue once overdosed on aspirin downed with half a bottle of Boone's Farm Strawberry Hill wine. She threw both up almost immediately and ruined her white shorts. Other than that, she was no worse for wear. Even so, my stomach knotted up thinking that my sister might succeed at suicide, and while I had cleaned the bathroom that morning out of boredom and knew the medicine cabinet was gutted of potentially dangerous drugs, there were sanitary napkins under the sink, and suicidal teenagers, if Sue was any example, were both clever and determined. If nothing else, the Kotex was a choking hazard.

Around me, the table had fallen silent and I could no longer stand it. "Mother? I think maybe Sue is smoking marijuana cigarettes. Those will make you crazy, you know." Suddenly I was worried that Sue was doing that very thing in the bathroom, trying to end her life using an illegal substance that could land us all in jail. "Maybe we should check on her?"

Just then, the bathroom door opened and Sue slumped out. She sat back and bit into her cold hamburger like nothing had happened. As far as I could tell my sister's mouth was empty of Kotex, and if she had been smoking pot it was of the odorless variety.

Meanwhile, Patty was sneering at me. "Has anyone told you what an annoying know-it-all you are?"

I shrugged, "Perfection has its price."

Mom stood and pushed her barely touched plate away. "Oh for heaven sakes' girls! Honestly, I might go drown myself in the bathtub, then you'll all be sorry, especially you, Nancy. If I go, who will pay for your nose job?"

I squirmed, hoping she was kidding. "No one, but you're kidding, right?"

"Not necessarily."

Patty moaned. "A nose job is a weird graduation gift, if you ask me."

"Nobody asked."

"Thuthie?" Marky dipped his burger in ketchup, like it was French fries. Chewing, he asked, "Why do wantha die?"

I said, "Don't talk with your mouth full, Marky. You know the rules."

Sue answered her brother, "It's none of your business what I want."

"Don't be mean to Marky. He's just a little kid."

"Shut up."

"You shut up."

Billy asked, "Why can't we keep Max?"

"Who?" Our Mother asked wearily. I knew she was thinking she was raising five misfits who had already shortened her lifespan. If she made it to sixty sane, it would be a miracle.

I pointed, "The dog." I looked up and caught my reflection in the glass doors of the maple hutch. "Mom, thank you again for letting me get my nose fixed. I know you had to get a loan and all, and Dad doesn't help out much, so I really do appreciate it."

"Show me by cleaning up, okay? I think I'm going to go lie down."

When Mom left the room, Patty said, "I'm asking for a car for my graduation. I think a nose job is stupid."

I ignored my sister as I gathered plates and took them to our kitchen sink, which was aqua and matched the oven and countertops. "It's called a septorhinoplasty, for your information. And what makes you think you're smart enough to graduate, Patty?"

Chapter Nine

"Sep-to-rhi-no-plasty: (sep"to-ri'no-plast'te): [*septo-* + *rhino* +*plasty*]: a plastic operation combining reconstruction of the nasal septum and correction of deformities of the external nose."

I set the Dorland's Dictionary down and leaned against the headboard of my twin bed. That I was reading a medical dictionary on a Friday night (the same night as Junior Spring Prom, where Patty and Dallas were no doubt smoking in between dances) spoke volumes (no pun intended) about my social life. It was the reason I was willing to take the risks of undergoing a *plastic* operation in the hopes it would make me pretty, or at least attractive enough to be invited to a prom. Heck, a barnyard dance might not be so bad, either!

Really, it was depressing not to have a boyfriend, or to never have been asked to a single prom, which meant that nearly every Friday and Saturday night, I was usually babysitting, earning the title of most dependable sitter for miles. Unfortunately *that* Friday, despite outstanding telephone networking to drum up some business, I couldn't find a single couple with plans to go out. Even Mr. and Mrs. Fisher, who always went out every Friday to dinner and a movie, leaving the care of their two boys in my expert hands, were heading out for a spring vacation to Montana, or was it Milwaukee? No matter, Joanie Fisher had sounded excited and in a big hurry to start packing, though when I joked she could leave the boys with her the entire two weeks (calculating mentally how rich I would be at fifty cents per hour for two weeks), there was a long pause and then a polite chuckle followed by Timmy and Tommy hooting in the background.

I called the Kellermans (sick with the flu), the Brights (yachting while Mandy, who was now three, was at her grandparents), and even the Jorgensons, whose odd and only child was obsessed with flour and truth be told, babysitting Johnny Jorgenson was worth a *dollar* an hour but I didn't push it. Someday, I might have a child displaying an abnormal fixation with baking products and would know exactly how to handle the situation: I'd hide anything that said Pillsbury and ignore the glazed eyes, finger up the nose, and unnatural desire to reorganize the kitchen cupboards. When Johnny did that, I was tempted to scream, *Get real Johnny! You're eight, I'm not! The flour isn't anywhere near the kitchen so stop snooping!* Nor was the baking powder or baking soda, items that could easily be mistakenly for flour if one were eight.

So here I was on a Friday night, alone in my room and contemplating a septorhinoplasty or, as my ignorant sister called it, nose job. As far as I knew, no other senior at my school was asking for a septorhinoplasty for graduation. A car was the top requested gift, followed by a trip to Hawaii, and then cash. No matter, I was getting a nose job and I was getting it in April so I'd look decent accepting my high school diploma in June.

On the morning of my appointment with the plastic surgeon, I giddily rushed through my morning routine and was sitting in our station wagon fifteen minutes before Mother walked out wearing a pink and green paisley wraparound dress with taupe knee-high boots. She looked like a fashion model. Actually, she looked like Sophia Loren.

Mom started up the car without buckling up, backed out of the driveway, and "California" stopped at three signs before turning left on a yellow light. When she approached the freeway on-ramp like she owned it, I discretely snapped on my seatbelt. The trip to the clinic should have taken fifteen minutes but we made it in eight. Once there, Mom walked to the office; I skipped.

Dr. Ross Berner, Plastic & Reconstructive Surgeon, examined my nose and sent me for x-rays. Upon returning from Radiology, I sat in the exam room thumbing through an album of "before-and-after" photographs, trying to pick out my new nose. I sort of liked the nose on page six, but the one on page nine was more sophisticated. Both noses belonged to girl patients. This was critically important.

A few minutes passed before Dr. Berner walked in holding a large x-ray jacket. He removed the films and placed them on a lighted reader board under magnets and pointed with his pencil. "See this? The septum is fractured." He turned and inquired, "Have you ever had any trauma to your nose, Nancy?"

"I banged it swimming lots of times." I glanced sheepishly towards my mother. "I guess I never told you about when Patty and I went swimming at the Holiday Inn in Woodland Hills. I banged my nose and it started bleeding really bad, right before Patty almost drowned when that little boy jumped on her back. Man, her face was bluer than your eye shadow! The lifeguard never even noticed."

Mom raised an eyebrow but didn't press for details. She explained to Dr. Berner, "My girls were tomboys. Nancy ran into a center post of our basement when she and her sisters were roller-skating. She was about eight or so. She also broke her arm climbing up an apple tree and her leg in two places while attempting to jump onto a rope swing. And don't even ask about Patty." She turned back to me. "I knew I shouldn't have let you girls go to the hotel pool alone."

Dr. Berner chuckled. "My girls are the same, always getting in—"

Forgetting my manners, I interrupted, "Doctor, does a nose job hurt?"

"Don't worry, you'll be knocked out." The doctor turned off the light and the x-rays went black. He said brightly, "Lois, this is actually good news, at least to your pocketbook. Since your daughter has a deviated nasal septum caused by a fracture, this is not considered elective plastic surgery and should be covered one-hundred percent by your insurance."

"Oh, thank God!" Mom clapped and accepted some papers to sign while Dr. Berner explained the procedure to me, using his thumbs to gently palpate my deviated septum.

"Your nasal turbinates appear inflamed on the films, so I will remove some of that tissue along with straightening the deviated septum, and I can try to do something with the dorsal tip, maybe take off some of the roundness and give your nose more definition." He reached for the book of noses and turned the pages. "Maybe like this?"

My head bobbed excitedly. "Oh yes!" It was the nose on page nine!

On the way home, I was gushing with gratitude. "Thank you thank you thank thank you, mother!" I studied my humped nose in the mirror on the back of the sun visor. "Wow, I have a deviated septum." Not to mention swollen turbinates. I closed the flap thinking about the condition of my nose. It sounded so *serious!* In fact, the more I thought about having a deviated septum and swollen turbinates, the woozier I felt. Maybe I had cancer!

"Mother?" The familiar sound of a police siren caused me to whip around. "Uh oh."

Mom glanced into the rearview mirror. "Oh shoot! Not again. Honey, get my license out of my wallet please." She checked her lipstick and pulled to the shoulder, where she parked the car and rolled down the window. This time, the officer was taller and younger than the last one. He bent over to look through the window.

"Mam." He tipped his hat. "Were you aware you were speeding?"

I watched the cop's eyes momentarily fall on two shapely thighs before returning north.

"Oh, dear, was I?" Mom purred through her pink lipgloss, "Well, it's because I was in a hurry, Sir." She reached over and patted one of my thighs, still speaking to the cop. "You see, officer, we were at the doctor. My daughter is having surgery. Her nose is broken."

The officer ducked for a better look. "Ouch. I'll bet that hurts."

"Not really." The cop was cute and I smiled sweetly. "It's been broken for aw—"

"Nancy, let's not waste this nice policeman's time."

The cop straightened. "I'll let you off this time with a warning. But I'd hate to see you pretty ladies get in an accident." He winked. "Slow down, okay?"

"Oh yes, I promise."

It took longer to get home on account of Mom obeying the posted speed limit, but once there I excitedly told Patty all about my upcoming nose job, especially the part about it being free.

My sister shook her head in disgust. "So I guess this means you get another graduation present?"

I squealed, "Maybe! I hadn't thought about that! Anyway, the doctor showed me pictures of noses. I picked a new nose that is very sophisticated. I can't wait to have a new nose!"

Patty rolled her eyes. "A new nose won't mean you'll get a boyfriend."

I felt kicked in the stomach. Sisters were so cruel! I stuck out my tongue and retreated to my bedroom. Never mind that the statement was true; the last boyfriend I had was Dallas' little brother, Randy, who broke up with *me*, shocking the entire neighborhood more than when we *started* dating because Randy was a dimwitted grease ball whose favorite thing to do was work on car engines so his jeans smelled of diesel. He was not exactly my type, if I had one.

Gazing into the hand mirror, I repeated over and over, "I'll be normal by April, normal by April..."

April arrived, and at the surgeon's office, a plump nurse lead me and my mother to a dressing room, where I put on a gown before being wheeled to the operating suite and placed into a padded chair that tilted back. Even with Mom standing nearby and holding my hand, my heart was pounding as I watched the nurse insert an I.V. into my arm. Her nametag read *Candy Jensen, RN*, and she said, "Dr. Berner will fix you up real nice, you don't worry. He has a lot of experience." Nurse Jett adjusted the tilt of the chair so I was lying supine and then she tucked me under a pink blanket. "As far as I know, he hasn't messed up one nose so I promise, you'll be beautiful. Now, start counting backwards from one-hundred."

I took one last look at my mother and then closed my eyes and began counting. "One-hundred, ninety-nine..."

The next thing I remember was looking up through a haze to find a masked man hovering over my face, and I heard a scraping sound like sandpaper being rubbed over steel. Whatever drug they gave me, it was strong because but I didn't feel a thing. The surgeon's voice sounded so far away and he was talking about golf. Or was it ghosts?

After that, the next thing I remember is Mom standing at my bedside.

Very groggily and gingerly, I touched my nose through the bandages. I tried to sit up and realized I was on my own bed. "I'm home? I don't remember anything."

Mom rearranged the pillows my head was elevated. "That's the drugs, but tomorrow you will probably be sore. Are you hungry?"

"No, just sleepy." I reached down to move Little Bit, who was burrowed into my side. The black cat woke, stretched, walked in circles, and plopped back down in the exact position she had been. She fell back asleep with a heavy purr, one paw over her cute button nose. What a life.

The day after the surgery, just as Mom had predicted, I was in pain but the painkillers kept coming. I had been warned repeatedly not to look in the mirror (yet) but when I got up to go to the bathroom, I peeked and nearly pooped my pants! My eyes were completely black and blue, and under the bandage my nose actually looked bigger! I would have cried had it not hurt so much. I crawled back into bed and fell asleep dreaming I died of complications from the nose job and came back as a cat. By the end of the week, I felt a bit better but didn't see much shrinkage in the hand mirror I now kept under my covers. Holding the mirror up, I studied my profile carefully. It looked exactly the same and I wanted to pull off the bandages, but a knock on the door kept me from doing that.

"Who's there?"

Patty peeked in with nylon stockings pulled over her face. "What do you think of *my* new facelift?"

I put the mirror down and rolled my eyes. It was obvious Patty's goal was to make me laugh and break my stitches, but it only made me groan. I asked her to turn on my T.V. for me and she yanked off the beige nylons.

"I can't believe Mom moved the extra television set in here. It's not fair." She reached to turn on the black-and-white T.V. and in the doorway said, "You don't look that good, you know. I'm glad I'm keeping my nose."

"Whatever, but close my door so I can have some privacy." On the T.V. was my favorite show, *The Mary Tyler Moore Show*. This episode was a repeat, where poor Chuckles the Clown gets trampled by an elephant during a circus stunt. It wasn't funny but for some reason everyone at the T.V. station found Chuckles' demise hilarious, even usually kindhearted

Mary. Watching the show, I giggled along softly, remembering I wasn't supposed to laugh. Besides, I had already seen the episode. Soon, however, I couldn't help it and my giggles became full-blown howls of laughter that brought tears to my eyes. And for unknown physiologic reasons, whenever I laugh *that* hard—where tears are flowing and my stomach and jaw muscles ache in protest—I get the urge to sneeze, and of all things not allowed following a septorhinoplaty, sneezing is number one.

I suppressed both urges during the funeral scene, where Mary Richards finally breaks down and begins sobbing. Why this was so hilarious, I didn't understand but now I was laughing *and* sneezing. "Ha ha ha….aaahhhhchoooooooooo! Ha ha ha…aaaachhhoooo!"

The next thing I knew I was back at the hospital getting stitched up. There, the stern doctor warned me to try not to sneeze. This is like warning someone not to breathe but I answered politely, "Yes, Doctor, I'll try, but if you want to know, it was Mary Tyler Moore's fault. That's what I was watching when I started to sneeze. Well, first I laughed and then I sneezed. I'm sorry."

We left the emergency room after I got another dose of painkillers and some antibiotics, and I went home and crashed. Fourteen hours later, I learned a lot had happened during that time: Billy had set the field behind our housing development on fire and endangered two old mares that were boarded there; Marky got "stuck" in the dryer and required professional extraction by members of the fire department; Patty and Dallas got engaged; Carol Bright called to check on how I was doing and mentioned again how upset she was that her nanny was leaving for college in the fall; and last but not least, Brad apparently ended things with Sue, who threatened another suicide before she met a boy named Brian at the A&W drive-in and was back in love.

Nothing ever changed in the Nash nuthouse.

Chapter Ten

I graduated from Hazen High School in June of 1974, and accepted my diploma wearing a royal blue hat and gown, and in possession of a cute nose. Even Dad noticed, who had surprised us all by attending the ceremony in the company of his mother, my only living grandparent, Willie Nash, all the way from Columbus, Mississippi. I was so nervous during the proceedings that I kept touching my nose to make sure it wasn't a dream. My partner was another honor student I had never seen on campus before. His name was Bill Vann, and finally he asked me if everything was okay.

"Yes, why?"

"Well, you keep touching your nose, like it might fall off."

I laughed and I told him about the septorhinoplasty, adding, "It was my graduation present."

Bill raised a bushy eyebrow. "Oh, I guess you already have a car?" This was followed by a polite trio of spaced-out guffaws: *Ha...ha...ha...*

I liked my partner's laugh and answered, "Actually, no, but I can borrow my Mom's car anytime."

Bill nodded. "My brother borrows my dad's car, too, except he forgets to ask."

I giggled, wishing I had met Bill sooner. He was handsome with a head of thick, curly brown hair, and big brown eyes. After the ceremony, we attended the Senior Party, which was a bus trip to Alpental Ski Lodge, where many members of the class of 1974 were drinking from bottles of booze hidden in socks and coat linings.

On the bus ride home, Bill sat next to me, holding my hand. I was nursing my first-ever hangover from orange juice and vodka, and despite my condition, he asked me out on a date, and of course I said yes.

Having a dainty nose was already opening doors.

In August of that year, President Richard Nixon announced in a televised speech that that he was resigning his presidency following the Watergate Scandal. It was big news sure to change the course of history, but more shocking news was my announcement that I had changed my mind and didn't want to go to college. I had practiced my speech, just as Nixon had.

"Sorry, Mother, but I've given this decision a lot of thought. I believe it is in everyone's best interests for me to stay here, plus think of the money it will save." The last was sure to convince as Mom was always looking for ways to pinch pennies. "So, I guess I'll start unpacking." I thought about President Nixon giving the peace sign to a stunned country. He said he wasn't a crook and didn't want to give up being president, but he had no choice. I felt the same way, resisting the urge to give Mom the peace sign. "I'm glad that's settled."

"I don't think so." Mom replied, unfazed. "You most certainly are going to college. I've already paid for your tuition at Central Washington State College for the semester. Besides, Nancy, why on earth would you change your mind? It's been your dream to go to college to become a schoolteacher since you were twelve."

Bill happened, that's what! In one magical summer, I had fallen madly in love and my heart was breaking at the thought of living three hours away, and over a mountain pass.

"But Mother, I can't leave Bill! Please! Don't make me or I'll die!" I collapsed into a heap on my lilac bedspread, crestfallen in the self-absorbed manner of a forlorn teenager.

Mom folded another sweater and put it in a box. "Don't worry about

Bill. You can visit him on the weekends and the holidays. Believe me, the time will fly by."

I cried myself to sleep that night, doubting my Mother's reassurances, though part of me knew going to college was a privilege and an honor, and something that was made possible only by a trust fund left by my late grandmother, Georgia Taylor. Everyone was proud of me, but going off to college felt like punishment, all because of Bill. Sweet, polite Bill Vann, who *asked* me if I wanted to have sex right after returning home from the Puyallup Fair. Mom already adored Bill but might have been even more impressed at such a display of decency, but how could I tell my mother *that?*

Nothing happened, but I still replayed that night over and over in my head.

"The Puyallup Fair was really fun, Bill. I *loved* those scones!" I was lying in Bill's lap on the sofa bed in the den of our house. I looked up, "And your friend Ben and his girlfriend Laurie seem so nice."

"They might get married when they turn twenty-one. Hey, I'm sorry about begging you to go on the roller coaster with me. I didn't know it would make you throw up."

I grimaced. "Sorry. I'm not much for carnival rides, especially after three raspberry scones." I paused. "Laurie is so brave to go on the roller coaster twice!"

"Laurie's a trooper."

"Boy, is she! She's the bravest girl I know, except maybe Patty." I turned my head over on Bill's chest and listened to his heartbeat, which seemed to be going inordinately fast. "Are you okay?"

Bill cleared his throat and asked nervously, caressing my long straight hair, "Do you want to have sex?"

We had been going steady for nearly three months, and I bolted upright and stammered, "Sex? You mean now? Here?" We were in an alcove of the den next to the laundry room. It was the furthest room from my mother's bedroom, but still, I knew from movies and books that sex was nothing if not noisy and my mother's hearing acuity equaled that of a bottleneck dolphin's. "I don't know. My Mom might hear."

Bill replied hoarsely, "We'll be quiet, plus I came prepared." He pulled out a pack of rubbers.

I stammered, even more nervous looking at the condoms. "Uh, well, um…how about we do it in your car?"

Bill grinned. "Okay."

In our driveway with the porch light off, Bill quietly opened the door to his Chevy Nova and the dome light came on, illuminating a back seat piled high with band equipment, including two speaker woofers and a leather case as big as me that held Bill's guitar.

"Darn it! I forgot I have all this stuff in here. My band is practicing tomorrow."

I suggested, "How about putting the band stuff in the trunk?"

"Can't, my mom's sewing machine is in the trunk. I was supposed to drop it off at the Singer shop to get fixed." He put his hands in his pockets and pulled out the condom. "Guess we won't need this tonight."

I averted my eyes from the rubber. This would be my first time, if we managed the technicalities of location, and I was overcome by insecurity. What if I did it wrong? What if Bill did it wrong? What if we *both* did it wrong and got seriously injured?

I nodded toward the trunk. "Is it one of those sewing machines that weighs a ton? My Mom used to have one. She doesn't sew much because she doesn't have time. I never was good at sewing. I once made a skirt for home ec but sewed the bottom together. The teacher said she liked my choice of fabric, though, so I got a C minus."

"Oh, that's nice." Bill put his arm around me and we leaned against the side of the car looking up at the stars. "My Mom can sew anything. She even made my Dad a suit."

"A suit? Wow."

"Yeah, it's blue tweed and the blazer is double-breasted with gold buttons. Dad wears it to church all the time."

"That's nice." I leaned into my boyfriend and said, "Want to go see *The Exorcist* again instead?"

Two weeks later, after our first sexual encounter, I immediately called Planned Parenthood to go on The Pill. I was seventeen and felt so grown up.

Chapter Eleven

During my first year at Central Washington State College in Ellensburg, I shared a dorm room (F-4) at co-ed Stevens-Whitney Hall with Brenda Landry and two other roommates. Each room in the dormitory had four of nearly everything: Four beds lined in a row across from four closets, a study room with four cubicle-style desks and four chairs, but only one toilet and one shower. There was a tiny living area with a futon-style couch and two end tables.

Brenda also brought with her a T.V. and several varieties of living plants; she was totally into houseplants and they had to be living, not plastic. Another roommate contributed beanbag chairs and a stereo. Unpacking and gossiping, I began to relax and a month later was adjusting to college life and being away from home for the first time in my life. Of course I missed Bill, but his constant (sometimes three in one day!) letters were a heartwarming consolation and, as promised, we saw each other every weekend, when either I went home by bus, or he came to Ellensburg.

In between, college turned out to be equal parts studying (which came easily) and equal parts partying (which took practice). Beer flowed freely and while I had never even tasted beer, soon I was sipping Olympia or Rainier from plastic cups alongside all the other coeds who used any reason they could find to throw a party: Passing grades, no homework, Taco Night at the cafeteria, I-finally-got-my-period. You get the picture.

For Halloween that year, my roommates and I hosted a costume party. For the bash, Brenda's boyfriend Lance, who was already twenty-one, delivered the keg he had rented to our room dressed as a dissected frog. Ropes of plastic innards hung from safety pins at a fake midline incision. Completing the costume was a green T-shirt and green shorts, and his stocky legs were encased in green tights but were not scrawny or bowed enough to look froglike. Overall, however, the costume was unique and might have raised eyebrows had Brenda and I not answered the door dressed as a pair of Paramecia bacteria.

Biology I, a freshman prerequisite, was the inspiration for the costumes, but since Lance Oliver was usually high during biology, he had no clue what his girlfriend and her roommate were dressed as, though he wagered a guess. "Alien cheerleaders?"

Brenda directed Lance where to put the keg. "No, silly, we're bacteria."

I clarified, "*Paramecia* bacteria."

Lance nodded in slow motion. "Bacteria. Very cool." Indifferently, he reached for his green gonads and began scratching. "I'll bet you are the only ones dressed as bacteria at the party."

Lance the Frog turned out to be correct, though most costumes were inspired by Biology I, including four freshmen who had cleverly (and cheaply) formed a sperm chain with ivory sheets and wire hangers, and their girlfriends were lab rats, two white, two black.

After Brenda and I painted our faces Smurf blue, we slipped into blue dancer's leotards painted with brownish-black globs to represent bacteria markings, put on blue plastic shower caps and voila, we looked exactly like the photographs in our Biology I textbook. We got First Place for Best Costume.

A couple weeks later, the much-anticipated Thanksgiving break arrived, and I wasted no time once home to reassert my powers as oldest by calling a family meeting. None of my siblings knew that fueling my enthusiasm, and considerably boosting my self-confidence, was the supercilious gloat of the sexually experienced. There was nothing more potent than being desired by the opposite sex.

Trying to push thoughts of Bill's anatomy from my mind, I used a ball peen hammer to tap the maple coffee table. I was also holding a Pee-Chee and ordered, "Okay, everyone come to order!" I set the makeshift gavel down and began, "You are probably wondering why I called this meeting this morning. Well, it's because—"

"This better be good." Sue moaned as she sat slumped in the La-Z-Boy wearing pajamas that were so big they hang off her hips. She glowered, thin arms crossed. "It's Saturday morning, and I can think of a lot better things to do than listen to you."

"Bear with me, please." Jesus, my baby sister was a brat! I ignored Sue and cleared my throat, flipping my long straight hair ala Cher, my favorite singer of all time, right after Karen Carpenter. "As you know, Mom hasn't been feeling very well lately, since the biopsy, so I thought we would make her a nice dinner. Remember, she's bringing Bob and Jill over after church." I opened the Pee-Chee and retrieved some papers. "I've also drawn up some contracts for each of you to sign."

"You've what?" Sue bolted up and her perky breasts followed. "You've been home one day and already you think you're the boss. I don't have time for this crap!"

Patty agreed. "Nancy, what are you talking about?"

"I'm calling a Truce Peace for Mom." I turned to both brothers, who were separated by Patty and two cushions from the sofa. "Marky and Billy, you will agree to remain apart the entire day, in different rooms, until suppertime. When you pass each other in the hall, you must look the other way and not say a single word, even if it is nice, which I am sure it won't be. There will be no fighting or weaponry used of any kind. If blood is drawn, there will be severe punishment." I handed over a piece of college-lined paper titled "Nash Family Truce-for-a-Day Contract."

"I can't read." Marky pointed and grinned. He was poster-child cute and knew it.

"Just sign it or no more cartoons for the rest of your life." I looked next at Sue. "You, Susan Kay Nash, will not bring up the subject of moving to Dad's all day. In fact, you can't even *mention* Dad's name. And you must agree you will not try to kill yourself, at least till Mom and you work out an agreement." I handed the contract over, shaking my head. "Why you want to move to Oklahoma is beyond me."

"It's my business." Sue grabbed the paper and crumbled it up.

I ignored Sue but smiled at Patty. "You and I, dear sister, will agree to put our sibling rivalry on hold for the entire day. I agree I will not make any snide comments about your rear-end, or Dallas." I paused, mostly to bite my tongue because my perspective on boyfriends had changed considerably now that I actually *had* one. Pre-Bill, Dallas had seemed attractively roguish but now I believed him to be nothing more than an overconfident thug whose peacocking masked an inferior intellect. Somebody should probably tell dimwit Dallas that substance was far more than sporting an arm full of chintzy tattoos. Perhaps if he had joined Debate Club, like my Bill, he might have had a chance. Then again, Dallas McMurtry probably couldn't debate the benefits of breathing oxygen.

Clearing my throat, I added, "And in return you must agree not to call me a bitch and stay out of my room without permission." I showed everyone where to sign. "One last thing."

Lots of groaning, but no one got up to leave.

"All of you must help me clean the house. Top to bottom, especially your bedrooms." I glanced first at Patty, then at Sue, but kept quiet on account of the agreeable nature of the meeting, even though my sisters' shared bedroom was a disaster zone where a maggot would feel disgraced. It was a room overflowing with decay and neglect while my room had fresh hydrangeas in a glass vase and a made bed. "This means we are going to vacuum, dust, wash all the windows, and if it applies, remove all food and dirty clothes from under the beds."

Sue snapped, "I guess, but only for Mom. I'd never do this for you."

Three hours later, the house was sparkling clean, and there was a homemade German chocolate cake on the counter and cheese enchiladas in the oven. We also had a blender of fake strawberry Margaritas waiting in the freezer. I was preparing to tell everyone how proud I was when Billy, who was allowed to ride his bike to the store alone, walked in with a box, inside of which were two adorable kittens. They were crawling over each other and mewling with alert eyes that looked up briefly before commencing with the wrestling.

My brother was always bringing home stray animals, especially if they were free.

Patty scooped up the gray-and-white one and it began purring and snuggled into the crook of her neck. I put the caramel kitten on the floor and it attacked my shoelace.

"Billy, don't you remember what happened in California with the kittens that had ringworm?"

Billy shrugged. "No, I was just a kid."

"You still are. Here, take this." I handed him a five-dollar bill from my jeans pocket and told him to go get kitty litter and cat food, but it was too late. Mom, along with Bob and Jill, were already pulling into the driveway. We hastily hid the kittens behind the piano, still in their box, and shut the den door. Much later, when the Mexican feast was over and the dishes were done, Billy decided to bring out his surprise, keenly aware that Mom's mood was considerably brighter when she was around Bob Adamson.

Mom groaned. "Oh dear, just what we need, more mouths to feed!" She picked up one of the kittens and put it to her nose. "You don't have ringworm do you cutie?" She set the kitten down and recalled for Bob and Jill the Nash Ringworm Incident.

"We were living in Woodland Hills, California, and the girls came home with three kittens from the grocery store. The kittens were darling but had ringworm and all five of the kids got infected! The boys had to have their heads shaved and they had to take this awful medicine. Bill was so mad he threatened to strangle the kittens." She sipped her Margarita and sighed. "We got rid of the kittens but should have got rid of the husband!"

Jill laughed as she leaned over to pick up the one I had already named Garfunkle (and the other Simon), who immediately tried to slip down her shirt. "Kittens are cute and I would love to steal them but I don't think Waggles would like that."

Bob agreed. "One pet is enough."

The phone rang and after Patty answered it, she held the phone out on its short cord. "Mom, it's for you. It's Dr. Harrison. He said it's important."

"Okay, I'll take it on the phone in my bedroom." She patted Bob's shoulder affectionately. "Hold down the fort, Bob, and don't believe a word my kids tell you."

Chapter Twelve

Hospitals had never bothered me. In fact, I had spent more time than the usual youngster in hospitals, beginning with fracturing my left arm when I fell from a tree while picking apples and landed on our concrete patio. It was Fourth of July and my parents had been hosting a neighborhood barbecue and had barely finished their first Harvey Wallbanger when the accident occurred. At the time, I was seven, and a few years later I broke my right tibia and fibula the Saturday before school started, when I jumped to land on a swinging tire and missed. Boys were watching that time and despite the pain, I insisted on walking home, which is why the break required surgery and I spent two months of fourth grade in a full-leg plaster cast.

Then, when I was twelve, my mother and I nearly camped out at Baptist Memorial Hospital in Oklahoma City after Patty shattered her left ankle jumping from a window onto a trampoline. I was supposed to be spotting her, but instead I was playing spin-the-bottle with a boy named Frank. We had snuck out our house way (jumping from our second-story window onto the porch roof) around midnight, explaining why Patty missed Frank's trampoline. Unfortunately, the compound fracture (where the bone fragments broke through skin) was just the beginning of that nightmare: Patty had a severe allergic reaction to the penicillin that was being given intravenously and this induced a coma. A week later, she developed a Staph infection from a cotton roll that had been left in the incision during the complicated surgery and amputation was seriously discussed.

Eventually, Patty made a full recovery, and litigation over medical malpractice was never discussed; Baptist Memorial was where Mom worked, and where I spent the occasional weekend helping her type radiology reports. I didn't get paid, but I did get to go shopping afterwards.

This time, however, things were different. My mother wasn't at her desk typing, she was lying in a hospital bed wearing an oxygen mask with tubes in her arms, and missing her right breast. A plastic bag dripped, a heart monitor bleeped, and sounds from the hallway were a brusque reminder this was a hospital: Moans from pain and wails of grief, the hushed but urgent murmurs, clicking of heeled shoes scurrying over the tile floor, and nonstop sirens.

Just one week earlier, Mom had sat all five of us kids down at the dining room table and announced she had breast cancer. "The Big C." It was devastating news, yet my mom managed to joke, "I'll lose a breast and my hair, but only one will grow back."

Later, when they were alone, Mom told me that the cancer was of a moderately advanced stage, using the medical jargon that bonded us: Infiltrating ductal carcinoma, stage II, with multiple lymph nodes that were positive for invasion. Translation: The cancer had already spread, which is why her surgical excision site was so large, including most of the deep tissues from under her right arm and down the lateral aspect of her chest.

The day after her surgery, I stood at the window of Mom's private room, a courtesy since she was a hospital employee, and looked out at the grounds, scattered with empty benches. My dorm has a similar area, but it was always packed with laughing coeds throwing Frisbees or playing volleyball, or studying in the fresh air. I focused on a large rhododendron tree lying dormant outside the window and wondered the color of its blossoms. Suddenly, a voice from behind startled me.

"Hope Dr. Pepper is okay."

I turned. "Oh, thanks, Patty." I pointed through the window. "I'll bet they're red."

Patty looked, popping the top to her own can of Coke. "What are?"

"The flowers on that rhody. Remember those deep red ones in Cougar Hills? Those were Mom's favorite."

Patty nodded. "They were the raccoon's favorite, too." She sat in a chair in the room and I did the same, watching Mom. Nearby, Sue was sitting onto the floor, slumped against the wall. I asked her, "Do you want something to drink? I can go to the vending machine."

"No! I'm not hungry, and I hate hospitals. They smell like pee." She had her knees pulled up to her chest, and her layered hangs across her pixie face. She mumbled, "I'm glad I'm moving in with Dad, then I won't have to deal with all this crap."

I shook my head in pity, not understanding why my baby sister was so miserable, when a soft moan came from Mom's bed.

We all rushed over. "Mother?" I grasped my mother's frail hand. "Mother?" I repeated, desperate for an answer to tell me she was alive. "Are you okay?"

Mom opened her eyes and licked her dry, cracked lips. "I'm thirsty."

Patty filled a water glass. "How do you feel?"

She lifted one weak arm and put it to her chest. "Five pounds lighter."

We all laughed and then we began to cry.

A few days later, Dad arrived in town get Sue, but no one would have guessed he would also show up in Mom's hospital, too. I honestly did a double take when I saw him. He looked so different from what I remembered. In fact, I hadn't seen my father since my graduation and we never talked on the phone. When he nodded my direction and offered a curt hello, his eyes looked less steely, and sad. He walked to the bed and gazed down. "How is your mother doing?"

I answered, "Okay, they just gave her more painkillers."

"Oh." My father's features were pinched, like he was trying not to cry, though I found this unlikely. He leaned over and patted his ex-wife's limp hand. "I'm sorry, Lois. Truly sorry." His voice was a raspy whisper and that was all he said before straightening and surprising me, his eldest daughter, with a tender hug.

I was speechless yet there was so much to say. *Daddy, why did God give Mom cancer? Daddy, do you still love us?* It was like I was eleven years old again and it was strange I was thinking these thoughts because this man was never my "daddy"; he was the enforcer, a man accustomed to being called Sir.

My father let me go. "You probably already know that Sue is coming back to Oklahoma to live with me and Kay. She's in the car waiting."

"Yes, Sir, I know. I guess it's for the best. She's miserable here."

There was a long, uncomfortable pause.

"Well," my father said, "tell your mother I came by."

I gulped back tears and forced a smile, wanting to prove to him how strong I was. "Sure." *And she'll believe I'm the Queen of England, too.* "Dad?"

"Yes?"

"Drive safely and good luck with Sue. She's a handful." It took every ounce of strength I had not to cry as I watched my father's back as he hurried down the hall, eager to get far from the hospital. When he was out of range, I closed the door and quietly sobbed.

Later, I would ask God how it was possible to love someone I hated, and I begged Him not take my mother when I had already lost my father.

Six days after surgery, Mom was discharged from Overlake Hospital with a Penrose drain in her chest. She was so thin her ribs protruded and the surgeon who performed the mastectomy ordered her to drink lots of ice cream shakes and Carnation Instant Breakfast. He also recommended radiation therapy, in addition to traditional chemo-therapy, but his well-informed patient refused, telling him her body has suffered enough, that she would do chemo, but refused to get zapped by radioactive waves.

The doctor told her it was her choice and she replied, "Damn right it is!"

Over the following weeks, Mom lost her beautiful auburn hair and this was the hardest part for us to watch, but especially for my brothers, who were too young to understand what was happening.

Marky wanted to know if Mom was really a boy and Billy punched his brother's arm, but only lightly; they were mellowing now that our mother had cancer.

"No stupid," Billy answered, "she's just bald 'cause of the medicine." His frightened eyes pleaded, "Right, mom?"

Mom nodded. "Yes, I'm bald today but I won't be soon because I'm going to buy me a sexy blond wig!"

"And a new boobie, too?" Marky asked with wide brown eyes.

Chapter Thirteen

Bill and I tried to see each other every other weekend when I was at college in Ellensburg, but on the rare weekends we spent apart, I hung out with Brenda and Lance and their friends. Sometimes we studied, but mostly we gossiped and partied the night away, usually in a haze of dope listening to The Eagles or Pink Floyd.

I now understood the term *higher education.*

The first time I smoked marijuana, I ate an entire jar of crunchy peanut butter with a butter knife. No crackers, no celery, no bread. Just the butter knife, and it was the best damn peanut butter I had ever eaten. While I was eating the peanut butter, Brenda was drinking Tequila Sunrises, and Lance (plus approximately fifteen people jammed into his dorm room) were drinking beer and grinning in front of a large-screen T.V. watching *The Wizard of Oz.* The volume on the television was turned off because on the stereo sisters Ann and Nancy of Heart were singing at the top of their lungs.

Brenda picked up a bag of Doritos and shouted over Heart, "Wow! Dorothy is so beautiful! Look at her dewy skin! Look at that golden hair!"

Lance nodded, yelling even louder because the Wilson sisters were trying very hard to make us all understand something about a Magic Man, "Dig those ruby shoes. Brenda, you'd look good in ruby shoes!"

Brenda glanced over at her boyfriend, who had a long blond beard and was cuddly in a big, bearish sort of way. "And nothing else?"

"Yeah!" Lance's gaze was transfixed on the T.V. "I never noticed how fuckin' real the witch's castle looks. And those flying guardsmen! Man, those are fuckin' amazing special effects!"

I giggled and shouted loudly, "Toto is so damn cute. I want a Toto dog."

"Nancy, you look like Toto."

Next, Pink Floyd's "Brick in the Wall" album began playing on the stereo and the entire room went into a PF trance, mouthing the words to "Dark Side of the Moon," while on the T.V. Dorothy was tripping out in a poppy field and Toto was kidnapped by flying monkeys. Smoke filled the room and the T.V. was a blur, and when the Doritos were gone and Dorothy was in the Land of Oz, we ordered pepperoni grinders to be delivered.

They were the best damn grinders I ever had.

For our second Halloween Party at college, it was a food theme that was pervasive at Stevens-Whitney, and Brenda and I dressed as a pack of Oreo cookies, proudly proclaiming on our black poster-board cookie shell (with white leotards for the cream filling): *"Please don't fiddle with the Oreo middle!"*

Lucky for me, Bill attended our party, too. After discussing it, he decided to transfer his community college credits to Central to study Accounting and Business Management and was assigned a room at the same dormitory as me. His roommate, who was also named Bill (so my Bill was Big Bill and the roommate was Little Bill) were the only ones at the party not dressed as a foodstuff and were Third Reich Generals.

Lance was supposed to be a Tootsie Roll, but he was so big and bulky and brown that he resembled something a dog left on the lawn.

During the party, and after I has three plastic cups of beer to Brenda's six beers and two shots of tequila, we decided to entertain the troops. I jumped up onto the futon-style couch. "Attention everyone!"

Near my feet, Brenda banged a bong against the side of a stein, but that wasn't loud enough so she did one of those whistles where you put two fingers between your lips and exhale. It sounded like a train coming to a screeching halt. The entire room stopped talking and looked up.

"Quiet!" Five-foot, nine-inch-tall Brenda Landry ordered and then announced, without slurring a word. "Listen up! My Little Friend and I would like to sing a song!" She looked at me and grinned. "In Spanish!"

"Si, Si!" I squealed. Brenda and I were in Spanish I together and while I was barely passing the course, I loved our professor, Miss Garcia, who took us on field trips to Mexican Restaurants. My arm was glued to one of Brenda's shoulders because the futon was flimsy, not to mention I was as drunk as a sailor. I said, "Yeth, tonith we wuth like to theeng a vewy thpecial thong!"

Brenda did one more shot of tequila and asked me, "Ready, Little Friend?"

Forgetting I was unable to sing in English let alone a foreign language in which I had had a month of study, I answered giddily, "Si Si!" What happened next might have been avoided had I flashed back to the time in third grade when, during "Show and Tell," I got up in front of my class and tap-danced a three-minute routine wearing a pink tutu. I had one week of tap lessons under my belt and knew I was a lousy tap dancer so I began singing the only show tune I knew, "Hello, Dolly." Third grade only went downhill from there, and Woodland Hills Elementary School would be just another bad memory.

I slurped more beer and said to Brenda, "Um weady!" And together, we belted out a drunken duet:

"El Sabado en el parke, we theenk it was el quatro de Hoo-leo!!!"

After getting through two verses mostly in Spanish, we began stripping and the last thing I remember was Bill helping me off the futon and tucking me into bed. He was at my bedside the next morning with seltzer and aspirin, when I promised never to drink beer again. I reached for my Afrin and did two quirts in each nostril. I was totally dependent on nasal spray to breathe, a side effect of the nose job. I sniffled deeply and told Bill, "I will never, ever drink beer. Just the thought of beer is gross, and I feel so bloated."

Bill pushed my limp bangs from my face. "Wow, you said you can't sing, and you really, really can't sing."

"I know. It's a birth defect that runs in my family." I eyed my Afrin bottle, which was almost empty. "I hate being stuffed up all the time."

"I could give you lessons."

"On what? Breathing through my nose?"

"No, singing lessons. Music is a vital part of life. I can't imagine not being able to sing."

I tossed the Afrin bottle onto the bed and took another sip of seltzer. "Don't waste your time, Bill. It's useless. I used to mouth hymns at church so I wouldn't embarrass my Mother."

Bill leaned over and kissed my forehead, "It's okay if you can't sing. There's still tennis, and your serve is getting a lot better."

"Sure," I agreed lamely. "There's still tennis."

My high school sweetheart was a "keeper" boyfriend, and the list of reasons why was long: Bill was chivalrous, athletic, polite, good-looking, funny, multitalented, and intelligent. He opened doors for women (risky during the growing popularity of the women's liberation movement) and didn't grope. The closest thing he ever did to breaking the law was dining-and-dashing at Denny's. Bill owned a car, a stereo, and had a record collection taller than Brenda Landry. His parents, Barb and Bill Senior, were happily married and owned a split-level in a nice quiet neighborhood near Lake Washington. The household also included another brother and a sister, both younger, as well as the proverbial cat and dog.

In addition, Bill was a straight-A student who could water-ski on *one* ski and before he even graduated from high school, had climbed both Mount Rainier and Mount Hood. His three-part laugh was genuine and infectious, and it always brightened my day.

Finally, to show his commitment to our relationship, he had transferred from community college in Renton to Central in Ellensburg. It was a huge sacrifice.

His only fault, in my opinion, was his obsession with playing tennis, which meant every available day it was not raining was spent at a tennis court. Bill was an excellent tennis player, not surprisingly, and looked quite attractive in tight white shorts, but even without that distraction, I loathed playing tennis and felt like I was holding a gigantic fly swatter, which despite its size rarely connected with a ball. Bill shouldn't have bothered keeping score (which had to be shouted for all to hear and was another reason to hate the game) because he always won, and by the end of the so-called "match" I wanted to swat Bill's 'fro into the next school district.

It was while playing tennis, in fact, that we had our very first argument, during which I tossed my brand-new tennis racket towards the park like a Frisbee. It bounced three times before it landed, and Bill blandly pointed out that was roughly the same number of times the tennis ball usually bounced when it was in my court. The remark made me cry, as did the stupid one-bounce rule. I told Bill if I was going to keep playing tennis, I wanted at least *two* bounces and silent scorekeeping.

"Practice makes perfect," Bill had answered. "Besides, it doesn't matter who wins, just who tries the hardest." Then he jogged over, picked up my racket and ran back, handing the Dunlop over. He wasn't even panting. "Tomorrow we'll practice your serve."

Tomorrow I'll be locked in the bathroom soaking my bunions. "I guess, but don't you ever get tired? I mean, of playing tennis and always being on the go? Rock-climbing, water-skiing…"

Bill shrugged his broad, well-muscled shoulders. "No, I'm used to it. My parents taught us early on to not be afraid to try new things." He cocked his head clearly hoping the message would get through. "They've raised us to be diverse individuals."

"You mean risk-takers, don't you?" I stuffed my racket into its cover. "By the way, do your parents still have Family Forum Night?"

"Sure. Mike keeps me updated. He said last week Sally told Mom and Dad she was on the Pill. I guess dad got real red in the face and had to leave the table."

I shook my head. If I had told Dad I was on the Pill at age fourteen (not that my father spent any quality time around the family dining room table, especially if the purpose was to allow his children to discuss important personal issues and voice their opinions on current events), I would have been disowned first and disemboweled second.

Bill said, "Mike thinks Dad went into the garage to smoke. I guess he's been smoking more lately. My parents aren't perfect but they are pretty open-minded and like to keep the lines of communication open."

Actually, I thought Bill's parents *were* perfect, which was part of a growing problem for me: The whole perfect-family idea incited antipathy (or was it envy?) and I began to fantasize about being with wild, flawed boyfriends like Lance and Dallas, guys who smoked and spit and lived on the edge. Bad, bad boys with lax parents who wouldn't dream of holding Family Forum Night but might entertain the thought of sleepovers with the opposite sex.

I thought about seven-year-old Stevie and wondered how he had turned out. Was he still a bully? Did he prefer tennis or Harleys? Good grades or cold beer?

I was growing restless and discontented with Bill, and I knew why: He was too normal and nice! Thus, I began creating my own excitement (read: chaos) by picking fights with him. The desired outcome of a Big Scene with lots of yelling and screaming would have been achieved with any member of my family, with the possible exception of my mother, but with Bill, it was a ploy that failed because his reactions were always perfectly thought through, and began with "I see."

I *saw* nothing and screamed and shouted even louder looking for some kind of reaction. Finally, I'd begin throwing things because that was the hallmark of an ace fighter, but Bill remained annoying calm. Even so, I couldn't admit to him that it was an addiction—like M&M's and puffed Cheetos—this craving of a good fight followed by breaking up and making up, because even I didn't understand this need. Countless times, I broke up with Bill but he wouldn't break up with me, even the time I said I was really, really breaking up with him for good.

"I can't go on like this!" I wailed, now in full Drama Queen mode. "You just don't understand! I hate having a boyfriend who's so smart and good at everything. And I hate tennis! It's killing me!"

Bill put his hands on my shoulders in a paternal gesture. "You're getting much better, especially your serve. Hey, how about some iced tea and you can rest on my waterbed."

I threw myself face first onto Bill's waterbed wishing Bill would forget about tennis and get a tattoo, or maybe, just once throw something back at me. For five minutes I sulked, listening to the gurgling sounds of his roommate's aquarium. Eventually I peeked up over my shoulder, the Drama Queen deflated and replaced with The Princess. "I'm sorry, Bill. I really don't want to break up. I guess I am tired."

Bill sat down, his hands on his thighs. "I know. Things will work out, don't worry." He paused. "Maybe tomorrow we can play doubles with Little Bill and Gina?"

Chapter Fourteen

To cover the costs of my textbooks and fashionable wardrobe, I found a part-time job before and after classes for the Advertising Department of the college, a job that involved filing, typing memos and letters, as well as writing ad copy for the school newspaper. I had my own electric typewriter, and my boss, Mr. Stillwater, would hand me three pages of copy to type and ten minutes later I would hand it back, asking for something else to do. This shocked Mr. Stillwater because most of the part-timers who worked for him were inefficient bubbleheads who couldn't wait to get off work so they could go party or make out. But I was different: I always stayed late when asked, brought him coffee and sometimes a snack or sandwich from the vending machine, and delivered a copy of the school newspaper to all heads of each department by 6:00 a.m., using a borrowed bicycle to do it, rain or shine.

Eventually I earned a reputation in the department as the most loyal secretary Mr. Stillwater had ever had. Most girls lasted two weeks tops, but I worked for Mr. Stillwater for the entire school year. Right before summer semester began, Mr. Stillwater announced he would be leaving Central Washington State College and moving his family to Spokane, but told me I still had a job working for his replacement.

Mr. Stillwater also offered me one last task—unrelated to department business—as minutes' keeper for the International Order of Job's Daughters, who were holding their Leadership Conference on campus in McConnell Auditorium. The pay was a flat fee of thirty dollars for "about two hours' worth of work" (including deciphering notes and typing them up), plus a formal dinner. His oldest daughter would be one of the attendees, and Mr. Stillwater told me, "Please wear your best dress, but nothing too ostentatious, and put your hair up or back. This organization is quite reserved and by-the-book."

The day of the conference, it was 98 degrees and hordes of young, allegedly reserved girls between the ages of eleven and twenty began filing into the auditorium, which quickly filled with a girlish, preadolescent trill. The hall was usually air-conditioned but this day the air-conditioning was out of order, and attempts by an overworked crew to correct the situation caused a delay of more than hour.

I sat patiently, wearing (in deference to Mr. Stillwater's advice) a beige skirt, buttoned-up white blouse, and taupe suede wedgies, at my designated spot on a bleacher, composition notebook and ballpoint pen at the ready. I was using my program to fan my face like everyone in the room, which was become more stifling by the minute. The doors were open but there was no breeze, unusual since Ellensburg was known for gale-force winds on cloudless days.

My hair was up in a tidy bun but perspiration pooled on my neck and between my legs, where my pantyhose threatened to cut off vital circulation. To pass the time, I reexamined my program and jotted down the Job's dogma, deciding this was probably important to include in the minutes: *In all the land were no women found so fair as the Daughters of Job; and their father gave them inheritance among their brethren. Job 42:15.*

I looked up and across the auditorium, picked out Mr. Stillwater when suddenly someone screamed and Job's Daughters from all angles began dropping like flies in the dark auditorium, whose lights had been dimmed so as not to add to the temperature. I watched in horror as Daughters toppled over in a domino of pastel frocks, and adults began yelling orders:

"Call an ambulance!"

"Call my mother!"

"Call Engineering to fix the damn air-conditioning!"

I scrambled to my feet but it was pandemonium, and soon the auditorium's occupants were evacuated onto the lawn, where finally there was an early evening breeze. I plopped on the grass, making sure my skirt covered my knees, and began making notes in her notebook.

The illnesses were later attributed to a combination of the heat wave and Salmonella poisoning, likely acquired from the catered luncheon that included tuna fish sandwiches and potato salad. Nevertheless, the conference continued without 22 of its delegates (Lucinda Stillwater among them) and when I typed up the conference minutes, I was pleased I had accumulated enough notes to fill four pages.

I mentioned in my report that there was a delay in the proceedings without over-reporting, as instructed by Mrs. Beverly, the Order's spokeswoman, who did not want the food poisoning to taint (her word) an otherwise remarkable conference.

Barely into my second year at college, I changed majors, deciding after one year of prerequisites that included the scourge of all subjects— mathematics—that I really wasn't really cut out to be a schoolteacher if math was involved. Spelling, reading, writing, *those* were subjects I could teach, but math was a mad mix-up in my mind.

Of course, my career counselor, as well as Bill (who could perform complicated math equations in his head!) were quick to point out that math was one of the basic studies, essential to any degree. Upon hearing this, I told my counselor, Mrs. Cooley, that math was a basic all right, a basic pain in the behind that should never have been invented.

Bill offered to help and said, "You can get better in math. We'll start with flash cards, but you have to try."

Trying was everything to Bill, and I moaned. "Great, that'll make me feel like I'm in kindergarten all over." I leaned over and murmured, "I'll pay you to do my math homework, if you know what I mean." I winked with the innuendo and tried to look sexy, but mascara streamed from my face from the crying jag at Mrs. Cooley's office, plus I was wearing Brenda's baggy sweats, which were two feet too long and being worn because my Swabbies were covered in vanilla pudding and chocolate sauce, a direct result of the emotional encounter in the aforementioned counselor's office.

Bill reached for paper and pen and asked quite seriously, "Do you want to graduate or not?"

"Yes, of course, but I also want Central to drop all math from their curriculum and replace it with something else, maybe a class called 'Lifetime Strategies for Avoiding Math Forever'."

"That would be redundant," Bill answered. "Lifetime would imply forever, and I think you mean curricula, not curriculum."

I rolled my eyes. My boyfriend was not being at all helpful, despite the smug look. I asked petulantly, "Can't you for once let *me* be the smart one?"

"Sure, but you'll have to try."

It turned out the change in majors was a no-brainer. My veins coursed with medical terminology, so it was natural for me to enroll in the newly formed Medical Transcriptionist Program at Central, a two-year course taught by a beautiful young teacher we called Miss Michele. There were only nine students enrolled that semester, and Miss Cooley was able to devote a great deal of one-on-one attention to her students.

Bill was proud that I studied so hard, bringing home index cards of medical terms every single night, practicing words with mostly Greek or Latin origins over and over: Achalasia (failure to relax of smooth muscle fibers of the gastrointestinal tract); anoxic encephalopathy (lack of oxygen to the brain), ectropion (eversion of the eyelid), hematochezia (the passage of bloody feces), hematuria (blood in the urine), lymphadenopathy (enlarged lymph nodes), pneumothorax (air in the pleural space, which was another word for lung), dyspareunia (painful intercourse), and so forth. It was almost like I was in medical school!

Chapter Fifteen

After I changed majors, I continued working for the Advertising Department, promoted from secretary to office assistant/receptionist, and began working for Mr. Stillwater's replacement, a 27-year-old man named Carl Callahan, who wore baggy khakis and didn't tuck his shirts in unless he had to go to a staff meeting. I liked Carl (though found it initially hard to call my boss by his first name), especially his easygoing manner. Mr. Stillwater had been a drill sergeant in comparison to Carl and because of this, I looked forward to going to my job after classes, where Carl began teaching me all about the fascinating world of print photography. In the darkroom, I learned how to process negatives into photographs, how to correctly mix the developer chemicals in large metal pans, how to shoot film in sunlight, how to cut-and-paste together a school newspaper, and how to actually compose advertising copy geared to sell whatever product it was promoting.

In December, with a two-week Christmas break looming, Carl asked me to stay on campus to work on the winter catalog, at premium pay, but I longed to be home and with Bill, and declined the offer for overtime. When I got home, waiting for me was a letter sent First Class from Carl, which was filled with flattery and accolades about my secretarial skills. Whimsical pencil illustrations of tiny cameras and typewriters and rolls of undeveloped film decorated the border of the handwritten note.

Two days later, another letter arrived from Carl. Excitedly, I tore it open. Unlike the other, this began, "Dearest Sweet Nancy." *Uh Oh.*

I locked myself in the bathroom with the package of Lemon Crème cookies I was eating for breakfast/lunch and began reading the letter:

December 19, 1975

Dearest Sweet Nancy,

I am compelled to write this letter before I am crushed with the weight of my unprofessed feelings for you. First, I must tell you these few days without you have been agonizing! The office is an empty shell without your beautiful smile and lilting laughter. I realized the moment you left that I am in love with you, and it is a magnanimous, unfiltered, blinding, heart-skipping, toe-tingling love for the most efficient and beautiful secretary on campus!

I nearly dropped the letter and wasn't sure whether she should laugh or cry; Carl was so melodramatic! I took a deep breath, double-checked the lock, and began nibbling on another cookie despite mom's off-the-cuff comment I "finally had some meat on my bones," and read on:

I will completely understand if these feelings are not mutual (but I fervently hope they are!) and I hope I am not coming on too strongly. Initially I tried to reign in my growing fondness but there was nothing I could do! Cupid's arrow has pierced my heart like a gold shank and I see your lovely face and nubile body in my every waking, breathing moment. Whether or not you feel the same way, I will miss you every second of every minute of every day till I see you again.

Love Always,
Carl

Under his signature was a caricature drawing meant to be Carl, with a large red heart pierced by an arrow.

"Omigod!" I sat down on the toilet and re-read the letter, focusing on the word "nubile." I had no idea what that meant so I put the letter in my pants pocket and in the den, retrieved the family dictionary, where I found nubile to mean "of suitable age to marry; marriageable." *Marriageable! Omigod! Omigod! My boss wants to marry me!* In a state of euphoria and near panic, I went back to my bedroom and told my reflection in the mirror: "My *boss* wants to *marry* me!"

Bill's handsome face suddenly appeared so I closed my eyes, not believing this was happening. I plopped on my bed and retrieved the letter, re-reading every word until I had memorized each page. Eventually I packed the letter away in my suitcase, and at dinner sat straighter and beamed broadly, feeling all-powerful in my nubileness. Mother noticed and thought the reason was Bill.

She said, "You and Bill make such a cute couple, and he's the nicest boy."

"Yes, he is." I spooned creamy potato soup into my mouth.

"So, will Bill be coming over later?"

Enough already about Bill. "I guess."

"That's good." Mom put a spoonful of the thick white chowder to her lips and blew on it. "Maybe someday you and Bill will get married?"

I nearly choked on my soup. "Married?" I'm not ready for that!" Inside, my stomach was in knots and all I could think of was that Carl thought I was nubile.

I fell asleep wondering if maybe it was Carl I was going to marry, not Bill? Or would I be torn between two lovers, just like in that Karen Carpenter song? How *cool* would that be?

Chapter Sixteen

Once I was back at college, Carl wasted no time teaching me, his nubile protégé, decidedly un-businesslike things, such as how to have really quiet sex on a rubber mat because the darkroom was in the center of the department, right next to the office coffee machine. I didn't consider what we were doing an affair but more an experiment, which began with a French kiss over a developing pan that left me dizzy, and it wasn't from the chemicals. Carl apologized for being weak and told me I was beautiful, and I reached for his soft shoulders and pulled him into me.

Carl would eventually share that he was a Cancer born on June twenty-sixth, who would turn twenty-seven on his next birthday, that his mother Beatrice was an advertising executive for Frederick & Nelson's in Downtown Seattle, and that his father had recently passed away following a stroke. He was an only child and was single, though had a roommate named Daisy, who "shared his house for free in exchange for cooking and cleaning."

Sounds like a wife, I had commented though Carl didn't respond. Nevertheless, I became infatuated with my boss, who wore his long blond hair in a ponytail and had green basset-hound eyes and a shuffling, careless gait, like it was too much effort to pick up his feet, which were always in Birkenstocks.

On a Tuesday night in mid-March of 1976, when I told my roommates and Bill that I had to work late to meet a deadline, Carl and I snuck out in his 1957 Bel-Air, which was painted aqua and nicknamed "Blue Baby."

Inside Blue Baby, I felt like I was in old man's car, especially tucked under a green wool blanket because the Chevy's heater was "finicky." I squirmed and lowered myself under the blanket and out of view until we were out of town. On the way, Carl talked about Mary Hartman. He was driving leaned back with one arm draped on the steering wheel and one arm around me. His voice was casual.

"*Mary Hartman, Mary Hartman* is the best show on T.V. right now." He slowed and then parked off a logging road, where he smoked a joint he had rolled himself. He turned to face me in the front seat. "You've watched daytime soap operas before, right?"

"Sure, *All My Children* is my favorite."

"Well, *Mary Hartman, Mary Hartman* is a parody of all the classic soaps. Nothing currently in the television media reflects the pathos and absurdity of life as well as this show. It's only been on the air a few weeks but I predict it will be a classic, just like Blue Baby." Carl patted the dashboard. "I only take this out on special occasions. The rest of the time, I walk. Of course, that's easy to do in Ellensburg."

"Not if you weigh a hundred and ten pounds." I hated that about Ellensburg's weather: It could be a beautiful sunny day but nearly every afternoon, strong winds swept down from the mountains and blew trees sideways and scattered leaves and scrawny coeds alike. Pulling the blanket tighter, I felt the darkness of the forest push against the old windows. I turned and said, "It's so quiet out here, Carl. How'd you find this place?"

"I've lived in Ellensburg over seven years now. I know all sorts of secret spots." Carl lit up the joint again, took a hit and handed it over. "Toke?"

"No thanks, my roommates would be suspicious. Remember, I'm supposed to be working."

Carl grinned. "We're working, in a way. I'm educating you about Mary Hartman."

I giggled, "Go on."

After another pull from his Foster's, Carl said, "Mary is a pigtailed housewife who lives in Fernwood, Ohio, and has a sister named Cathy. Cathy's a blond bimbo but she has a good heart. Anyway, Mary's husband Tom is sexually repressed and dimwitted. I think he could be a closet homosexual. Mary is surrounded by bizarre characters, including a streaking grandfather, but what I really appreciate is that this show raises your conscience about the ordinary and makes you see nothing is ordinary, not even yellow buildup." He leaned back dreamily with me at his hip. "So what *do* you watch?"

I answered easily, "*Saturday Night Live* on the weekends. I also like the *Sonny and Cher Variety Show* and *The Waltons*. Actually, *The Waltons* is my favorite show but it usually makes me cry. The Easter episode was the saddest, when Olivia gets diagnosed with polio and then at the end of the episode, she can walk because she thinks she hears Elizabeth calling her, even though the doctor said she would be in a wheelchair for the rest of her life. Stuff like that makes me bawl like a baby. It's embarrassing."

Carl gave me a sideways glance. "You are a most remarkable but strange combination of woman, both passionate yet unsullied. I've never met a woman like you." Carl bent to look up through the windshield. "Wow, look at the all the stars."

I craned for a view, wondering how he could think me unsullied considering what we had been doing an hour before, something that was over before it began with Carl apologizing profusely, saying he had no control. I thought that only happened to guys my age, like Bill.

As soon as thoughts of Bill popped into my head, I felt overwhelmed with guilt. The only thing that helped this feeling was to remind myself that what Bill didn't know couldn't hurt him.

Carl reached over and kissed me. "You taste like…"

"Chocolate?" I pulled a candy bar from my sweater pocket. It was a half eaten Milky Way candy bar. "I snuck a bite before, you know, *before*." I may have been a woman, but I was blushing like a schoolgirl.

Carl's hound dog eyes fluttered. "See, that's what I mean. You're a delicious nineteen-year-old conundrum."

"Conundrum?" I snuggled into the fold of my boss/lover's arm and murmured, "So, does this mean I get a raise?"

Carl kissed the top of my head. "I'll do my best." He whispered hoarsely, placing my hand on his crotch. "First, do you want to touch me?"

The next day, I found a folded note on my typewriter from Carl, who thanked me for brightening his life both in and out of the office, and signed it *"Hugs, Kisses, and Much, Much More, Carl."*

Hiding the note in my purse, I propped up the newest copy for the Central Washington Bookstore onto a metal clipboard, readjusted my chair, and began typing when a woman with a long, thick, gray-brown braid walked into Carl's office. Her face was free of makeup and she was holding a *Happy Days* lunch pail. She said politely, "Oh, hi. You must the new secretary. Where's C.C.?"

"C.C.?"

The woman smiled. "Carl Callahan. C.C. is my pet name for him."

"Oh." I smiled from behind my desk. "Well, Carl is at a department meeting. May I help you?" I glanced down and saw the woman was wearing, under a long flowing skirt, the exact kind of leather sandals as C.C. I had no idea who this woman was but my stomach twisted into knots and instinctively, I crossed my legs under the desk.

The woman sighed. "Oh, well, I'm his wife Daisy and this is C.C.'s lunch. He forgot it this morning, along with his pills." She handed over the lunch pail and turned to leave. Her smile was very kind and she said, "You're prettier than Carl said."

The woman left and I took a quick peek inside the lunch pail and discovered the pills were Dilantin, an anti-seizure medication, and C.C.'s sandwich was whole wheat with bean sprouts and something inside that was white and foam like. My first thought was, if Carl was a vegetarian, and the sandwich would indicate this to be the case, then how come he was so pudgy in the middle?

Secondly, Carl was really C.C. and he was a married epileptic!

I confronted Carl, who told me Daisy wasn't his legal wife but his common-law wife, and this was *way* different than a regular wife, and besides, they hardly ever slept together. He said the relationship was more an arrangement of convenience, plus Daisy was always out of town teaching women about organic gardening. Last week she was in was Walla Walla.

"Orgasmic gardening?"

Carl grinned. "No, silly, *organic*. Don't worry," he cooed," Daisy is more like a sister than a wife. You, however, are my bewitching, nubile lover."

Being called bewitching and nubile was flattering but it didn't overcome my increasing discomfort with Carl's kinky sexual appetite, especially when he invited me to watch porn while Daisy was out of town. I did, once, and felt like a whore. I practically ran back to the campus afterwards and showered for twenty minutes. Carl wasn't even thirty but to me he seemed much, much older, and was definitely over-the-hill.

It wasn't long after that I ended the affair with Carl and went back to being Bill's full-time girlfriend, and the truth was I loved Bill, despite my dalliance with my boss. Proving I wasn't eager to cheat on him again, when his roommate Little Bill came on to me, crawling into my bed at the dorm, drunk and horny, I politely turned him away and told him I couldn't because I loved Bill. Later that year, Bill contracted food poisoning (the source bad roast beef at the school cafeteria) and ended up one of several students confined to the infirmary on IV fluids and antibiotics. I was worried sick, and in the infirmary, I held Bill's weak hand and promised I would always love him.

The promise came from the heart but it was made by a girl who had learned at an early age that promises rarely were kept.

Chapter Seventeen

After I graduated from college, I temporarily moved back home to Renton, where a lot had changed: Laurie and Ben had called off their wedding because they agreed their goals weren't the same (she wanted kids; he wanted a high-tech stereo system), while Mom and Bob had become engaged. Now, it was Patty and Jill who had become best friends, as had John and Billy, and Tom was dating a girl named DeeAnn.

Earlier that spring, while I was still in college, Bob had taken the blended families camping at his favorite spot on Priest Lake in rural Idaho for a week. When they came home, they talked endlessly about their adventures: The big brown bear they had encountered, the fun they had camping and floating on inner tubes in the hot Idaho sun surrounded by unspoiled wilderness. I was envious and missed my family, especially the closeness I once had with Patty, who by this time disliked me so much she played the song "The Bitch is Back" whenever I visited.

I didn't blame my sister. We were complete opposites: Patty was a free spirit who preferred to go barefoot and wasn't afraid of anything. She was a girl who was liked equally by boys *and* girls, and was someone you could take camping without worrying she'd freak out if she saw a snake or learned there was no toilet or shower in the woods.

In contrast, I was the frail, dainty type who not only refused to go barefoot but used a special cream at night to soften my soles, removed my face makeup religiously before turning in, and brushed my long straight hair exactly one-hundred times every day. My overwhelming fear of snakes meant I refused to participate in anything outdoors where the potential of spotting a snake was high, including hiking, camping, even swimming in rivers or lakes, something that drove athletic, adventure-seeking Bill nuts.

I tried to explain to Bill how I was traumatized at age eight when I stepped on a snake while running away from home in search for new parents, and about Charles, a king pet snake owned by a cute French boy named Maurice, who I thought I was going to marry, until I met Charles.

Bill finally comprehended the depth of my fear of snakes the afternoon I was relaxing in a scented bubble bath in preparation for one of our dates. It was midsummer and the bathroom window was ajar, and outside I heard Stu laughing uproariously. When his husky voice was below the bathroom window and way too close for comfort, I sunk lower into the tub and covered my breasts, warning, "Stuart Lynn McGuinn, don't you dare get any closer or I'm calling the police!"

It turned out Stu was mad that I used his stupid girl's middle name and *that's* why he dropped the snake he was holding through the window, even though he said later his original plan was to let it go under the rose bush. From the tub, I watched in slow horrified motion as the snake (a garter species, but does it really matter?) sunk under bubbles and touched a thigh. My screams were so loud and persistent they summoned the police.

Even after that, I think Bill was still holding out hope I'd get over my silly fear of snakes so we could enjoy the outdoors and go on hikes together, but there were other things fighting to put a wedge in our relationship, and that was me, and I didn't even know *why*. I was moody and temperamental, and things came to a head following my mother's wedding to Bob in July of 1977. We had gone back to my house and Bill sensed I was about to deliver bad news, probably because I was fondling the promise ring he gave me.

I sat on my bad and asked him to do the same. "Bill, we need to talk."

Bill remained standing and began nervously chatting. "I really enjoyed your mother's wedding. She looked so beautiful, and healthy. I'm glad the cancer is gone. That was scary. And you can tell—"

"I want to break up, Bill. It's not working." I could not offer any other explanation, though I tinkered with bringing up tennis.

Bill put his head down and was silent.

"I'm so sorry." I removed the dainty diamond promise ring he had given me for Christmas, even after we got in a fight over how to properly decorate the X-Mas tree. "I guess you can have this back."

Bill looked down at the ring and when he looked at me, his eyes were heartachingly kind and pure. "No, that's yours to keep." His voice cracked as he put the ring back on my finger. "I understand that you need to spread your wings. I read this poem about setting something free; if it doesn't come back, it was never yours in the first place. Maybe someday you will come back, I. If not, it wasn't meant to be."

I lost my composure and began wailing, "I'm so confused, Bill! What's wrong with me?"

Bill said, "You're just trying to find yourself."

"But I'm so messed up! And, Bill, I haven't been honest. I mean, I should have told you—" I put my head in my hands and began bawling.

"About you and your boss, Carl?"

I looked up wide-eyed. "You knew?"

"I figured it was just a fling and nothing serious. Carl wasn't your type."

I squeaked through tears, "I'm so sorry."

Bill stood off the bed. "Well, I guess this is goodbye."

"No!"

Bill sat back down. "Nancy, you need to do this for you. Honestly, the last couple of months have been really hard on me, too. I love you, but I can't seem to make you happy."

"That's not true! It's just that…I don't know. I do *care* about you, really."

"I know." He stood and left, closing the door softly behind him. I waited until I heard his car start and then drive away before I threw myself onto my bed feeling ashamed I had just broken the heart of the nicest boy on earth, and not sure why I had done it.

In a daze, I put on my favorite Carpenter's album and when Karen began singing in her velvety smooth voice, "On the Day that You Were Born," I knew Bill was the boy in the song, the one so pure and sweet the angels got together and sprinkled stardust in his hair.

Many years later, I would understand why I had broken up with him: I didn't believe I deserved such a nice boy like Bill.

Chapter Eighteen

My first real transcription job was for Group Health Eastside Hospital, an HMO located in Redmond, Washington. With the income I could finally afford my own one-bedroom apartment, but I quickly discovered the acute-care hospital setting was a lot different from the classroom, or even the radiologist's office where I briefly worked as a receptionist. After nearly eight hours of wearing earphones, my earlobes ached and itched, and my lower back ached sitting in a rolling chair and bent over a typewriter all day. These complaints, however, paled in comparison to how bad my *brain* hurt from the intense concentration required to understand doctors who dictated at warp speed or with their mouths full, not to mention the physicians with foreign accents.

I was entering week three on the job and moaned for a countless time, rubbing my temples. My eyes closed, I asked no one in particular, "What on earth are you saying Dr. Connelly?"

Sheila Marino peeked around the corner of her partition. "Want me to listen?"

I removed my headsets and stood from my desk. "Yes, please!"

I watched over her shoulder as Sheila, my trainer-auditor, listened before handing back the headsets. She stood. "He's saying synechiae."

I grimaced. "Sneaky eye?"

Sheila shook a head of overprocessed hair. "No, *synechiae*, the pleural of synechia, which is an adhesion of the iris to the cornea."

Of course it is. "Oh." I rubbed my temples. "Dr. Connelly is so hard to understand. Are all the doctors this bad?"

"Some are, some aren't, but don't worry, you'll catch on. Ophthalmology is the most challenging, but your work looks excellent."

Thirty minutes later, I was stuck again on a different doctor. *Anatomic snuffbox? That can't be right.* My index cards and college education were failing me miserably! But it was correct, confirmed by Sheila, the office whiz kid, who pointed to her wrist. "Somewhere in there, that's your snuffbox."

I took her word for it. Really, despite the challenges, I found my new career fascinating, and by the end of my first month I was dreaming about hypertrophied prostates, twisted ovaries, cerumen-impacted auditory canals, and detached retinas. I would learn that medical reports usually began with the patient being introduced by an identifying statement:

The patient is a 71-year-old balding, edentulous black male in no acute distress.

The patient is a 22-year-old thin white female in no acute distress.

The patient is a 54-year-old morbidly obese Caucasian gentleman in no acute distress.

Patients were never in acute distress, even when they were balding, missing their teeth, or hideously fat.

After the reports were transcribed, they were placed in the appropriate chart and those charts were placed in a bin. When the bin was full, it was picked up and filed by a clerk from Medical Records. Some reports were "stats," which were high-priority reports, such as preoperative history and physicals or inpatient consultations, which the doctors needed right away. Each transcriptionist had a day when it was her turn to deliver stats. Wednesday mornings it was my turn, and among my stat reports one day was an infectious disease consultation on a twelve-year-old boy with fever of unknown origin, and another five-page report on a woman needing emergency cardiac catheterization.

In the Intensive Care Unit on the second floor, I handed the reports over to the unit nurse and looked up to see Tim Joseph, one of the more popular hospital engineers, standing on a ladder. He was using a flashlight to peer into a hole in the tile ceiling above the nursing station. He called down, "Hey, I think I just found Jimmy Hoffa!"

The charge nurse guffawed. She was a large woman with cropped red hair. She would have been pretty had it not been for all the weight compressing her features. She thanked me for the reports and turned to answer the phone while I looked up at the uniformed legs.

Sheila had introduced me to Tim, who had a reputation for being the hospital Romeo. Rumor had it that he was simultaneously dating a chart-filer in medical records, as well as a nurse on 3 West. Sheila also was pretty sure the charming engineer dated his daughter's third-grade teacher, at least on-and-off. "Tim likes to play the field," Sheila had explained, "And I was one of the players, briefly."

I looked up and joked, "Well, Tim, if you find anyone single and still breathing up there, let me know."

Tim climbed down the ladder, his uniform covered in dust and particles of ceiling tile. He had bright red hair and wore long sideburns and a mustache, and his face was covered with freckles. He was as Irish as one gets. He pointed to the ceiling. "Heck, if I find anyone single and breathing in the attic, I get first dibs!" He brushed off his shirt and then pointed. "I like your skirt. It shows off your legs."

I smoothed my tight-fitting, short yellow skirt and adjusted the wide macramé belt that made my 22-inch waist look even smaller. "Thanks."

"You dress very nice."

"Oh, do I?" I blushed, even though I was fully aware I dressed well. It took me an hour the night before work to gather my outfits, accessories included. That day, my straw-heeled wedges were also yellow, my peasant-style blouse was white with ruffles, and my earrings were white, yellow and black plastic dangles that tied everything together. Dressing smartly was as important to me as doing a good job at the hospital, and being a size two only made that job easier. I waved. "Well, see you around, Tim." I turned and started walking down the corridor. I bypassed the elevator and was approaching the stairwell when I heard someone behind me. It was Tim, who was panting.

"Man, you walk too fast!"

I laughed. "I'm always in a hurry."

Tim reached for the door to the stairwell and allowed me to pass. "Well, I was wondering. Would you like to go out for dinner Friday?"

I didn't hesitate to answer, despite his roving reputation. "That would be lovely." There was *something* intriguing about Tim, and I wanted to know what.

For our first date, I dressed entirely in pale blue, including Revlon eye shadow, a shimmering bell-sleeved blouse, and wide-flared slacks. When I answered the doorbell, I glanced at the clock and was surprised my date was thirty minutes early. I rechecked my appearance and opened the door, but it wasn't Tim at my doorstep, it was Carl Callahan.

"Carl?" It was his second unannounced visit in a month and I regretted giving him my new address, which was a Bellevue condo-converted apartment on the top floor. Like always, my apartment was spotless but I didn't invite Carl in. Last time I did that, we ended up in bed, and when I awoke Carl was nowhere around, having left a note on my pillow apologizing for leaving to "take care of some business." There was something weird going on with Carl Callahan and I wanted nothing to do with it.

"So, Carl, what's up?" I noticed hopefully that this time Carl brought no box of chocolate or flowers.

"Hey, Nancy." Carl had his hands in his pockets and looked stoned. "Remember me?"

"Very funny." I swallowed hard but the lump I developed earlier in the week was still there. "What are you doing here?" I pulled the door behind me and went out to the entryway, hoping he'd get the message.

Carl answered, "Well, I was in town visiting Mother and thought I'd stop by. You look great."

"I have a date." I looked at my watch. In approximately twenty minutes, unless I got rid of Carl, this could get awkward. "Which means I'm kind of busy."

"I guess this means I don't get to come in?"

"Well, like I said—"

"Please?" Carl asked. "I miss you. Not a day goes by that I don't think of you and wish you still loved me." Carl's eyes were green pools full of hope. "I thought, after what happened a few weeks ago, you might, you know."

"I'm sorry, but that was a mistake." How could he not know I had just gone through the motions? In fact, I had to resist the urge to laugh when Carl begged to be spanked for being such a "naughty boy." It was embarrassing, and I got more pleasure from the caramel candies he had brought. Slyly, I asked, "So, how's Daisy?"

"Okay. She started her own aromatherapy business so the house always smells like bergamot and jasmine. It's cool, though. I had this killer migraine but after a lavender and rose-hip treatment, the pain was gone and I slept like a baby. Daisy knows her exotic oils."

I wondered what I ever saw in Carl. "That's nice."

"Yeah, let me know if you're ever constipated. Daisy brews up this all-natural laxative."

"That's nice." I needed to be firm, but I just couldn't. The man looked like a kicked puppy. "But I'm pretty regular."

Carl nodded. "So, can I come in? I need to use the little boy's room."

I sighed, "Sure, but maybe you can hurry?"

"Don't worry. I only have to go number one." Carl winked as he passed on his way to my tiny bathroom and after a long interval finally came out just as there was a knock on my door. I opened the door with Carl by my side. He introduced himself and Tim looked charmingly beleaguered.

"Nice to meet you, Carl." He turned to me. "Am I here at a bad time?"

"No, of course not." I swallowed hard and gently pushed Carl out the door. I waved goodbye. "Bye, Carl."

Tim turned to watch the balding man shuffle off on "Jesus" sandals. When Carl rounded the corner, Tim asked, "Did he smell like pot to you?"

I sighed. "Yes, bean sprouts and pot. Anyway, come in." I opened my front door, wondering if our first date was too early in the relationship to ask Tim to install a deadbolt. I explained, "Carl's an old friend from college. He's here visiting his mother in Seattle."

"Friend? He looked love struck." Tim stepped in and handed me a fresh bouquet of flowers. His eyes swept the room. "Wow, very nice place. It's neat and tidy. I like that." He walked over to the slider to gather in the view of Old Bellevue below. "I'm glad you're on the top floor. It's much safer." He turned. "You look fantastic. You'll blow them away where I'm taking you."

I thanked him and went to my kitchenette to put the flowers in the only vase I owned. Minutes later, we were seated in a vinyl booth under a ceiling decorated with baseball bats and sports memorabilia, plus peanuts on the floor. The place was Tim's favorite watering hole, a tavern called "The Mustard Seed."

The tavern was cool and dark, and most patrons were in jeans. One woman standing near the bar was holding a cue stick in one hand and a large mug of beer in the other, dressed in a flannel shirt three sizes too big, and a baseball cap. Unkempt bangs hid most of her face. She could have been thirty or sixty; it was hard to tell. She bent to break and the pool balls cracked. Some even landed in the pockets and I was tempted to clap. Across from me, Tim was filling me in on his life.

"Well, I should tell you I've been married twice. I'm Catholic and knocked them both up, so what's a guy to do? Plus, my Mother would have hung me by my fingernails if I didn't make honest women out of them." Tim stubbed out one cigarette and lit another, talking through a haze of smoke. "I was only eighteen the first time I got hitched to Rusty. Anyway, she gave me custody of our daughter, Angela, moved to Alaska, and is shacked up with some guy in the woods with no running water. I guess they trap fur for a living, in between growing dope."

While other girls on such a first date would have been dreaming up excuses to end the date early, I was captivated. Our pizza arrived and I accepted a small piece, which I ate with a fork. "Tell me about your kids."

"Angie turns eight in a week, and Mark will be four this October. He lives with his mother in Des Moines and I only see him when Carole lets me, which isn't very often. She's remarried and is someone else's problem now."

"So your daughter's name is Angela? That was my favorite name growing up. I promised myself if I ever had a daughter, that's what I would name her. I even have a doll named Angela Jean." I was convinced this wasn't a coincidence but a sign of something good.

"Really? Well, my Angela is the apple of my eye, but after Mark was born, I was done with kids and got a vasectomy. I heard it hurts like hell but my doc gave me morphine. Like I told him, 'Doc, you gonna mess with my balls, I need to be out like a light.'" Tim extinguished an unfiltered Marlboro into a plastic ashtray. "Didn't feel a thing for a week." He was grinning like a Cheshire cat.

"Good drugs will do that." I smiled just as a bad case of heartburn set in. I put my fork down and pushed my half eaten piece of pepperoni pizza away. "I usually don't trouble with spicy food, but I seem to have heartburn all of a sudden."

"Hope you don't have an ulcer."

My eyes went wide. "An ulcer? I'm only twenty-one!"

"I was too the first time I got one. Divorce does that."

I swallowed. "I don't think it's an ulcer, maybe just nerves." I looked down to examine the broken peanut shells at our feet. I was glad I wasn't in charge of cleaning the tavern's floor.

"Hey," Tim reached over and patted my arm. "I've been doing all the talking so now it's your turn. What's your story, Nancy Nash?"

"*My* story?" I sat back, not sure what to say. "I don't have a story. I'm just a regular gal." Of course, "regular" in my case meant someone who dabbled in witchcraft as a teenager, loved ghosts, feared snakes to the point of phobia, and never, ever stepped on spiders, believing them sacred reincarnations of my grandparents. I was about as regular as a constipated pigeon.

Tim quipped, "A regular gal, huh? That might have to change. So, tell me about Carl."

I shrugged. "He was my boss at a job I had on campus. I went to Central in Ellensburg to study to be a teacher but changed my mind. Anyway, Carl and I had a fling, but it's over. He's just having a hard time accepting it." I swallowed a lump in my throat. "He's way too granola for me."

"Your boss, huh? I would think the college would have rules about managers fooling around with beautiful young co-eds."

I suppressed a burp. "I'm sure they do, but we kept things low-key." I sipped my beer hoping the carbonation would help. It did, to a slight degree. I didn't want to talk about Carl any more so I changed the subject. "So, Tim, tell me more about your life. It's much more interesting that mine, I'm sure."

It was more than interesting, it was Hollywood fascinating: Following graduation from high school, Tim and his best friend Danny spent the entire summer traveling through Europe with backpacks and not much else. In Amsterdam, he said they smoked hashish in open tents from huge brass bongs (one of which he brought home as a souvenir) and hopped from hostel to hostel. In Spain, they both paid for hookers, and Tim later drank homemade red wine from a street vendor and danced in the streets all night. Unfortunately, whatever was in the wine was bad and landed Tim in a Madrid hospital with a severe case of encephalitis, from which he said he narrowly escaped death. He used the layman's term, "water on the brain."

I enjoyed the way Tim told his stories in a spirited, tangential manner, and hung onto every word despite the waves of nausea. Eventually, however, I had to end the date early. At my apartment doorstep, Tim told me to feel better, kissed me chastely on the cheek, and asked me out on another date.

"Sure," I answered, "And I have just the place you can take me: My sister's wedding."

Tim replied without hesitation, "As long as it ain't *my* wedding, I'm game."

I was still laughing when I locked my apartment door. I walked to the bathroom for some Pepto-Bismol, where I found a manila envelope with my name sitting on the toilet seat. Gingerly, I opened the envelope and out fell a set of photographs.

The color photos were of Carl, or more precisely his uncircumcised genitalia. Accompanying the lewd, albeit professional photos, was a handwritten note that read, "Here's something to remember me by." The photos were up close and personal, and in them Carl's erect penis bore a striking resemblance to a Twinkie. Gazing at the pictures, I realized the full impact of Carl's heavy reliance on boasting about his girth rather than his length. Poor man was hung like a chipmunk!

Quickly, I gathered up the envelope and its contents and dumped them all into my apartment complex's dumpster.

Chapter Nineteen

Here's the good news: Patty was not marrying Dallas McMurtry, although he had asked her to marry him (when she was seventeen) and she sort of said yes, but that was before the robbery.

Really, Dallas' story was a sad saga, and began when he told Patty he was going to Montana to visit his dying grandmother in a nursing home, but in reality was there for the sole purpose of holding up a jewelry store in Missoula in order to procure a properly expensive diamond engagement ring for his teenaged girlfriend. It appeared the 20-year-old outlaw had thoughtfully planned the robbery, picking a familiar shop near a vacant lot, armed with a fake pistol and a mean scowl. Unfortunately, the owner of the jewelry/pawn shop was a crotchety old fart with poor vision and a .38 Magnum, which he used to effectively abort the crime (missing Dallas's head by a mile, he would later brag), allowing him to escape unscathed. Then, two days after his twenty-first birthday and while in a highly intoxicated state, Dallas stole a Toyota Celica low on transmission fluid. Stuck on the side of the freeway, he was arrested and ordered to serve thirty days in jail.

Her outlaw boyfriend doing jail time was the straw that broke the proverbial camel's back, and the first person Patty turned after she broke up with Dallas was Bob's son, Tom, whose consolation was so complete it was *he* she marrying. It was kind of like Greg Brady marrying Marcia Brady, but then kind of not, because we never actually lived under the same roof as a family, and most of us viewed it as a match made in heaven.

Their wedding took place in the backyard of a rented rambler on an unusually warm and sunny April afternoon. For the occasion, Patty wore an ivory-and-lace Gunny Sax dress, Tom wore a borrowed blue suit, and I wore a white polyester pantsuit accessorized with a red silk blouse and matching fringed scarf, plus red sandals. In pictures, I look like a short, blond John Travolta in *Saturday Night Fever* and can't believe it was *on purpose*.

Stirring things up was Patty's bride-of-honor, a 19-year-old hottie named Tiffany, who wore a cream gauze dress that in direct sunlight revealed she had nothing on underneath. For this reason, some of the guests had difficulty attending to the matrimonial proceedings, officiated by a Justice of the Peace named Marigold in front of a raised garden of yellow rhodies. As soon as Marigold announced the happy couple husband and wife, guests scattered, some heading for the keg, others to the punch bowl, still others to Tiffany's table.

It was at the punch bowl where Tim asked me in hushed tones, "Okay, so let me see if I have this straight: Tom is Bob's son. Bob is married to your mother so he is your stepfather. So your sister just married her own stepbrother?"

My heartburn was back and I burped as ladylike as I could. I gave him the explanation I would give any one who asked the same thing. "Yes, but it wasn't a *Brady Bunch* scenario. See, Mom and Bob got married after us kids were all grown and out of the house. Well, except for my baby brothers, and John."

"Oh." Tim used a ladle to scoop up pink punch. "Just one more thing. If they have kids, won't that be weird?"

I was spared from answering when Mother walked up. She didn't look too happy.

Nancy, can I speak to you...alone?"

"I guess." I glanced nervously at Tim, who smiled. "Excuse me, ladies. I'm going to mingle."

I watched my date as he headed for the keg, where Tiffany, whose honey-colored hair fell like a waterfall down her back, was the center of attention. Then I turned back to Mom. "What is it? Is something wrong?" Whenever she looked worried, I immediately thought it was her cancer coming back. The possibility loomed with every ache and pain she shared, and until she reached the five-year mark of being cancer-free, I would constantly worry.

"Nothing's wrong, but honey? Where on earth did you find that guy?" Mom pointed towards the keg. "Tim looks too old for you, and there's something, well, funny about him. I can't put my finger on it."

I relaxed. "Jeez, Mom, I thought it was serious! Yes, Tim *is* funny. That's what I like about him; he makes me laugh."

Mom arched an eyebrow. "I didn't say he was funny. Anyway, the guy smells like a tobacco factory and looks like Howdy Doody! I'm telling you, he's not your type. You're smart and beautiful, and you can do better than Tim, trust me. He has the same cheating eyes and mannerisms as your father."

"Mother, please!"

She sighed. "Nancy, you should have stuck with Bill. He was such a nice boy."

"Yes, he was." I was getting irritated and eyeing an escape. "But he wasn't for me."

"Well, please consider my advice: Leave the bad boys for the bad girls. You'll thank me later."

I did an eye roll, resisting the temptation to remind my mother this is exactly what *her* mother told her when she started dating Dad, but the only thing that would prove was that mothers were always right. I took a sip of punch and said, "Don't worry, Mom, we're just casually dating. Tim's not ready to settle down." I didn't mention two failed marriages was the reason. "Guess what? Tim has full custody of a daughter named Angela, just like my doll! I haven't met her yet and have only seen pictures, but she is so adorable!"

"He has children? Oh dear! You're headed for trouble if you get mixed up with that."

I joked, "Define trouble." Out of the corner of my eye, I saw Linda and her new husband Aaron Kelso chatting with some guests. "Oh, sorry,

Mom, I hate to cut you short but I need to go talk to Aunt Linda. I haven't seen her since she got married!"

Mom's hands shot up in the air. "I can only offer advice, not live your life for you."

For our next date, Angie's 8th birthday in late April, Tim picked me up from my Bellevue apartment and thirty minutes later we were approaching a small town called Duvall, nestled in the Snoqualmie Valley of East King County. My window was down and I resisted the urge to pinch my nostrils. The smell of manure was stifling.

Tim grinned. "Welcome to God's country."

I fanned my face. "Well, Tim, if Duvall is God's country, He's missing a complete set of olfactory functions."

"English, please."

"Our Lord can't smell." The valley smelled like a manure factory mixed with an odor I didn't recognize and to get there we had traveled down a two-lane road that cut through a forest and down a winding hill that ended in a valley.

Tim turned over a bridge and slowed, pointing. "That's the Snoqualmie River. Right there is where Tom and I put in our raft last year for the raft race during Duvall Days. Halfway through, we ran out of beer and then our raft got a leak and we dragged it out and ran through the field. We got disqualified but we reached the Duvall Tavern in record time."

"Duvall Days? This town has its own days?"

"Yep, third weekend in May. Town goes crazy. Last year Angie got her face painted by a clown and Tom dunked me in one shot. Later, after all the kids go home, the real party ends up at the Duvall Tavern, but only if owner is in good mood."

"Who's Tom?"

"My roommate. He's up in Alaska working on the pipeline. Every week, he sends me his paycheck, which I cash and put into a pair of cowboy boots. Tom doesn't believe in banks."

"Tom sounds interesting."

Tim nodded. "He's getting richer by the week and only digs fat chicks.

Not me; I like my women skinny. Anyway, that's why Tom gets along with Bricks. She's one big ton of fun."

"Bricks?" My head was spinning from stimuli, most prominently the noxious fumes wafting up from the fields.

Tim lit up another cigarette and explained, "Bricks is the owner of the tavern. She's called that because she's built like a brick shithouse and will eighty-six anyone who doesn't follow the rules at her *fine establishment,* which is the only place in town where you can get pickled pigs' feet."

"You're kidding, right?" A belch passed my lips and I patted my chest. "Sorry."

Tim reached over and patted my thigh. "Don't tell me you have never tried pickled pigs' feet?" They were now passing a turn-of-the century house with spires and turrets behind a field of llamas. He pointed, "Back by the woods is the haunted house. It goes up for sale almost every year."

I turned in my seat to get a better glimpse. "That house is haunted? By who?"

"A ghost, I guess."

I laughed. "I know a ghost, but whose ghost? Most ghosts are the spirits of murdered people who can't let go. My sister Patty saw a ghost but it was our Grandpa Taylor and he didn't get murdered, he just died of cancer so he was an exception. I think he meant to visit me but I was in the basement practicing to be a witch." I paused. "I was twelve and obsessed with wanting to be able to cast spells. Making my boobs bigger and my nose smaller were at the top of my list, along with making a few younger siblings disappear."

Tim nodded. "I wanted to be Spiderman." He flicked his cigarette out his window. "Actually still do."

I giggled. "I'm rather fond of spiders, so we'll get along just fine."

Minutes later, we were within Duvall City Limits and Tim turned up a hilly street directly across from the Duvall Tavern and into the driveway of a yellow rambler. "Welcome to my pad. I hope you're hungry."

I *was* hungry, since the only thing I'd eaten all day were breath mints and a Kit-Kat candy bar.

The birthday girl turned out to be a shy befreckled redhead with green eyes framed by perfectly arched red brows. For the occasion, her father had prepared her favorite meal, an unusual Korean dish made with beef and radishes in a sugar-vinegar sauce. At the dinner table, I took a tentative bite and was surprised by its rich, flavorful taste. Tim said the secret was the sauce and to not overcook the radishes. I didn't even know you could *cook* radishes. I glanced at Angie, who hadn't said a word. "You have good taste in birthday dinners."

"Uh huh." Angie was eating slowly and methodically, starting with her rice, which she kept far away from the beef and radishes so they weren't touching, while Tim and I had poured the beef and radish mixture directly on top of the rice.

I said, "You're pretty lucky to have a gourmet cook for a dad. Most men don't know how to boil water."

Angie peeked up through auburn bangs. "I guess." Her face looked as if it had been sprinkled with cinnamon. There was no doubt she was Tim Joseph's daughter, but whereas he was goofy-looking, she was adorable.

"By the way, Happy Birthday, Angie. What did you get?"

She said softly, "A bike."

Tim said, "After work, I'll put it together."

I effused, "Oh, a bike, how nice!"

Angie's eyes were focused on her plate as she chewed her food carefully, sipping milk in between bites. "Yeah, but I need training wheels."

There's nothing wrong with that. You have to start somewhere." I lowered my voice and leaned over. "Want to know a secret? My sister Sue needed training wheels until she was ten, but we don't talk about her." I did finger circles around my ear. "She's, you know, a bit looney-tunes."

Angie giggled. "Really? What else does she do?"

I mused, "Well, my baby sister thought she was a gypsy when she was your age and she flushed my pet turtles down the toilet. Oh, she also had invisible friends named Yvonne and Yvette, and liked to run around with no shoes, even to church."

"Really? Even to church?"

"Yep!" I was proud I had finally engaged Tim's timid daughter and already had developed a nurturing fondness for her. I continued, "But Sue isn't the weirdest one in my family. That would be my Dad. If he tried to cook anything, he'd probably burn the house down. That is, if he even *found* the stove."

Angie had one elbow propped up, which she leaned into. "You're funny."

"Elbow off the table, Squirt." Tim stood and walked to the stove. "More beef and radishes anyone?"

After dinner, and after Angie had been tucked into bed by us both, Tim said, "That's the most Angie has ever said to one of my dates she has just met. I think she liked you."

"What's not to like?" I joked before burping. The heartburn was concerning and I had already had made an appointment with my doctor.

The following Friday, the three of us went to the drive-in to see "*Grease.*" We had sex for the first time on our third date, but it was our fourth encounter that would change everything. Tim was lying on my sofa bed, having shown up there after a trip to the emergency room, and was trying to explain how he hurt his back and wrecked his Bronco. I had news of my own, but waited.

Tim grimaced. "Well, hon, I went over to Nori's to break up with her and she wasn't exactly a happy camper about the news. In fact, she made a big scene and threw a goddamn bookend at me! Damn thing must have been made of brass! Anyway, I jumped in my Bronco and she came chasing after me. Her hill is steep and then I guess I just lost control and hit a tree."

I questioned, "Nori?" I could see Tim's temples were visibly throbbing, and he definitely looked in acute distress.

He answered, "She's the nurse I've been dating but I've been thinking maybe I don't need so many old ladies in my life. In fact, I already cooled things down with Gail. That's Angie's teacher." Tim shifted and winced. "I usually go for tall brunettes but I picked you, babe. I don't know why, really. I guess there's just something about you. Maybe I should have asked if you felt the same way about me, huh?"

I felt my face flush and swallowed hard. "I do, actually." This was despite my predicament, which was growing, literally, by the hour: I was nine weeks' pregnant by the only person who could possibly be the father, and that was Carl Callahan. I was still in shock and disbelief over the news and could never tell anyone, except the man on my secondhand sofa.

Tim groaned. "Angie likes you best, too. Anyway, the reason I'm in so much pain is a ruptured disk. Got it diving in Puget Sound trying to catch an octopus. Anyway, I've had a few injections, cortisone and some kind of pineapple juice, but they didn't work. The doc said I really tweaked it bad this time and may need surgery. Can you get me another pillow?"

I returned with *two* pillows. "You were diving for octopus?"

"Sure. Puget Sound has some of the biggest in the world. I have pictures somewhere."

Tim was full of fascinating surprises, even in extreme distress. I fluffed both pillows and placed them gingerly behind his back. "There, that should help."

"Thanks." He then leaned back with a Darvocet in his palm. "Maybe you could get me something to wash this down. A beer would be nice."

"You're in luck." I walked to the kitchen and came back with a can of Olympia beer, plus a glass. I handed the beer to Tim and looked around my tiny apartment, thinking of what else I could do. After all, Tim had picked *me*, and I was going to repay him by spoiling him for all other women. "Do you want me to turn on the T.V.? Are you hungry? I have soup. Oh, let me close those drapes."

At my apartment window, I heard Tim groan and whipped around. "Are you okay?"

"Once the pills kick in, I'll be fine, but do you mind if I crash here for the night? Angie's at the neighbor's house so she's in good hands."

"Of course, Tim." I tucked the blanket around him and eventually plopped into an antique rocker (on loan from Brenda). Soon, Tim was fast asleep and my news would have to wait.

Chapter Twenty

When I learned I was pregnant, I demanded that my doctor repeat the test. Getting pregnant at twenty-one had not been in my plans, especially not getting pregnant by a pervert! I suspected Carl may have drugged me the night it happened, either that or I blacked out on too many caramel candies and Diet Dr. Pepper, my current beverage of choice. When the test was confirmed positive, I cried all the way home, and once there I where was so angry I began throwing things, screaming No! No! No! I could not possibly have Carl Callahan's baby! The thought was sickening and once I calmed down, I did the only right thing: I called Planned Parenthood to schedule an abortion.

After being told the news, Tim was nonjudgmental and insisted on taking me to the clinic and bringing me home to his house so he could take care of me. I had planned on a taxicab and good drugs to do these things, in that order, but Tim would have none of it. The most agonizing part of the ordeal was waiting the proper time before the procedure could be safely performed. When it finally did happen, the only thing I remembered was being given an I.V. and being told to relax. Afterwards, I had slight cramps but no more than usually occurred with my periods.

That night, lying in my new boyfriend's queen bed being treated like a queen by Tim and Angie (who thought I had the flu), I had no regrets about my decision, no regrets I hadn't told Carl. It was my body, my life, my choice. Not once did I cry. For his part, Tim was unbelievably supportive during what could have been an awkward and lonely time, and it wasn't long before I willingly gave up my Bellevue apartment to move in with him and Angie. Shortly thereafter, I met Tim's mother, who was dying.

Nervously, and holding Angie's hand, I followed Tim up the stairs of the California-style split-level, passing a kitchen whose countertops were spotless. The house smelled piney, and in the living room, the first thing that caught my eye was the hospital bed set up next to the fireplace with a woman lying on it. Nearby was a portable metal tray that held numerous prescription bottles alongside a plastic cup with a straw. The room had vaulted ceilings and other than the hospital equipment, it was spacious and tastefully decorated. The woman in the bed had a square face with almost no hair. She held up one frail hand and beckoned her granddaughter. "Angie, come say hello to Grammy."

Angie walked over and bent to hug her Grammy. "Hi, Grammy. How are you?"

"Things could be better, dear, but I'm hanging in there." She peered around Angie at me. "So, you must be Nancy. Tim has told me about you." Her voice was ragged. "Sit down, make yourself comfortable." Mary-Jane sat up to take a sip of water before laying her head back against her pillow. Tim had said she was fifty-two but she looked much older.

I joked, trying to lighten the mood, "So, Tim told you about me, huh? I hope he didn't tell you about my cooking!"

Tim explained, "Nancy made us dinner last week but I think she left out a few key ingredients." He walked to a sliding glass door, which he cracked open. He was smoking and exhaled onto the balcony. Without turning he asked, "Hey, Ma, I thought Pop was going to stain the deck?"

I thought it was cute the way Tim called his parents Ma and Pop.

Mary-Jane answered, "He's been too busy caring for me."

Tim's eyes darted back and forth before they settled. I could tell he was agitated.

He said through a smoke ring, "I see the bluejays are back."

"Damn things never left. What a racket those birds make. I told your father to—" A coughing fit seized her and she clutched her chest. "Sorry."

"Please, don't apologize." I was aware that Mary-Jane had breast cancer that had spread to her bones and lungs, and I asked politely, "Can I get you some more water?"

Tim blurted, "I'll get it! You gals chat." He grabbed his mother's water glass and scurried down the stairs of the split-level, where I presumed there was another bathroom.

Mary-Jane shook her head. "My son can't handle illness. Just wait until he has a cold. He'll act like he's got the pleurisy and you'll be waiting on him hand and foot."

I giggled. Mary-Jane was charming and funny, even in her debilitated condition. "Most grown men are babies. My Dad is the worst of all."

Mary-Jane nodded. "Do your parents live around here?"

"No, my parents are divorced and remarried. Dad lives in Oklahoma with his wife Kay and my Mom and stepdad live in Eastern Washington."

"Oh, I see." Mary-Jane's voice cracked and there was a long pause so she could gather strength. "Nancy, you seem a nice girl. What are you doing dating my son?"

Angie yelped, "Grammy! That's not nice!"

I reached and put an arm affectionately around Angie, who was seated next to me on a cream-colored sofa. "What can I say? Your son has grown on me."

Mary-Jane deadpanned, "Fungus grows on you, too, but that doesn't mean you have to like it."

Angie groaned. "Dad wouldn't like to be called fungus, Gramma."

Mary-Jane waved a dismissive hand. "Your father has thicker skin than a rhinoceros, except when he's sick." She coughed into a hankie and asked me, "Are you Catholic?"

"Almost, I'm Episcopalian. You know, Catholic Light?"

Mary-Jane chortled. "I see. Do you attend church?"

"On Easter always, but the rest of the time I have to be forced. Blame that on my mother."

"Mothers always get blamed for everything. It's why we're so guilty."

When we were preparing to leave, Mary-Jane called me to her bedside. She held my hand. "Nancy, I have a favor: Straighten out my son so his father will be proud. He's got a good heart, he's just, well, I think he needs direction. It wouldn't hurt if you made him go to church once in a while, too."

I answered honestly, "Yes, I will." It seemed like an easy promise, one full of hope. "You can count on me."

"Yes, I think I can." Mary-Jane's eyes fluttered before they finally closed and for a terrifying moment, I wondered if she was gone, but Tim returned with a glass of water and his mother reopened her eyes. She waved a pale hand. "You kids get going. I know you have better things to do than hang around a sick old lady."

I saw Mary-Jane only once more, before she died at home in August, and I reacted like it had been my own mother who had passed away. I called my boss Lorraine sobbing, and at Tim's mother's funeral was inconsolable as I grieved for a woman I barely knew. But the grief was real and the loss reminded me of another death when I was only eight.

My beloved maternal grandmother, Georgia Taylor, had died of a blood clot following elective surgery at age 75, and I would never forget the ringing phone in the dead of night, or my mother's sorrowful wails and her frantic packing. It was the night before Halloween, my favorite holiday, and I had planned to dress as a ghost like all my siblings, but not that year. That year, my sisters and I accompanied Mother to Geneseo, Illinois, while the boys stayed home with a live-in caretaker and Dad.

Eleven years after Grandma Taylor's passing, the death of a woman named Mary-Jane Joseph would leave an indelible impression on me, and I would struggle magnificently to keep the promise I had made to her.

It turned out that loving Tim was a bigger challenge than I thought possible.

Chapter Twenty-One

On paper, it sounded like fun: River-rafting and camping on the sandy banks on our parents' waterfront property in Plain, Washington, on a Saturday in July that promised to be hot. For the trip, the gang was well prepared, *if* one counts among preparedness enough alcoholic beverages to intoxicate an entire army platoon. In addition to the coolers full of ice and alcohol, we had packed life vests, suntan oil, cameras, and waterproof watches. We also had a schedule: Get in the river at 11:00 a.m., be back home by 5:00 p.m., just in time for a barbeque. Unfortunately, what should have been a five-hour trip max was delayed considerably by a slowly leaking raft, the unrelentless and scorching August heat, and flaring tempers coupled with too many wine coolers and empty stomachs.

The outing had consisted of Patty and Tom, Tim, Angie, and me, a seven months' pregnant Sue, Joy and her boyfriend Big John, and Little John and his girlfriend Cheryl. We had all started the trip excited and in pleasant dispositions but arrived at our designation at dusk, covered with mosquito bites. In addition, we were all cold, wet, tipsy, and in the case of Tim and me, barely speaking.

Later, inside our tent, I couldn't control how mad I was. "I can't believe you were flirting with my pregnant baby sister. She's only eighteen and that was disgusting!"

Tim narrowed his eyes in confusion. "Flirting? Is *that's* what's bothering you?"

"Don't deny it. You took Sue's side." I climbed fully clothed on top of the sleeping bag. It was a message: Don't touch me tonight.

Tim said, "That's ridiculous. I didn't take sides." He pulled at yet another beer, despite it being midnight.

"You did so." Jealousy, and wine coolers, turned me irrational, and I was glad Angie was sleeping in my parent's spare bedroom and not camping with the rest of us. "I suppose you have a crush on her?"

"No, but you don't have to be so rough on her. She's just a kid."

I sniffed imperiously. I knew I was right and was going to make Tim admit it. "Well, I saw you staring at her boobs. Everyone did. You can be a real womanizer who has no respect—"

Tim suddenly slapped me hard across the cheek and I reeled back, stunned.

"Shut up! You can be such a bitch." He pitched his empty beer can out the tent. After that, he farted inside the tent to show I was the one not worthy of respect.

Really, the farting wasn't unusual. Tim was a champion producer of flatulence, farting loudly and proudly, blaming it on everything from Pop-Tarts to pistachios. The worst ones were cheap-beer farts, so nasty they could chip paint from the walls.

I choked down tears and tried to breathe through my mouth. I muttered asshole but very, very quietly.

What seemed like hours later, he said with his back to me, "I'm sorry."

I muttered, "You should be."

"It's just that you just get on a roll and don't shut up." He was at the opening of our tent smoking a joint, and blew a smoke ring. Finally, he turned and in the glow of the moon, he looked boyish and harmless. "Let's just forget about this, okay?"

I hardly had a choice. What was I supposed to do, abandon the tent and the following morning explain to my mother and stepfather that the reason I was sleeping on their sofa was because the boyfriend they despised had gotten physical? I had done nothing but praise Tim's accolades in their presence, trying to convince them he wasn't *that* bad, and now he had hit me.

"Fine," I hissed from under the sleeping bag, "but I wish you wouldn't smoke pot at my parents' house. It's disrespectful."

"Stop worrying." Tim did a buttock tilt heralding the passage of what could be deadly fumes, and claimed, "Your parents are clueless." He farted and I wanted to stab him in the back.

The next day, I forced myself to be civil towards Tim (who acted like he didn't remember what happened) as I gave him a tour of my parent's property, fifteen rural acres on which they had erected a mobile home with a cedar deck, a huge shop and a garage, as well as a log cabin studio where Bob could paint overlooking a bend in the tranquil river. Mom showed off her vegetable and flower gardens, as well as their horses. I could tell she had never been happier.

The day after we got home, I admitted to Mom over the phone that I was living with Tim and Angie. By then, Tim and I had made up and I was sure he was sorry. The flowers and night of passion proved it. We hung up and I thought things were fine, until I received this letter two days later:

July 8, 1980

Dear Nancy,

First of all, I love you very, very much. Second, I am very concerned about your future, and very displeased about your living with Tim. You have so much potential to offer a man that I can't understand why you have settled for this situation. I often wished my mother had talked to me a little more and perhaps I wouldn't have made the bad decisions that I did—ones I see you are making too, and which will ruin your life.

This is such a beautiful place here and we love to have you kids appreciate it and not come here to sit and smoke pot and drink and play loud music...you can do all that at home. It breaks my heart to see you kids ruin your health and spend hard-earned money on marijuana. And don't feel picked on; Patty and Tom are getting a letter, too.

I know I can't live your life for you, I, all I can do is share some wisdom that comes from making mistakes. It doesn't mean I don't still make mistakes, only far fewer and not so big. Tim is nothing but trouble. I know his type; I married one the first time around...your father.

Please think about what I have said; God will show you there is a better way.

Love Always,
Mom

P.S. My blue plaid shirt followed you home on your last visit.

I came very close to ripping the letter into shreds but instead placed it into my scrapbook, which I tucked away in a secret box in the spare bedroom. I really didn't blame Mom, who was just being motherly and certainly wasn't the only one who didn't approve of my relationship with Tim. Even our friends referred to us as the Beauty and the Beast, while Patty called us an odd couple. Neighbor Melanie (and ex-girlfriend of Tim's) rudely joked we were "Mr. Right and Miss Take."

Looking at the scrapbook, my thoughts turned to nice and normal Bill Vann. I wondered what his life was like now. Was he happy? Did he think about me? Was his new wife Diane a proponent of Family Forum Night, or did she snicker as I had done? Not a day went by I didn't think of Bill, wishing him well, and had even kept the stack of love letters he had sent me while I was away at college the first year. I couldn't bear to part with the letters even as I feared what Tim would do if he found them. Perhaps burn them in the backyard as her own father had done to her mother's precious box of memorabilia.

I sensed the truth and wisdom my mother's letter contained but could only focus on Tim, who I viewed as a messed-up man who just needed a good woman to straighten him out, and I, Nancy Anne Nash, would be that woman. Driving this decision were two promises: The one I made to the dying Mary-Jane, and the other I had made to myself not to abandon sweet Angela Marie.

Chapter Twenty-Two

Patty conceived her first child in the back seat of Tom's '72 Rambler in the parking lot of the Factoria Drive-In. They had gone there to watch a first-run showing of Woody Allen's *Everything You Always Wanted to Know about Sex but Were Afraid to Ask*. Patty told me was pretty sure she knew all she needed to know about sex, though she did have questions regarding Woody Allen's frame of mind when he made the movie, especially the part where a huge set of breasts with legs gets chased by Woody's character. After that, other than the sound of a sheep baaing loudly, she recalls the movie was a blur.

Patty suspected she was pregnant a few weeks later, when she began craving chocolate and pizza together, making Tom order two pepperoni pizzas, one for each of them. The Shakey's Pizza delivery truck would pull into the driveway of their A-framed duplex and Patty would answer the door with cash, chomping on something chocolate, favoring fudge brownies. Finally she took a home pregnancy test, which was positive, and told Tom. Then they gave the happy news to Mom and Bob, who would be first-time grandparents. That night, they celebrated with Frozen Pizza Rolls and German chocolate cake.

Patty particularly craved chocolate milk she made herself, and Tom estimated his wife was consuming close to four gallons of milk a month, costing them a small fortune and running their milkman Dennis ragged. Because her chocolate milk was equal parts Hershey's Chocolate Syrup and whole milk, Patty gained sixty pounds by her second trimester, most of which settled in her rear end, but Tom loved every pound, every dimpled inch, and called her his One-Ton Honey Bun, especially when she waddled out in his boxer shorts because her own underwear no longer fit. Truly, it looked like two gigantic meteors had landed on my sister's behind! And her breasts were melons!

At six months' along, Patty quit working at the Albertsons Bakery since the smell of donuts made her hurl, and in one afternoon completely renovated the spare bedroom into a baby's room, complete with "new" curtains and yellowish walls, although the paint can she found in the carport under a tarp had read, "Snow White." They were on a tight budget so basically the room was a mishmash of donated items and Value Village specials, including the crib. Tom was pleased about the baby-room makeover and to show his appreciation offered to cook dinner, choosing his father's Famous meatloaf. The meal was a big hit with Patty, who accompanied her portion with a tall glass of chocolate milk and retired early. The next morning, speculation was wildly varied whether it was the meatloaf, the chocolate milk, the desert of two Ding-Dongs *and* a theatre-sized box of Good 'N Plenty's, the pregnancy itself, or a combination thereof that had caused such severe nausea and vomiting that Patty ended up in the emergency room for dehydration. I thought the culprit was the licorice candy, while Mom diagnosed hyperemesis gravidarum (later confirmed by a comprehensive metabolic profile).

Poor Tom thought it might have been the dash of extra horseradish he added to the meatloaf at the last minute.

Whatever, two things *were* clear: Patty promised that this would be her first, last, and only pregnancy since it was pure agony in a foreign body the size of a house, and second, she would never eat meatloaf again, no matter whose freakin' recipe.

(Of note, Patty kept neither of these promises. Three-and-a-half years after her son Robert was born in October 1979, Patty became pregnant while on the Pill, this time with a baby girl and this time craving chipped beef in gravy over toast or potatoes with a ton of pepper, also known as "shit on shingles," but gained only thirty-two pounds. Her daughter Brianna was born in May 1983 bald as an eagle, and the next time Patty ate meatloaf was not until 1994.)

In stark contrast to Patty's pregnancy, our baby sister Sue had very little physical symptoms while carrying her first child, other than morning sickness and increasing headaches. She was unmarried and the baby's father was a divorced man who wasn't all that keen on being a dad, and certainly had no desire to be tied down but another loveless marriage. Sue didn't care and planned on having her baby regardless of Lenny's intentions. It was a decision made from stubbornness and based on the Nash motto: *Act now, pay later.*

Single parenthood would complicate her life tremendously but Sue had practically been handed a set of blueprints on "How to Complicate Your Life" at the impressionable age of fifteen, when she had moved to Burns Flat, Oklahoma, to live with dear old dad, our stepmother, and four stepsisters. Living with Dad Sue would later recall was in its own bizarre way an educational experience, and one that would shape her future.

There in Oklahoma City, under the auspices of self-absorbed, narcissistic, 18-year-old identical twin sisters Sara and Tara, Sue learned in one short summer how to smoke pot, play poker, drive without a permit, and hitchhike, the latter of which always lead to adventure, once even a detour to nearby Midwest City. In that case, the driver who picked Sue and the twins up turned out to be a 17-year-old boy who was driving his older brother's pickup. A couple miles later, Tara ended up driving because Calvin was clearly more interested in flirting with the bodacious Sue and since Sara's 19-year-old boyfriend lived in Midwest City, that's where they ended up for an afternoon of swimming, smoking, and making out. When Calvin needed to get the truck back, the girls decided they weren't ready to go home and hitchhiked again, this time being picked up by an old farmer, who warned them about the perils of hitchhiking.

Sue said the old geezer let them out a mile short of their destination when it became clear Sara and Tara, who were impossible to tell apart and lovely in appearance, had insufferable personalities marred by a nonstop competitiveness fraught with overplayed bitchiness.

Particularly entertaining were Sue's summers spent at our father's house, when Dad would get drunk and chase the five girls all over the house like he was the "big bad boogieman." Sometimes he'd throw them in the pool, but his favorite thing to do was play golf on the lawns of vacationing neighbors. Drink in hand, he'd swing wildly with the other until the lawn was butchered and the irons were flung haphazardly into the woods. Sue, Sara, Tara, and their older sister Audrey, a print model, would pull up lawn chairs when Dad began golfing, ducking at regular intervals, smoking in between.

When Sue told us she was pregnant, I told her she should give the baby up for adoption, thus sparking a sisterly feud that would last for years. This is why Patty was chosen as Sue's birth coach, who was at her side during nineteen hours of labor. Her bouncing baby boy was named Anthony and had perfect Apgars. The father was there for the birth.

The very next day, Patty and Tom's son Robbie turned one year old. The following March, Jill and Big John gave birth to their first son, Justin.

It seemed the only one not having babies was me, and I wondered if I would forever remain a gravida 1, para 0.

Chapter Twenty-Three

I wasn't really looking for a new job when I spotted an intriguing ad in the Sunday employment section of *The Seattle Times*. Working for Eastside Hospital had its perks, like being able to have lunch with my boyfriend, who gave me secret tours of the bowels of the hospital. There were many other things I disliked, however, especially the union rules that restricted my pay, even though I was producing twice the work as anyone else. I also was scheduled to work the 9:00 a.m. to 6:00 p.m. shift, Tuesday through Saturday, and tried unsuccessfully to change it to match Tim's schedule of Monday through Friday, 6:00 a.m. to 3:00 p.m., so we could have even more time together, but at the hospital, I was at the bottom of the tier in my department.

The ad had been placed by a company called Professional Dictation & Secretarial Services, who were looking for full-time medical transcriptionists. Reading on, they offered benefits and a retirement plan, but the kicker was the last line of the ad: "Join the only company in town who pays their transcriptionists by the word!"

By the word! Now I was ecstatic! I typed 120+ words per hour. I was going to be rich!

Immediately I scheduled an interview with Lucille Byrnes, owner of Professional Dictation, located in Seattle's so-called University District, and after acing the typing and spelling tests, as well as transcribing the dictation on an entire 30-minute cassette in record time, I was hired on the spot. I immediately gave the required two weeks' notice to Group Health, where I had worked not even fourteen months. This was a bold move. "Green" transcriptionists—those with less than two years' experience—didn't ordinarily leave jobs where they were paid no matter how much work they did, to work for a company that paid them based exclusively on how much they typed, i.e., produced. But I was confident in my abilities, and with Tim's blessings and assurances, I joined the growing ranks of Professional Dictation (P.D.) in March of 1979.

A year later, I was making more money than I thought possible at P.D., racking up production bonuses and earning the "Flying Fingers" award month after month. Production figures were posted every month on a clipboard, calculated by a part-time college student who used a plastic see-through grid placed over the carbon copied text of all work transcribed by each transcriptionist, which were stapled together and marked with that transcriptionist's ID number. I was number 26, and number 26 was always at the top. Even Tim was impressed.

The money I was now making burned a hole in my pocket so for Angie's tenth birthday in April of 1980, I splurged and took her on a shopping spree, offering to buy her an entire outfit, and afterwards we would dine on Godfather's Pizza. Angie could barely conceal her excitement and was ready in ten minutes.

At the mall, my surrogate stepdaughter picked out red pants, a pink sweater, and new underwear. I bought myself the newest edition of *Grays' Anatomy*. We shopped some more and after enjoying a Hawaiian-style pizza, we split a malted milkshake. Later that night, Angie asked for help with her homework. It was late Sunday afternoon and I was bothered that Angie was just admitting she had unfinished homework. Tim had a strict rule about doing homework before anything else, including shopping, but I hoped if we hurried, Angie's homework would be done before Tim even got home from the store.

We sat at the oak table with Angie's assignments scattered. She began, "I don't like Mrs. Baxter. She told me I was dumb."

"Dumb? Are you sure she actually said you were *dumb*?"

Angie nodded, "Well, it was the other word, the one that starts with 's'."

"Stupid?"

Angie nodded. "Yeah, it's 'cause I can't tell time or read very good."

"You can't tell time?" Disbelieving, I pointed to the clock above the sink that had hands. "You are sure you don't know what time the rooster clock says?"

Angie glanced up and studied the clock intently. "One four?" Her eyebrows were scrunched into a single nutmeg dash across her pretty forehead.

The hand clock actually read "4:25" and I stood up and changed the hands of the clock to read "1:00." Surely she would get that. "Now what time is it?"

After a long pause, Angie queried, "Eleven o'clock?"

I pulled out a piece of paper from Angie's schoolbook and wrote: *The cow jumped over the moon.* I pointed. "Can you read any of this, Angie?" It was a simple sentence taught in first grade; Angie was in third grade.

"The...woc...I dunno, Nancy, the letters are mixed up. I got a problem."

Angie's "problem" was starting to sink in as I attempted one more assignment. I handed over paper and a pencil. "Angie, I will give you a couple of words and you try to spell them. Okay?"

Angie had her head resting in one propped up hand. "I guess."

"Cat."

Pencil poised, Angie began writing cautiously, "c-a-t."

"Very good! That's right! Now try spelling 'stop'."

This proved more difficult for Angie, who after a long time concentrating, finally writes "s-p-o-t."

Next, Angie misspelled "dog" as "g-o-d" but got "big" correct. After fifteen minutes, her answers were hit-and-miss, with approximately half the words spelled right and half wrong, but it was unclear to me if she was guessing or not.

"Don't worry, Ang. I'll talk to your Dad tonight and see if we can do something about Mrs. Baxter." I was sure Angie was dyslexic like her father and if that was the case, a rash of questions came to my mind:

Why didn't Angie's teachers pick up on the dyslexia, especially Miss Lee, who had intimate contact with Angie through her father?

Why wasn't Angie in special education classes?

Did Miss Baxter cause permanent damage by calling Angie stupid?

Did Tim know about his daughter's learning disability and choose to ignore it because of his own experiences? He admitted he had struggled all the way through Catholic grade school, being taunted by the nuns (though I suspected it was the other way around). In fourth grade, his family moved to Honolulu where his father was stationed in the navy, and there, the teachers considered being left-handed taboo so Tim was repeatedly punished for not using his right hand for tasks.

And what about Carole? She was Angie's stepmother for a few years; surely she knew something was amiss?

How could Angie fall through so many cracks?

Right then and there, I decided to be in charge of educating Angie. Never mind I had failed miserably at this same task with my own struggling siblings long ago in a red playhouse in Woodland Hills, California. I'd succeed this time because I had connections, and one was a formidable psychologist named Wendy.

Chapter Twenty-Four

Like many of P.D.'s clientele, Wendy L. Irwin, M.D., PhD., was very particular about the appearance of her final reports. She provided her own template that the transcriptionists were required to follow exactly, including underlined and bolded headings, and indented paragraphs. And she absolutely prohibited editing of any sort. What she dictated was what she wanted transcribed. Her detailed reports were lengthy, often ten pages or more long, and filled with unfamiliar syndromes, acronyms, and names of diagnostic tests used in her comprehensive evaluations. The day I was handed Dr. Irwin's tapes because the transcriptionist who usually did this account was on a leave-of-absence with a lupus flare was the day I knew I had found the answer to Angie's school-related problems. Dr. Irwin was a child neuropsychologist who specialized in diagnosing learning disabilities in children. I was sure Angie was such a child, though the public school psychologist claimed after her evaluation a few weeks earlier that the only thing wrong with Angie Joseph was "lack of motivation and some degree of dyslexia."

"Some degree?" I had asked. "What does it mean? And does it matter? Dyslexia is dyslexia." I was close to losing my patience with the weary school-appointed psychologist, who wore oversized glasses and had a high degree of halitosis. "And if Angie lacks motivation, it's because her fourth-grade teacher told her she was stupid."

Dr. Plutz had tilted her head. "Clarice has apologized. What she meant was that Angie didn't apply herself and therefore was not as bright as she could be." She paused. "At least she's cute."

Tim and I exchanged looks of incredulousness. "At least she's cute?" It was true, but irrelevant. "Cute won't cut it in the real word, and Clarice's comments hurt Angie's feelings and were inappropriate." I leaned back irritably with my arms crossed. It had been decided before the meeting I would be in charge and I continued undeterred.

"Look, Dr. Plutz, this back-and-forth nonsense has gone on long enough. Tim and I want a second opinion from another psychologist."

Tim nodded, though he looked unsure.

I added, "We have endured months of nonproductive testing and Angie is still not in special education classes. Time is running out."

"The system moves slowly."

I replied, "But a child's future is at stake!"

Tim's jaw was twitching and his legs bobbed, not from nervousness but an hour of nicotine withdrawal. He knew I was willing to pay out of my own pocket for the private appointment with Dr. Irwin, and while he wasn't against it, he often volunteered at the elementary school and had seriously dated Angie's third-grade teacher. As a result, he said it felt like treason to be so contentious against a school with fond memories. Eventually, he saw it my way.

I looked first at Tim and back at Wanda Plutz seated next to me. Her breath really did smell like fried skunk. "Well?"

Tim finally spoke. "Nancy is right. We just want to make sure Angie gets the help she needs. It seems like you guys have been dragging your feet and Angie is slipping further behind. I'm not trying to cause trouble, but I agree with her." He pointed to me.

"Oh?"

"Yeah. We want to consult another doc, and hopefully we can get the ball rolling in the right direction. Angie is my daughter. I gotta do what's best."

Dr. Plutz shut the file folder and expelled fetid breath. "You'll have to pay for an outside evaluation yourself."

"We know," I answered with my hand to my mouth.

Wanda Plutz stood and said to Tim, "It's your child and your choice, Mr. Joseph."

Tim smiled affably. "Me and Nancy are in this together. I trust her when it comes to school stuff. She went to college to be a teacher, you know. She isn't really a dumb blonde."

I hated backhanded compliments, but sometimes I had to settle.

Chapter Twenty-Five

Tim had a self-deprecating, keenly offbeat sense of humor combined with the ability for making others feel protected (or coddled, in some cases), and used this combination to talk his way out of all kinds of predicaments, including traffic tickets, bar brawls (even those he started), and neighborly disputes. Once, he got me out of a signed contract for a brand-new Mazda I bought on a whim, a car he claimed on inspection was overpriced for a piece of imported shit. I didn't argue with Mr. Fix-Up, though I did wish he'd do something about his chronic flatulence. I even made him a doctor's appointment, citing an article I read that said people with chronic bad gas had a problem with improper digestion.

Tim had looked at me like I was an idiot. He said everyone farts. "It's natural," he said. "If you don't fart all those toxic fumes collect inside your gut and could blow a hole in your stomach."

How does one argue with that? Nevertheless, the farting problem aside, nothing mechanical-wise stumped Tim: He tackled home projects and repairs, his leather tool-bag at his hip, including retrieving dishrags stuck in the garbage disposal and tampons clogging the septic. He once permanently disposed of the snake our cat Fluffy had brought in through the cat door and dropped on a new peach satin comforter under which I had been sleeping, right before I screamed bloody murder.

So, when Tim mentioned he someday wanted a boat and didn't care if it was a fixer-upper, I decided to find one as his Christmas present, and I didn't have to go far. Right next door, an 18-foot wooden open-style skiff had been sitting under an apple tree and partially in the alley for months. A quick peak when no one was around revealed the boat was filled with some ratty-looking life preservers, stinky fishing poles, and lots of junk, but otherwise seemed intact, though admittedly my knowledge of boats was nonexistent.

I knocked on the Birdsong's door and offered Earl Birdsong a hundred dollars for the boat "as-is."

Earl cocked his head, which was bald. "A hundred bucks?"

I nodded, "Yes, it's for Christmas for Tim. I can get cash if you want."

"No, a check will be fine. You sure we's talking about the boat out back?"

"Yes, I notice you never use it, and well, it looks like it has potential."

Earl grinned. "It was a beaut back in its time before I got the gout. Tell ya what, you can have the boat and all the accessories, too, for that price."

What he meant was all the junk but I accepted. "Great, a bonus!"

On Christmas morning, after Angie was done unwrapping her presents, I told Tim we needed to go see something in the Birdsong's backyard.

"Blanche Birdsong naked again?"

"No!"

Angie was examining her Cabbage Patch doll, a gift from me, and commented, "Thank goodness. Once was enough!"

Tim asked, "*Earl* Birdsong naked?"

Exasperated, I replied, "No! Nobody naked, but if you want, later I will get naked and run around the backyard, something I am ashamed to say I have prior experience doing."

Angie's eyebrows knitted. "You do? When?"

"When I was twelve and living in California. My best friend was weird and took every chance she could to get naked, but enough about Lynne. Come on, both of you follow me."

Tim said, "I want to hear more about Lynne later."

"She's probably dead. Hurry, to the alley."

In the alley, the boat that used to belong to Earl Birdsong was under a clean tarp with a big red bow. There was no card. I said, "Well, pull off the tarp."

Tim pulled off the tarp. "Oh, wow. That's Earl's boat."

"No, it's *your* boat. Merry Christmas!"

Angie giggled. "You're kidding, right?"

Tim, who had his coffee cup with him, cracked up laughing and Irish coffee splashed everywhere. "Earl has been trying to get rid of this boat for years!" He walked around the boat, stooped to look underneath, and said, "Well, there's no motor."

"Oh."

"Other than that, I think this boat has potential." He gave me a hug. "I really didn't expect a boat." He finished off his coffee and said, "So, tell me about your naked friend."

Chapter Twenty-Six

Tim gave his "new" boat a complete makeover, thanks to a coworker from the hospital named Walt Parks, who previously owned a boat-building company on Elliott Bay. Together, they sanded off the cracked layers of old white paint down to raw fir and varnished the wood with a cherry finish. The interior of the boat was completely gutted and replaced with new vinyl seats. They installed an outboard motor and named the vessel *Park's Place* in Walt's honor.

Our maiden voyage aboard *Park's Place* took place midmorning on Sunday, May 18, 1980, in the relatively secure and calm waters of nearby Lake Sammamish. We agreed to go childless in case there were problems so Angie stayed with our neighbor across the street, Melanie Dickerson, and her two kids.

On Lake Sammamish, Tim navigated *Park's Place* cautiously around the perimeter of the lake, not going too far out because its seaworthiness was yet to be proven. When the engine sputtered and quit, it took Tim five seconds to figure out the problem (a faulty spark plug), and soon we were cruising towards the middle of the lake, where Tim killed the motor and lit up his pipe prefilled with pot. After taking a deep hit, he handed over the smooth wooden pipe, a birthday gift from his ex-roommate Tom.

"Here, take a toke. We're celebrating!"

"Sure." I took a tentative hit and handed the pipe back over. Immediately I began hacking a considerable amount of phlegm and part of a lung. My eyes watered and then I sneezed. "Good stuff," I managed to wheeze.

Tim held up his Rainier. "Have a sip of beer."

I drank some beer and from the cooler fished a Diet Pepsi. I sat down and turned my face to the sun. "Boating is fun. I can't believe how nice it is and it's only ten o'clock in the morning." I wondered if we would become fair-weather boaters like so many people in the Pacific Northwest. A few minutes passed and I said dreamily to Tim, "I'm glad we forgot the radio because it's so peaceful out here on the water with nothing but the sound of slapping water."

"Yeah, ain't this the life?"

Minutes later, I asked, "Tim? Are you high? I don't feel high. I think that pot must be old."

"Nah, I just bought it." Tim looked at her and grinned. "Got a deal, too."

"So are *you* high?"

In answer, Tim continued grinning and it certainly looked like his "high" grin but then again, Tim grinned a lot and was high a lot, so it was hard for me to tell if the grin was a pot-induced euphoric grin or the grin of a pleased new captain at the helm of his vessel, given to him by his scantily-clad first mate. Then again, it could have been his "I-want-you" grin, which was both goofy and flattering.

I finally decided on all of the above and stripped off my halter-top and stood with the goal of seducing the captain but due to the lack of anything to eat all day (a routine practice to keep my weight at or below a hundred pounds), I became lightheaded and slumped back down, covering my small breasts. "Oopsy doopsy!"

Tim was clearly annoyed. "Have you eaten anything today?" The subject was a sore one because when I didn't eat I usually got cranky. And while he was the first to admit he liked skinny women, he didn't like skinny *bitchy* women.

"Yes, I ate breakfast." I replied, wondering why my voice sounded so far away. In fact, it seemed to echo off the lake. "I had two cups of coffee and a muffin." Actually it was the top crunchy crust of the muffin; the rest went to Angie.

"And what else?"

"That's it. You know I'm not a big breakfast person." Or lunch person, though dinner I usually devoured, eating so fast I was finished before Angie even touched a single item on her plate. It was my reward for starving myself all day, though I still counted calories.

"You're anorexic, you know. Skinny is one thing, but skin and bones is another."

I rolled my eyes and put my top back on. "I am not anorexic and I ought to know. It was the subject of my term paper in Health 101. I got an A minus, and my professor said I had nearly perfect grammar and spelling."

"See, you just proved my point. You got an A because you have firsthand knowledge of it."

"No, dear, I just watch my calories and have the metabolism of a hummingbird." Possessing the arrogance of youth, I believed I would never battle the bulge, even when I was old and fifty. "You know what they say: A moment on the lips, forever on the hips."

He cocked his head, "You'll never have to worry about your hips, which by the way *do* look good in those short shorts." He sat back down on his swiveling vinyl captain's seat and turned the key, igniting the engine. "Let's go exploring."

"Okay." I relaxed and leaned against the seat with my hands atop my flat stomach. We were approaching the state park and I told Tim, "Me and Brenda were at the state park the day Ted Bundy was here with the fake cast. We didn't see him or anything but you've met Brenda. She's tall and thin with long brunette hair. That description fits his victim profile, you know. When we were at Central, after that girl disappeared, we weren't allowed to walk on campus at night alone. You always had to have an escort. Safety in twos, that's what they said. Anyway, it's weird how close our paths crossed, me and Ted Bundy. I wonder if Brenda and I would have helped him that day? A person in a cast would be hard to say no to."

Tim asked over his shoulder, with one hand on the wheel, "You were there that exact day? Wow."

"Yep. We had to do one of those human chains because they thought someone drowned. I always hated doing those because the last thing I want my legs to touch was a dead kid."

Tim shrugged. "That brings back memories."

"It sure does." I felt like I was floating and leaned back with my eyes closed. Growing up, Lake Sammamish was a popular choice for my family to hang out, swimming or floating on inner tubes, or sunbathing slathered in baby oil to see who could get the darkest. Only Mom cheated with Q.T. because she thought too much sun exposure was aging.

One summer day, Patty, Mom, and I went to the state park, choosing a less traveled dirt path hidden under a thick canopy of trees that lead to a secret cove on the lake. There on the path, we encountered a longhaired hippie. The hippie was smelly but polite and stepped aside to let us pass. Mom said thank-you and the hippie wedged one filthy hand down the front of her bikini bottoms before taking off running. My sister and I squealed, "Perv!" and turned in quick pursuit of the creep, but he was agile and disappeared into the woods. We reported the incident to the park authorities but who knows if he was ever caught. After that, we weren't allowed to go to the park without an adult, which was disappointing only if you forgot the park was full of crotch-grabbing hippie perverts and good-looking serial killers.

Tim looked at his watch and said, "Well, it's one o'clock. We should probably head in." He steered the boat to the public dock, where we loaded *Park's Place* onto the trailer behind the Bronco.

Driving home, Tim pointed to the southern sky. "Why is the sky so black down there?"

I craned to look. "I have no idea but let's go home so we can eat. I'm starving!"

Tim rolled his eyes and turned on the radio.

Only then did we learn that at approximately 8:45 a.m. that morning, while we were cruising Lake Sammamish and smoking fifty-dollar-a-bag Maui pot, long-dormant Mount Saint Helen's had erupted with unrelenting fury. The statistics were quickly reported: The explosion of the eruption possessed the equivalent power of a hydrogen bomb and with the eruption went 1300 feet of mountaintop and thousands of acres of forest. The Tootle River was all but erased from existence, and Harry Truman, the elderly curmudgeon who lived near the mountain and had been recently interviewed on the news because of his steadfast refusal to leave the area, and his home, despite the increasing seismic activity and warnings to leave, was undoubtedly buried under a mountain of mud.

The day of the explosion, the winds had been from the east and strong, driving the cloud of ash and debris towards Yakima, where one minute, children were playing under a shining sun and the next, it was snowing ash. Residents could not see their own porch lights and the ash was so heavy it sank swimming pool covers and caved in old roofs. Businesses and schools were immediately closed.

The direction of the wind explained why to the north, in Duvall, there was hardly any ash fall and no clear sign of the natural disaster, but the pictures on the news told a different story: The gray and dreary aftermath, people wearing surgical masks to keep from breathing in toxic ash, others sweeping ash from their cars and rooftops.

Like our neighbors, we were glued to the T.V. coverage for the weeks following, asking ourselves how we could have not heard such an explosion, but we weren't alone. The real devastation was to the southeastern part of the state. Surprisingly, only 62 people had perished thanks to the evacuation orders and news alerts.

Two weeks later, Tim and me, along with Brenda and Laurie, both suddenly single at the time, decided not to postpone our long-planned camping trip for Memorial Day weekend, but when we got to Crescent Bar Resort, like all other campgrounds in Eastern Washington, it was vacant and covered in ash, and the weather was anything but warm.

Further north, Lake Chelan was even worse, where there were gale-force winds blowing across the mountain-wrapped lake. Back at the campsite and wearing a parka, Tim used his hand and pushed a layer of ash from a picnic table into a baggie. He explained, "This is a keepsake because you never know. Someday, this shit might be worth something."

Chapter Twenty-Seven

Tim and I spent two summers vacationing in the picturesque and peaceful San Juan Islands on our next boat, an 18-foot Dorset we christened *The Novice*. This boat had replaced *Park's Place*, which sadly caught fire while Tim was showing it to a potential buyer (who declined on the purchase but helped extinguish the fire). The Dorset could best be described as "cute," especially after I added red-and-white checkered curtains and a hammock for storage. With its tiny cabin, it was a far cry from Earl Birdsong's old boat.

I was happy with the Dorset but one September day, when boating season was already over because we lived in Western Washington, Tim developed a raging case of "two-foot-itis," a fast-attacking malady in which a boat owner simply must replace his current boat with one better and bigger by at least two more feet. In his search for a bigger boat, Tim began scouring the "Little Nickel," read all the "Boat For Sale" ads posted at the grocery store, and followed every lead on an affordable boat. Nothing turned up so one day we decided to go to the Edmond's marina. It was blustery and gray outside, a perfect day to get a deal.

After a brunch of crab omelets and Bloody Mary's at Arnie's, we walked over to the boatyard of used boats for sale, and the minute he laid eyes on a 23-foot Bayliner "Skagit" with the big red "For Sale" sign, he knew it was The One.

The boat's sleek body was made of fiberglass, not wood, had a front berth with a teak galley, an enclosed head, and aft sleeping quarters big enough for two tucked away under the spacious top deck, which had an L-shaped seating area with storage underneath. I had to admit, it put the Dorset to shame.

There were only twelve hours on the engine, the reason being that the seller's new wife became violently seasick whenever she was on it. He was asking $10,000 and Tim bought it for $9,500.

Naturally, a party was held to celebrate the acquisition, during which many traditional female names were suggested for Tim's boat: *Nancy Anne, Angela Marie, Mary-Jane,* not to mention *Cheryl Tiegs, Christie Brinkley,* and *Blondie.*

Others were more creative and had sexual themes: *High Tide, Master Baiter, Naughty Girl, Wet Dream, Dripping Wet,* and the worst by far: *Smelly Clam,* thought up by next-door neighbor Mike Strange, whose own boat—a 1930's wooden tugboat that ran on diesel—was unnamed.

Angie's idea for the boat's name was *Boring.*

Tim's Dad had a suggestion that was practical, *The Money Pit.*

I favored *Tranquility* because whenever me and Tim were on the water, whether it was aboard Mike Strange's holey, leaky tugboat, on more seaworthy *Novice,* we got along famously while cruising, sightseeing, sunbathing, and photographing the scenery (mostly sunsets and seals lying on rocks, which fascinated me). We had an unspoken peace truce when we were on our boat, at least at the beginning of our relationship, and one of my favorite stories to tell regarded our first summer aboard *Park's Place.* We had launched from the public marina in Anacortes on a cloudless but windy day. The boat seemed to do fine moving along at a good clip, but our first night, anchored in East Sound off Orcas Island, we awoke to the sounds of splashing water and the foot of our sleeping bags were soaked. Frantically, I began bailing while Tim barely saved the battery from drowning, and got the boat started.

On his orders, I crawled to the front and held a spotlight as Tim maneuvered the boat with only the light of a half moon and the weak beam of my flashlight. The night was terrifying; these were unfamiliar waters, which by day had been azure and refreshing but by night were sinister and the color of steel. Shivering in the salty air, I prayed for our safety as Tim moved slowly lest they hit a deadhead. An hour later, we were ashore. *Where* we had no idea, but land was land, and we built a bonfire out of driftwood and hoped we weren't trespassing.

The next morning, we awoke to children laughing and seagulls squawking. When I peeked cautiously from under our makeshift tent (a patio umbrella), the morning beach was covered with clam diggers and beachcombers. The tide was hours from coming in.

A leaky boat was no reason to call off the vacation off, so we simply shortened it to a week and beached *Park's Place* every night as we slept, and then waited for the morning tide to rescue them. We tried to anchor for short periods but even this required bailing, and the floral-patterned umbrella was great for protection from the elements but such an eyesore the marina at Roche Harbor kindly pointed us to "free mooring" in the mudflat bay around the corner.

The Dorset had been a welcome change, but now we had a *Bayliner*. We were definitely movin' on up.

Bragging to his friends about his new boat, which we eventually named *Sindrome*, Tim joked I was the first mate on good days, fish bait on in-between days, and dead weight on bad days, but he was thankful he at least *had* a boat.

"Carole wouldn't let me get a boat. Said they were too much trouble, but the real trouble was that bitch. Hell, if we had a boat, she'd be at the bottom of the fuckin' lake feeding the fishes."

All of Tim's friends laughed knowingly, but I was in the dark. Getting Tim to talk about Carole was like trying to get Tim to give up farting.

Chapter Twenty-Eight

In order to find out the details of Tim's breakup with his second wife Carole, I enlisted the surreptitious help of the only other person in the household who might hold some answers: Nine-year-old Angie. As soon as she came home from school, I greeted my hopeful source with hot fudge sundaes, beaming like Aunt-Bea. "Welcome home from school sweetie! I made fudge sundaes! Hurry and sit down before they melt!"

At the table, Angie sat rod-straight with her bowl in front of her. She bit her maraschino cherry off its stem. "Did I do something special?"

I cooed, "You *are* special and I know school has been rough with the new tutor and classes, so I just thought you might want a treat."

"Oh." Angie scooped up a spoonful and took a dainty bite. "Thank you, this is very good."

"So, how's school? Any better?" I felt bad that I had stirred things up at Angie's grade school but viewed it as a necessary evil. I didn't feel sorry for challenging the incompetent Dr. Plutz, who visibly shrank and went pale at the mention of Wendy Irwin, who made sure school districts met and maintained the mandated standards. I wished I could have framed that moment, or the one when Tim and I informed Dr. Plutz that because of the delays in Angie's placement, we had also hired the services of a Seattle attorney by the name of William Dressler, who had co-written several key state disability laws. Mr. Dressler and Dr. Irwin were big guns, and it showed on the startled face of Wanda Plutz, who clearly wanted to wash her hands of the entire Angela Joseph matter.

Angie replied, "School's okay, I guess. I like Dr. Irwin and she's really nice, but I don't want to take any more tests. They make my brain hurt."

"I know, honey, but it's in your best interests, really. Your dad and I want you to have the best education possible and to be in a classroom tailored to your needs."

"But I don't want to be in a class of retards."

"You are *not* a retard." I paused in an effort to get back to the purpose of the sundaes and began my redirect. "You know, I heard Carole loved maraschino cherries. Your Dad said she could eat an entire jar of them."

Angie gently swirled her chocolate syrup with her whipped cream. "I don't remember."

"Oh. What do you remember?"

"I dunno."

I grasped for something that would nudge Angie's memory and release a flood of juicy details. "Carole sure was pretty, don't you think?"

"Sure, I guess. You're pretty, too."

"Thanks." Not wanting to get off track, I continued. "Boy, your half-brother Mark is so adorable with that blond hair. I wonder why he only eats macaroni and cheese? And what a coincidence his birthday is the day after mine. Another Libra! I wonder if Carole—"

"Nancy," Angie set her spoon down. "If you wanna know what happened with my Dad and Carole, all you have to do is ask."

I felt my face redden. "Oh." I finished my sundae and looked up smiling sheepishly. "Well, only if *you* insist."

Angie rolled her eyes. She then told me her version of what happened. "I came home from school and Carole was packing her stuff and Mark was crying."

"Oh?" I glanced nervously at the clock, hoping Tim wouldn't walk in. "Go on." *Details, dear, details!*

"Well, Carole said Dad was being too nice to her best friend Cindy and this caused a huge fight. They were screaming really loud and I had to turn the volume all the way up on the T.V., but that didn't help so I rode my bike to the elementary school to see if Miss Lee was around because she was someone I could talk to."

Her again. "Oh, I see."

"Miss Lee was nice. She gave me good grades because of my Dad but then they broke up and Dad started going out with Nori the nurse." Angie hesitated briefly. "Dad said Nori had something wrong with her elevator."

I clarified, "Oh, you mean Nori's elevator didn't go to the top floor." It was one of Tim's favorite maxims.

"Yeah, I guess. Did you know Nori came over here once and sat down in the grass in her bikini without a towel to get a suntan but she got bugs in her you-know-what? She smelled funny and had hair under her arms. It was so gross." Angie finished her ice cream and added brightly, "My dad has lots of girlfriends but you're the normalest."

My eyes widened. "Really? Wow." It was the nicest compliment I could possibly receive. "So, was Carole nice?"

"To me, but she didn't get along with Dad." Angie took another bite of ice cream and asked, "Did you know my real mom lives in a shack and pees in the woods?"

"Yes, I heard about your mother. That's too bad."

Angie licked her spoon. "She likes living that way. Anyway, I only peed in the woods once, when Dad and me were camping. He forgot the toilet paper and I had to use a leaf. It scratched."

"Ouch." I stood to take our bowls to the sink and turned on the faucet with Angie at my side. She couldn't reach the sink but was eager to help. As I rinsed the dishes, Angie loaded them into the portable dishwasher. "Well, Angie, I've only camped once in my entire life right out of high school and for the occasion wore yellow suede sandals and white jeans, with a cute yellow blouse. My friend Brenda will never let me live that down. She says I need camping lessons."

Angie giggled and looked up. "Hey, Nancy? Will you buy me some sandals?"

"Absolutely, and white jeans, too!"

Chapter Twenty-Nine

We all pay a price for our parents' shortcomings. In the case of my family, we use humor to replace the pain of a dysfunctional childhood, ranging from the sardonic (Mark), wry (Bill), blithe (Patty), self-deprecating and docile (Sue), to droll and lighthearted (me).

Mom was cleverly amusing and witty, while Dad was scathingly acerbic, viewing the world as a corrupt society filled with too many weirdoes *and* Democrats.

Each of us in our own way shared a compelling need to make people laugh.

Tim, too, used humor, but in a more disdainful way and I could only speculate what happened in his childhood to make his sense of humor so edgy it was often mean-spirited. From what I gathered, his Catholic parents had a good, solid marriage. The first time I met Bob Joseph, he was so polite and kind it had me wondering if Tim was adopted.

Of course, Tim could be kind, *if* he wanted, and was highly altruistic. He didn't hesitate to save a drowning boy from the Snoqualmie River and donated his universal and rare type 0- blood regularly. In December of 1980, he took two vacation days and spent them helping a family down the street clean up after a Christmas Eve fire destroyed most of their home and killed a cherished pet. He routinely picked up hitchhikers and changed flat tires for people stranded along the side of the road.

Playing a large role in his paradoxical life was the female influence: A dead Catholic mother, an estranged older sister, an emotionally blunted daughter abandoned by her own mother, two ex-wives, a naïve girlfriend, and now a new stepmother, Gwendolyn.

Gwendo, as she was called, was a multitalented lady who enjoyed many music-related avocations, including singing in the opera and playing a variety of musical instruments. She was particularly gifted on the piano, and performed with gusto in leading roles for various musicals, including the part of Bloody Mary in a Seattle production of *South Pacific*, for which she was rightly cast.

Gwendolyn loved to be the center of attention but only on stage. Otherwise she was a homebody, preferring the company of Bob and her bevy of animals: A five-year-old Shih-Tzu named Sasha Girl, a parrot called Pavarotti, and a pair of cockatiels, Bach and Beethoven. Gwendolyn's nature was doting, especially on Bob, but it was mutual. In fact, it was sometimes hard to tell who had the bigger heart.

I instantly admired Gwendolyn and grew to adore Bob Joseph, sometimes feeling envious that Tim had such a kind-hearted father. Interestingly, over the years and without trying, my relationship with my father had begun to mysteriously change course for the better. I would never forget his tender display in the hospital when Mom was sick with cancer. It was moment etched in my mind, but there was another turning point.

On August 10, 1981, I wired Dad a bouquet of sunflowers with a card saying I was thinking of him because just days before, President Reagan (having survived an assassination attempt just months before) had fired thousands of striking air-traffic controllers. Dad was then Chief of Air Traffic Control at O'Hare International Airport in Chicago and I worried how this might affect him. My father responded with this heartfelt, and most surprising, handwritten letter:

8/11/81

Dearest Nancy,

I can't express how thoughtful your gift was! I came home after a particularly difficult day and felt like a million dollars when I read your card. Thank you so much. I'm sure that you have been following the news. However, some of what you see in the news is not a true portrayal of the situation.

The air-traffic control system is operating better and safer than ever, regardless of the PATCO statement. I say this not only from a personal observation standpoint, but from comments I hear from flight crews and others.

I have been supervisor in charge since the day the strike started (and leave it to a Republican to do the job right!) Never has Reagan been more popular with me nor have I ever enjoyed work so much. The union just doesn't realize how good and how tough we old guys are. Saturday I worked my 11th day in a row and had Sunday off, and next week we are going back to 8-hour shifts so conditions are practically back to normal.

The problem, which has not reported in the news, is the threats and actual incidents of violence directed towards us and our families. We have had 24-hour police guards at the tower and police patrol cars watching our homes. Unfortunately things will get worse, as soon as the fired controllers realized they have lost everything, especially financially, but we can handle it, so don't worry about us.

Kay is fine but doesn't particularly like it here, but I don't have too long to go before retirement and we are going to find a home in some lovely mountain like New Mexico or Arizona, when hopefully I'll get my health back (diabetes just like mama).

I know I am a very poor communicator, so this letter is a rare item, but I hope you are well. Give my love to your sisters, too. (By the way, Mark is now working at the Holiday Inn and making good money, and he is also thinking of joining the navy!)

I love you very, very much, and thank you again for your kind thoughts.

Love Always, Dad

My tear-filled eyes were glued to the words, "I love you very, very much." Up until that letter, I couldn't remember my father ever saying he loved me. Was it possible he had always loved me but just couldn't express it? During my childhood, he was a strict, unlovable, unapproachable man. Because of this, he was, by most standards, not a good father. This did not mean he was not good in other ways. For example, he was a very good air-traffic controller or he would have never made it as Chief Controller at O'Hare International Airport, the busiest airport in the U.S., and it was his salary that paid for the luxury houses my family had lived in during my childhood, each larger and fancier. The drawback was the length of time spent in these houses—two years max and usually only a year.

As a father, his disciplinarian techniques, while cruel, were effective: Standing in the corner of a darkened room for lengthy periods without meal or bathroom breaks had, at least for me, guaranteed I would not repeat whatever offense got me in such a corner. He whipped us with the belt and washed our mouths out with soap. He demanded we call him "sir."

I may have feared my father as a child but I could honestly say now I loved him, and *he* loved *me*. I shared the letter with Tim, who knew almost nothing about my father by my choice. He looked at the letter without reading it. It would have been mumbo-jumbo to his dyslexic eyes.

"So, tell me about your old man."

It was time, so I told him. "My father was one of four kids born in Columbus, Mississippi. Dad was raised on hushpuppies and black-eyed peas, and his daddy, my Grampa Nash, supposedly ruled with an iron fist. Bill Senior was always drunk, according to Mom, and meaner than a cobra. He was a railroad detective so I guess he had to be mean."

I actually didn't recall Grampa Nash being mean or a drunk, just someone who kept to himself and was not particularly affectionate. I also knew he was in frequent pain from an on-the-job injury when he was chasing some thieves that had robbed one of the freight trains on his duty and miscalculated the distance between two moving boxcars. His foot was nearly severed, and he was forced to retire. That's when my Gramma Nash began designing and sewing wedding gowns to make ends meet. On

Christmas Eve of 1967, Grampa Nash died in the hospital of a heart attack during recovery from surgery.

"If your dad was from Mississippi and your mom lived in Illinois, how the hell did they hook up?"

"Well, Dad was standing at a street corner in Columbus when Mom and her sorority sister, June, were driving through on their way to Fort Lauderdale for spring break. They needed directions and handsome Bill Nash was happy to oblige. A couple weeks later, he showed up in Geneseo. I guess he had taken he bus and walked right up to the porch of my grandparent's house and rang the doorbell, looking like something the cat drug in. Mom said her mother nearly fainted at the sight and wouldn't let him set foot in the house. He had to wait on the porch."

"No shit?"

"Yep, Dad had taken the bus all the way from Mississippi just to see my mother. They got married in Colorado Springs a few months later and moved to Peoria. There, Dad got a job as a baggage handler for TWA but a couple weeks later, he decided he wanted to be *landing* planes, not loading them." I paused. "It was good girl falls for bad boy, and the rest is, as they say, history."

Tim put his arm around me. "Kind of like us, huh?"

I shrugged. "Yeah, kind of like us. The last time my parents set eyes on each other was when Dad came to the hospital when my Mom had breast cancer."

Tim's jaw dropped. "*Your* mother had *breast cancer?*"

"Yes, when I was in college."

"And you never told me?"

"Why? She's okay." I hadn't thought it important to bring it up since Mom survived, especially in light of the fact Tim's mother had not. I suppose looking back it was guilt that kept me quiet. "Anyway, it was a long time ago." I folded up my father's letter and put it back in its original envelope. It was a letter I would never part with.

"Nancy? Don't you see?"

"See what?"

Tim widened his arms with his palms up, like an attorney delivering his closing arguments. "The *reason* you were so upset at Ma's funeral even though you hardly knew her. It's because you were actually grieving for your own mother because it could have easily been *her* that died. See? It was transference of grief." *I rest my case*, his expression said.

I was momentarily speechless but his theory made perfect sense. I walked over and put my arms around Tim. "Sometimes you surprise me, Tim. You literally knock me off my feet."

"I've been told *that* before." Tim grinned and cracked the top of another beer can.

I would learn to hate that sound.

Chapter Thirty

Petitioning a lawsuit against Snoqualmie Valley School District was supremely satisfying because it demonstrated, at least to Tim and me, that we were doing something about an unjust situation rather than pissing and moaning about it. For months following filing the suit, we discussed strategy and immodestly described for friends how intimidating yet necessary it was, all for the sake of educating Angie.

It was also very expensive. Already we owed Mr. Dressler thousands of dollars in the year that had passed of negotiations for the mounting correspondence documents between Mr. Dressler, Dr. Irwin, and the school district's legal representatives. Along the way, we encountered enough bureaucratic red tape to circle an entire city block. Slowly, our disenchantment with the legal process turned to hostile intolerance, so when we were asked if would prefer to go directly to mediation, also called arbitration, rather than wait for a jury trial, we didn't hesitate to say yes. It would mean putting an end to idle and tense meetings that got 12-year-old Angie no closer to a proper education.

The day of the arbitration hearing, Tim was upbeat and had on his boxing gloves.

I was less upbeat. In fact, I was a nervous wreck and downed a Xanax tablet Tim produced from the medicine cabinet with my morning coffee.

Unfortunately, I reacted poorly to the powerful anxiolytic and as soon as I was called to testify, I froze. All the preparations for my testimony, based on months of reviewing carefully typewritten notes and copies of every scrap of correspondence that was sitting in chronological order in a file folder in front of me, vanished in a Xanax stupor. I had never taken Xanax before, which was part of the problem, especially on an empty stomach. The other was that I was a wimp when it came to confrontation. In fact, Tim put it best and in characteristic jargon later when we were alone: *Hon, you talk a big game but as soon as the cards are laid on the table, you're the first to fold.*

And *cry*, which I began doing copiously right after the mediator asked me if I was okay, leaving Angie's fate entirely up to her father.

Teary-eyed and dazed, I watched helplessly as Tim endured hours of grueling questioning and cross-examination, frequently referring to my notes for his testimony. He never faltered, although smoked heavily during breaks. When it was over, Tim assured me he wasn't worried about the outcome, even without my support. "Don't worry. Did you see me in there? I was on a roll."

I sniffled. "I can't believe I wimped out." My chest was a fiery blotch of nervous hives. "It was like my brain froze, all those strangers' eyes focused on me. If only—"

"Don't worry, there're worse things than being lily-livered, just don't take no more Xanax." Tim inhaled deeply on his cigarette. "Besides, how can we lose? Our attorney is the man who *wrote* the fuckin' law on special education. Besides, did you see Dr. Plutz squirm when Wendy grilled her? Poor woman is probably puking in the can as we speak. Anyway, we're not asking for millions, just justice."

It was true; our lawsuit sought simple, reasonable things: For Angie to be placed in a school district that would meet her needs, would endeavor to meet those needs free of charge as was guaranteed by state law, and we'd be reimbursed for legal costs incurred as a result of the lawsuit. In addition, we also wanted to be reimbursed for what it had cost to hire Wendy Irwin, which would not have been necessary if the school psychologist had been more qualified. Or alert.

During our appointments with her, Wanda Plutz yawned

continuously, which started a chain reaction. The yawning did not instill great confidence, but her lethargy could explain why she had failed in six months to find what two days of testing by Dr. Irwin had discovered: Angie was not only dyslexic, but had cognitive deficits in nearly all areas of learning, including written and verbal language. This was a child who would not succeed in a regular classroom and this conclusion strengthened our resolve to fight even harder. I knew despite our good intentions, Angie was embarrassed to be the center of such unrelenting attention and told me she wished I'd never said anything about to her Dad about Ms. Baxter calling her stupid. Convincing her we were doing the right thing wasn't easy, but that night I couldn't sleep and imagined us winning our lawsuit and being in the news. I mentally picked out an appropriate outfit for the interview and could see the headlines: *Local Couple Fights School District and Wins Big!*

Meanwhile, Tim was imagining a new state law named "The Angela Joseph Law."

Bright and early the next morning, we drove to the Public Administrative Building, where the verdict was delivered: The mediator ordered the school district to place Angie in a specialized program in nearby Woodinville (which had a bigger budget for special education), including bussing her there, and they had to use the Individualized Educational Plan, or IEP, formulated by Dr. Irwin. Unfortunately, the district was not held accountable for our legal expenses, which by that point totaled $6,500, nor would they have to pay for Dr. Irwin's fees. Since we had chosen arbitration, appealing the decision wasn't an option.

The news, while mostly good, devastated me because I was certain if I had testified along with Tim as planned, we would have won on all counts. After all, *I* was the mastermind of the lawsuit, or at least the one in charge of the paper trail, and had been instrumental in filing it.

Tim was more disappointed there wasn't going to be an Angie Joseph Law after all, one which would, as he so ineloquently put it, "Protect kids with learning troubles from being called stupid by stupid teachers."

Chapter Thirty-One

Mark Corbin Joseph had the longest eyelashes on any child I had ever met. Even with a department store eyelash curler and Estee Lauder mascara, my lashes would never achieve the length of Mark's. He also had piercing blue eyes, which at the moment were fixed on mine.

"How come you don't have kids of your own?" Mark, like his father, got straight to the point.

It was October 5, 1982, and Mark, Angie, and I were seated at a booth in Redmond's *Las Margaritas* restaurant celebrating Mark's ninth birthday. I answered honestly, "I guess the timing hasn't been right."

Angie said, "She's like *my* mom. I even call her Mom."

"I know," Mark replied, blond eyelashes fluttering. "My Mom wants lots of kids. That's why she's having another baby. She said it's going to be a girl and already painted the spare bedroom pink. My stepdad helped." Mark's arms were resting properly at his sides, his posture straight.

I asked, "Are you excited about having a baby sister?"

"Not really. I already have one stepsister. That's enough." He grinned at Angie, showing off deep dimples.

Angie groaned, "Very funny, Mark." She turned to me and said, "I wouldn't mind having a sister."

I scooped up pico de gallo with a crisp warm tortilla chip. "Oh?"

"Yeah, but I know my Dad can't have no more kids. I guess that's probably good."

I laughed nervously. Tim should have been with us at the restaurant for his own son's birthday but he was at home nursing a major hangover from my birthday celebration the night before. I, too, had overindulged but after downing two Extra Strength Tylenol with a large glass of orange juice, I felt good enough to go, and there was no way I was going to disappoint Mark on his birthday. In a way, I didn't mind Tim's absence and enjoyed my "alone" time with Tim's kids. They were delightful to be around. Plus, Mark was a Libran. That bonded us.

"May I please have another glass of Coke?"

"Sure, Mark, it's your birthday."

"Me too?" Angie inquired.

"Everyone can have as much Coke as they want."

The manners in these children were impeccable, including at the mall earlier, where Mark and Angie behaved perfectly. In fact, when I bought Mark a pair of Nike tennis shoes, he looked on the verge of tears, asking me why I would buy him something even though I wasn't his mom. Then he said his Mom didn't really like me, but that's because she didn't know me. He thanked me for the shoes *twice*.

"So Mark, is your mom going to have a big party for you after you get home tonight?"

Mark nodded and after wiping his mouth with his napkin, said, "My grandparents are actually throwing me a party. I already know what I'm getting. The helmet dad gave me kinda gave it away."

I knew Mark was getting a three-wheeler and that Carole had asked Tim to buy him a helmet. I asked innocently, "Really, what?"

"A three-wheeler but I'll act surprised. I can't wait!"

Their food arrived and Mark bowed his head and said grace. He finished and grinned through full lips, his blue eyes seeming wiser beyond his age. "Mom wanted me to wait until I was twelve to get a motorbike but I got good grades. That's why I'm getting one even though I'm nine, but I'll be very careful."

"I'm sure you will be." Remembering my gift, I retrieved a birthday card from my purse and slid it across the table. "I almost forgot. This is for you."

Inside was a ten-dollar bill and Mark's piercing blue eyes widened even more. "Money? Wow, thank you." He sipped his Coke through a straw and looked up. "You're really nice *and* rich. Does my Dad know?"

I giggled, and sipped my own Coke. "Yes, he knows, and I'm not rich, just well-paid."

When Professional Dictation landed the Harborview Medical Center account, I didn't have to beg to be assigned the challenging yet lucrative account. Many in our office preferred typing mundane "S.O.A.P." chart notes, called so because of their format: Subjective, Objective, Assessment, and Plan. I personally hated the often repetitive and always boring family practice SOAP notes and welcomed an account like Harborview, which presented an opportunity to transcribe some of the most fascinating (and odd) reports of my young career, and I was paid a premium rate for my skill and efforts.

Located in Seattle's First Hill district, Harborview Medical Center is a trauma and burn center where the lonely, neglected, uninsured, homeless, drug-addicted, and/or just plain weird ended up. The patients there were victims of fires, car crashes, suicide attempts, near-drownings, domestic violence, gunshot wounds, and AIDS, a new diagnosis accompanied by misunderstanding and disgust.

The first time I heard the terms "Kaposi's sarcoma" dictated in a report (in 1980), I had to look it up, but by 1983, anyone who watched the news or read the newspaper was familiar with Kaposi's sarcoma, a skin disorder common in patients with HIV infection or AIDS, which stood for Autoimmune Deficiency Syndrome. The "gay cancer," it was called.

Over the course of transcribing the Harborview account, many reports would stand out in my memory: A middle-aged black female who presented to the emergency room complaining that the ringing in her ears was so loud customers sitting behind her at the I.H.O.P. complained.

Another woman's chief complaint was that she had been raped, as had her Doberman, by someone wearing a green vinyl jumpsuit. In that report, I tried to detect the slightest catch of disbelief in the dictating doctor's voice, but his delivery was monotone and matter-of-fact, no doubt a result of years of practice.

There was the man who complained of intense abdominal cramping and on x-ray had what appeared to be a cucumber-shaped foreign object lodged in his rectosigmoid colon. It was indeed a cucumber, and while the mechanism of how it got there was clear, the *reason* was left for wild speculation.

I transcribed reports on 7-year-old child who swallowed a toad whole and another concerning an ICU nurse whose breast rash turned out to be a malignancy so advanced (and neglected) it had necrosed through skin. The diagnosis was Stage 4 inflammatory breast carcinoma, a rare and lethal form.

My shift flew by, filled with dictations about fascinating human tragedy.

Chapter Thirty-Two

When your office building is located on "The Ave," in Seattle's University District, the potential for police activity is high. From our fourth-floor office inside a converted condominium building built in the fifties, the sound of sirens was nearly constant and would eventually not even been noticed. Below us, we didn't need to watch to know somebody on that long stretch of blacktop peppered with everything from tattoo parlors to Chinese takeout to porn was up to no good.

It was a secure building, so inside I felt relatively safe, though it wasn't paradise. The building was poorly maintained and P.D.'s office smelled like mildew and old people, and the carpet was of the indoor/outdoor variety and the color of snot. There was one bathroom and two offices with doors that locked. The rest was an open space sectioned off with partitions in primary colors that offered little privacy. My desk was near the Lanier workstation, from which we regularly gathered cassette tapes to be transcribed after they were spit onto a tray.

Despite the building having a locked entryway, strays from The Ave occasionally made their way inside, like the homeless man found sleeping soundly under our proofreader's desk. The following fracas put most of us, but particularly Susan, who had been at that desk in a short skirt for hours, into a panic state.

I was afraid of The Ave, unlike my friend and coworker, Moira Batista, an exotic beauty with an edgy look and even edgier personality. Moira was a confident woman who always wore black, even in the heat of summer, often accessorized with gold. One December, Moira bought a two-hundred-dollar black sweater threaded with gold from Nordstrom and wore the sweater three times every week. By March, the sweater was showing its age, even paired with new black slacks and gorgeous black leather boots. In July, the sweater still made an occasional appearance.

In addition to being beautiful, Moira was fiercely ambitious, and soon after she started working at P.D. as a transcriptionist, she began dating our boss, Rick Greene. There was a lot that could be improved at P.D. and Moira set out to make those improvements, eventually being promoted to office manager. No one said no to Moira, though her in-charge attitude didn't mean things always went smoothly at P.D. She and Rick butted heads constantly over policy and procedure, payroll and marketing. Her job was extremely stressful trying to meet important client deadlines with staffing problems that were ongoing. By the time Moira was office manager, I couldn't count the number of people who had worked at P.D., some for just days, one woman less than an hour because the office smelled like "cheap perfume" and made her nauseous.

The few that outlasted the critical six-month mark included Sunday school teacher Paula Shores, who a year after being hired was discovered sleeping in the basement storage room and sporting a huge black eye. Paula claimed she only dated black men and drove red cars (until the latter were impounded and/or repossessed) and was a knowledgeable transcriptionist when she wasn't nursing the aftereffects of an all-nighter. In that case, she'd spend her shift with her head slumped on crossed arms atop her typewriter snoring until Moira noticed and woke her up. By then, I had already snatched the cassettes sitting on her desk and was dutifully finishing them. It didn't matter to me because the more I typed the more I got paid, while Paula was living off advances until eventually there was no paycheck due her. Right before she got fired, Paula said proudly of her current boyfriend James, "Once you go black, you never go back." My interest was piqued but that's where it stayed.

After Paula's departure, Moira hired a young woman named Ursula, who was a part-time journalist who proclaimed on her resume that she was "a great speller, an excellent writer, and a decent typist." On that same resume under "Hobbies," she listed "scrapbooking, yoga, pelvic tilts, and studying the Bible." We were skeptical since the resume was printed on rainbow-lined paper, but Ursula Timmerman was called in, and during the interview, conducted near my desk, Moira asked, "Pelvic tilts?"

Ursula nodded excitedly. "Oh yes! It helps keep things in place. I do them when I'm watching T.V., or reading the Bible." She smoothed the front of a yellow calico dress eight sizes too big. "So, am I hired?"

Moira's beautiful features became pinched and she glanced my direction. She was either constipated, having a spontaneous orgasm, or contemplating jumping off our fourth-floor balcony. "Well, Ursula, pelvic tilts are not a skill P.D. is looking for, but the backlog of dictation is growing like wildfire, and you seem eager." She took one more glance over the newest applicant's resume, removed her glasses, and in a display of optimism unsupported by any credible work history yet bolstered by desperation, hired Ursula on the spot. It didn't matter that Rick had already perused the resume and said no; Moira rarely valued Rick's opinions to any great degree.

Ursula was handed over a book of training materials and a test cassette, and told good luck.

"Thanks, but I won't need it."

I doubted that, but smiled. "Well, if you do need help, please ask."

Ursula smiled back. "Thanks, but I'm a quick learner. Besides, how hard can it be?"

Harder than you think, granola girl!

It was so annoying when people said that about my job. Everyone who could type thought they could do medical transcription (NOT!) and the chances that Ursula was going to be another Trish Elliott were about as likely as Moira going celibate. Trish was a rare treasure in this field, a young mother with a background in science and research. She was frank during her interview about having never done transcription but begged to be given a chance. Rick had sensed more than steely determination and agreed to hire her, and Trish did not disappoint. Within months, despite the stress of raising a toddler and in the midst of a divorce, Trish was already transcribing hospital accounts, which usually were reserved for us "old-timers."

Ursula was no Trish, proven a couple days later when Ursula refused to do the very first report for a new account, an Ob-Gyn Clinic in Shoreline. She handed the cassette tape to Moira, saying she couldn't possibly type the report, which was an elective termination of pregnancy.

"Abortion is against my religious beliefs. Sorry, but you'll have to give this tape to someone else."

Moira shot daggers at Ursula and threw the tape onto her desk. It landed directly on her typewriter with a loud crack. I would have been quivering and offering to work overtime. Ursula was picking at a scab near her nose.

Moira told her, "Sorry, Ursula, but that's part of our job. We *type* reports, we don't make judgments."

"Supporting baby killers is our job? I don't think so." Ursula sniffled. "I'm sorry but I cannot and will not type a report detailing the murder of an unborn fetus. Why can't I be a *specialized* transcriptionist who types only certain reports?"

"Oh, you mean happy reports?" Moira's tone was dripping with sarcasm but Ursula's eyes widened with delight.

"Yes! Exactly!"

"Jesus, Ursula, I was kidding. If you want happy, go apply at the fuckin' Jack-in-the-Box. I am sure they are hiring idiots today."

On the other side of the partition, Trish and I were listening. Clearly, Moira was reaching her boiling point so I stood and said soothingly, "Actually, Ursula, what Moira means is there is no such thing as just happy medical reports. It'd be nice, but that's not how this job works."

Ursula turned. "That sucks."

I shook my head. "If you want to learn to do this job, you must distance yourself from the patients you are transcribing about, and not get involved personally. It takes time and practice."

Ursula whined, "But if doctors can be specialists, why can't transcriptionists?" Her ponytailed braid swung heavily across her bony back and she held her chin up, like she was onto something *big*. "I'll bet

Mr. Greene would agree with me." She turned to Moira, "Unlike you, he seems nice."

Moira snorted, "You don't live with him, and Rick would fire you on the spot, which is what I'm going to do if you pick and choose what you will and will not transcribe. That's unacceptable."

"Here, I'll do that tape." Trish walked over and reached for the cassette. She asked patiently, "So, Ursula, out of curiosity, what kind of transcription would you specialize in, if you could?"

"Maybe delivery notes? I adore babies, you know, even though I don't have any kids but I'm sure that will change."

Moira snapped. "Not if all you're doing with your pelvis is tilts. I'm sorry, but you can't pick and choose in this office."

Tears began to flow down Ursula's thin face. "But…"

Trish said patiently, "Ursula, not all deliveries have wonderful outcomes. What are you going to do if the report is about a complicated birth or cesarean section?" She was the mother of a healthy son named Thomas, though the pregnancy had been difficult, and for her first trimester she lived on saltines and club soda.

"Complicated?" Ursula's gray eyes grew wide.

I nodded. "I can think of a few: Nuchal cord wrapped around the infant's neck, breech delivery, uterine atony. That always leads to postpartum hemorrhage and is often fatal. Really, there are all sorts of gory, unpleasant things that can happen during deliveries. Babies don't always pop out with perfect Apgars."

Trish agreed. "Just the other day I did a report where the surgeon had to dislocate the infant's shoulder to get it out of the birth canal and afterwards—"

"Never mind." Ursula picked up her duffel bag and said, "I guess the job isn't as easy as I thought it would be."

"Famous fuckin' last words," Moira hissed, and it was true. Our job required a long list of skills, among them mindreader, detective, secretary, interpreter of English spoken as a second language, syntax specialist, and last but not least, one had to learn how to use the exact amount of Wite-Out so mistakes, if any, would not stand out like a sore thumb. Our new Selectric typewriters, which could store text in a limited capacity, had reduced the office's need for correcting fluid, but not by much.

Ursula slumped out and, sure enough, headed in the general direction of the Jack-in-the-Box at the corner.

Looking out the window and watching Ursula walk down The Ave, I said, "It *would* be nice to specialize. We could really make big bucks doing just one primary account, and I'd pick neurosurgery."

Trish, who had a Bachelor of Science in Medical Technology, nodded. "I'd pick oncology or hematology."

Moira was back and said, "It'd be ophthalmology for me. Eye diseases fascinate me." She reached for her can of Diet Coke, poured it down her throat, and threw the can into the trash, along with Ursula's resume. "What a waste of time."

I suggested, "Maybe Ursula was pregnant? That would explain a lot."

"Maybe *I'm* pregnant. My period's twelve days late."

My jaw dropped and Moira read my mind. "Yes, Rick knows, and like always, he barely showed any emotion. Sometimes I think that man is made of wood."

Trish asked, "Have you gone to the doctor to get a pregnancy test?"

Moira cocked her head in a manner that suggested she had just been asked to give up her left breast for a donut. She asked derisively, "Do I *look* like I have time to go to the doctor?" She walked back to her desk, retrieved her Steno pad, and picked up her phone. "I better call our next lucky contestant, Sylvie Happner. At least she has experience."

At the mention of the missed period, Trish and I exchanged a knowing look, one that said *Uh Oh* loud and clear. Rick and Moira was a couple constantly at odds, probably because they were both too damn smart for their own good. And Rick seemed to have a knack for poor timing. He had been gone all afternoon and now was just walking into the office, loosening the knot of his tie. His tone was bland but his eyes were triumphant, as if he already knew the answer to his question. "So, Moira, how did the training go with Ursula Timmerman?"

I cringed as Moira reacted with typical drama: She threw the entire in-basket of proofreading and cassettes into the wall and then she started yelling.

"Rick, has anyone told you you're a clueless idiot?" She rubbed her stomach through a black tunic. "This job is killing me, and I probably have a fuckin' ulcer the size of a watermelon but you don't care!" She pulled open a drawer and retrieved a bottle, which she threw across the room. "I'm eating Tums like candy!"

The office was empty other than Trish and me, and since it was next to impossible to transcribe complex dictations through earphones when Moira was in the throes of theatrics, we watched intently from our chairs. The only thing missing was popcorn and an usher.

Rick said calmly, "Well, then, this couldn't have come at a better time." He was holding a flyer.

"What the hell are you taking about?" Moira spit through sniffles, hands perched on ample hips.

Rick waved the flyer into the air. "This one-day seminar at the Seattle Sheraton, 'Managing Stress at the Workplace.' I just got the information in the mail today. I'll pay for you to attend." His condescending tone was hard to miss. He continued gratuitously, "It will be held on May 12. Parking is validated and lunch is catered." He tilted his head waiting for what he expected was a positive response.

I knew what was coming because Rick *was* clueless, at least when it came to reading the body language of the opposite sex, particularly that of his live-in girlfriend/office manager. A long string of expletives, not completely in English, filled the air, interspersed with references to Rick's anal-retentiveness.

Rick continued rubbing his beard, obviously unperturbed at the outburst. "Moira," he appeased, "It would behoove the office if you would refrain from obscenities. Perhaps we can discuss this matter in my office?"

Moira screamed. "Perhaps it would *behoove* you to get a new fuckin' office manager!" She grabbed her black leather hobo bag and black leather jacket, and stormed out in a dark whirl, but not before spewing a few more "assholes."

Rick shrugged, placed the flyer on Moira's desk, and walked into his office, closing the door.

Trish leaned over. "Maybe if Moira doesn't go to the stress seminar, we could go?"

"Sure, but I don't think a one-day seminar will do the trick, not for *this* job stress."

Trish sighed. "That was quite a scene. Is Moira going to be all right?" She had formerly worked in a laboratory and was unaccustomed to such emotionally charged office exchanges.

I replied, "Sure. After a pack of cigarettes, she'll be fine."

Chapter Thirty-Three

Sylvie Happner was a forty-something bleached blond with fifteen years' M.T. experience, who ended up working the weekend shift. On the day of the interview, she wore brown combat boots, camouflage-print parachute pants, and hadn't bother shaving. I was guessing she was pushing two hundred pounds, which was mostly muscle, and was close to six feet tall. Work wise, Sylvie was knowledgeable and productive, and a couple months after she was hired, things were looking bright for Sylvie and Professional Dictation's working relationship. Then, on a Monday morning, Moira walked into the office and discovered all the tapes she had left at Sylvie's station for her to do during her weekend shift were exactly where Moira had left them, untouched. Five minutes later, Moira's phone rang.

She picked it up and answered harshly, "P.D. " She then said, "What? You're in jail?" A long pause followed before Moira said, "Sylvie, what happened?" Her gorgeous eyes narrowed as she massaged a temple with one hand. A short pause was followed by, "Hello? Sylvie? Are you there?" Another short pause preceded, "But why are you in jail?" This time, there was a very long pause, during which Moira was multitasking, going through a file folder and organizing the cassettes on her desk.

I was dying of curiosity and mouthed, "What happened?"

Moira shook her head and turned into the phone, with one hand over her nonlistening ear. "Sylvie, I can't hear you. What is going on?" Moira glanced my direction and put her hand up, motioning me to be patient. She slumped against her desk. "Omigod. Okay, well, um. Thanks for calling, I guess." Moira hung up the phone just as Rick walked in.

"What's going on?" The beard was getting a workout.

Moira quipped, "Oh, nothing serious, Rick. It's just that Sylvie Happner has been arrested for killing her husband."

Trish visibly paled. "Sylvie killed her husband?"

"Yep." Moira was gulping her breakfast of choice, Diet Coke. "He's dead and she's in jail."

"Omigod, how? Was it with poison?" That seemed the cowardly way and Sylvie didn't look like a coward, but poison was an easy choice. Anybody could get hold of rat killer, especially if they looked like a Nazi. "There was something creepy about her. Maybe it was premeditated?"

"Who knows? I'm not the fuckin' coroner." Moira turned a digusted look towards Rick as if Sylvie's homicidal actions were his fault. Her eyes were slits. "Well?"

"Well, that's too bad." Rick picked up a newspaper and asked Moira to rerun the help-wanted ad in the *Times* for another week. He turned to his stunned staff and said, "You know, I met Sylvie's husband, Chuck, one night. He was your size, Nancy, probably didn't weigh more than a hundred pounds." Rick bent in front of a file cabinet, retrieved some files, and stood. "Chuck acted skittish and it was clear Sylvie ran the roost. The man probably couldn't shit without permission."

The office fell silent, not sure what was more surprising: That they had worked in the midst of a cold-blooded (my assumption) murderer, or that their old-fashioned, straight-laced boss had just cussed.

The next day, Moira had an Erase-Board hanging from the wall above her desk that read:

REASONS FOR ABSENTEEISM

1) Sick.
2) On jury duty.

2) Hung over.

3) Sick and hung-over.

4) In jail:

    a) Minor offense (keep on birthday rotation).

    b) Felony (clean out desk).

5) Sick and hung-over *and* in jail (keep an open mind).

6) Dead (wire flowers and card to family).

Moira could have added another: "Attending 'Managing Stress at the Workplace' Conference at the Sheraton."

Moira was supposed to go but at the last minute decided the office couldn't function even one day without her, so it was me who attended. I had found the morning lectures not only unhelpful but boring, and the only thing I was learning was how to manage staying alert. Finally we got a 10-minute break and I scurried to the ladies' room to empty a distended bladder of two Grande nonfat vanilla lattes. I was first there and first to leave being in the big hurry that I was. Unfortunately, the big rush resulted in my inadvertently bunching my cute purple skirt inside my pantyhose, but only in back where I couldn't see.

The stress levels I had come to abolish reached skyscraper heights when an elderly lady approached me in the bustling lobby (where I wondered why people were staring and pointing), and offered me her sweater. She escorted me to the ladies' room, where I unbunched my skirt behind a locked stall door. I remained there for thirty long, humiliating minutes, just enough time for all the people who had been in the lobby to disperse. Then I rushed to my car and cried. I would never wear that Liz Claiborne floral-print skirt again, even though it cost sixty bucks.

Chapter Thirty-Four

My brother Billy bounced around a lot in his younger years, alternating between our mother's house in Washington and our father's residence, wherever that might be in any given year. When he was fifteen, Billy moved to Albuquerque, New Mexico, where Dad and Kay had just moved from Oklahoma City. The arrangement lasted less than a month because two hotheads in one house was one too many.

Billy ended up living with friends but did not drop out of high school, and after graduation, moved to Oklahoma City to enter a technical and repairman apprenticeship program paid for by his new employer, AT&T. It was a job for which he would be well suited. After all, this was a kid who, at age six, was discovered replacing the spark plugs on the family lawnmower, and by age ten had rewired our grandfather's antique radio so it actually worked again. There was no explanation for this skill; our father couldn't change a flat tire or unclog a toilet on his own, and boasted that he did not know the difference between a wrench, a winch, or a wicket, nor did he care. Dad's approach to home repairs was to let his fingers do the walking. Six months later into his new job, Billy was promoted to Senior Technician and soon thereafter met his future wife, Debi Dudley, a fair-skinned, curly-haired native of Oklahoma.

Our brother's wedding took place in March of 1984, and was preceded on the part of his sisters and mother by a long list of preparations. First and foremost, we needed new outfits, including dresses and shoes. Next, because it was the Year of the Poodle, Patty and I got matching perms. My sister also added a few sessions of tanning to her preparations, and had her ears repierced again (the reason being the original piercing was done under less than sterile conditions in an attic by a friend using a knitting needle, a chunk of cheddar, and ice cubes. Patty was twelve at the time and has battled earlobe infections since). My earlobes were fine, but I did have my eyelashes dyed.

Unbeknownst to our mother, Patty and I also got Valium for the trip (our first aboard a commercial airplane), which we took at the airport with our coffee. When we boarded, we sat in the first row behind First Class, where I tried to convince myself the Valium was working but this proved hard to do when next to me, Patty had both hands glued to the armrests and her eyes were squeezed closed.

"Patty, why are you so nervous? We haven't even taken off yet." Mom was sitting between us and reached over to pat Patty's rigid hand. "Relax."

"I am relaxed," Patty said with her eyes closed, "Really."

I buckled myself in tightly and leaned back, moving only my lips lest I tip the plane. "Me, too, Mom. This is going to be so much fun." I would have rather undergone a root canal without Novocain. I ventured a quick peek behind me. "Where's the beverage service?"

Patty finally opened her eyes but didn't move her head. "Don't worry, I packed mini bottles of Kahlua in my purse. Just order coffee."

Mom rolled her eyes. "Girls, it's going to be okay. I've flown half a dozen times, all the way to the Caribbean with Bob twice and I'm still in one piece. You'll see."

I wondered how many Valiums one could take without O.D.ing, and asked my mother, an apparent aeronauticals expert, "Is it safer to be in the front, back, or middle of a plane?"

"Honey, if this jet crashes, we're all toast." Mom picked up a magazine. "We'll be fine. Here, read this magazine with Mel Gibson on the cover. That will keep your mind occupied."

I accepted the *People* magazine. I agreed wholeheartedly that Mel Gibson was the "Sexiest Man Alive." I sighed. "Too bad Mel isn't on this plane. I'd probably relax then, especially if I could get him alone in the cockpit."

Patty leaned over and whispered. "Yeah, I wouldn't mind fondling his lethal weapon!"

Over a speaker, the pilot announced it was time for takeoff and I had never been so nervous in my entire life. I was frozen in my seat with Mel Gibson's gorgeous mug folded between my knees. Sadly, my Styrofoam cup of spiked coffee was gone and I dared not move to pour another. I squeezed my eyes shut and prayed: *Please God, we spent a lot of money to attend Billy's wedding so please, please don't let us crash. Please!*

The Boeing 727 began taxiing down the runway and after a loud rumble of engine its steel nose rose and began ascending into a gloomy gray sky. I kept my eyes closed even when the plane leveled off, briefly peeking up to catch a glimpse of an unsettling demonstration by a stewardess in a blue dress on emergency exits and proper use of oxygen masks in the event the cabin lost pressure. The lady was describing potential disaster yet was beaming like a newly crowned Miss America. Finally, she finished and headed to the rear of the plane, doing a quick assessment of each aisle on the way.

When she passed, I whispered, "Mom, why would the cabin lose pressure?"

"It won't, don't worry."

"But—"

"Relax."

"I'm trying." I glanced out the tiny window. "Wow, we're above the clouds. I've never seen clouds from this angle. It's kind of scary." I looked at Patty, who was in the window seat and now reading the *People* magazine, a smile plastered to her face. "Patty, aren't you scared anymore?"

"Nope, I just took another Valium."

"Hand them over." I held out a shaking hand, noting my mother's disapproving glance. "Just one, I guess."

Mom shook her head. "This is going to be a long trip. I hope your brother knows the sacrifices that are being made."

By the end of the three-hour trip, my sister's and my full attention was on our dimpled male flight attendant, whose nametag read, "Travis."

I whispered, "Push the call button again."

Patty asked giddily, "What are we going to ask for now?"

"Peanuts, and maybe a blanket."

"Girls, leave the poor man alone. He has other passengers, you know."

Ignoring our mother, Patty pushed the button, which lit up and dinged, and a few seconds later Travis appeared. "What can I get ya'll?" He had long sideburns and an accent exactly like Kay's.

I murmured coyly, "A blanket please, and some more peanuts for my sister."

"Sure. Anything else?"

Mom interjected, "No, they're fine. My daughters have never flown before, so they're a bit nervous."

"Oh, that explains it." Travis smiled even wider and I wanted to kiss him.

Patty inquired, "So, Travis, where are you from?"

"Dallas."

"Oh!" I yelped, "I've always wanted to go to Dallas, you know, to see where President Kennedy was shot."

Mom rolled her eyes but Travis nodded and offered to bring us complimentary drinks since this was our maiden trip. Once he was out of earshot, Patty murmured, "Travis is cute, and flying is a lot more fun than I thought it would be."

"I know!" I was considerably more relaxed by the time our plane landed safely at Oklahoma City's Will Rogers Airport. We disembarked and Travis reached out his hand. "Have a wonderful trip and we hope you will fly Continental Airlines again real soon!"

I contemplated hugging Travis but the passengers behind me seemed restless, probably cause I hadn't shared my Valium, so I settled on a handshake and hoped he was on our flight back. At the airport, we rented a car and drove straight to our hotel in a blinding rainstorm with winds blowing so hard they knocked the traffic signals nearly horizontally. From one of the double beds at the Ramada, my sister and I sat watching the storm while Mom settled in.

"I cannot believe we're back in Oklahoma. Honestly, I would have bet money I'd never set foot in this state ever again." Mom pointed through the window. "Nothing has changed. This state is still ugly. Just look at that black sky."

I reached for the phone between the beds. "We better call Billy and Debi and let them know we didn't crash, and then let's go eat. I'm starving."

The clock read 9:36 p.m. and Mom yawned. "I'm fine. You girls go eat and I'll call Billy. I think I'm going to take a shower and relax before the big day."

At just past midnight on the day of our brother's wedding, Patty and I were pulling into the hotel parking lot. The storm was still raging and branches and tumbleweeds rolled across the pavement.

Patty exclaimed giddily, "I can't believe this night!" She wasn't talking about the storm.

"I know." I parked and cut the engine. "They were such nice gentlemen. Besides, how could we turn down a limousine ride to a *private* club?"

Patty yawned. "Do you think they were really congressmen?"

"Absolutely. Those were Italian suits, plus they knew everyone at the club."

We entered the hotel room quietly. In the darkness, we hurriedly changed into pajamas and were just ready to settle into the extra double bed when a gust of wind came up, so powerful the glass on the window buckled and the lights flickered. Sirens screamed in the city.

Mom reached to turn on the light. "I was worried about you girls. On the news, they said there was a tornado watch near Tulsa." She yawned and glanced at the clock, and my heart sank. "Goodness, look what time it is! You girls must have gone all the way to Baton Rouge for dinner."

I fibbed, "Traffic was bad downtown."

"Yeah, and we got lost," Patty lied. I never got lost, at least not while driving. Unnecessarily she added, "*Really* lost." Embellished lies were a Nash specialty.

Three days later, on the flight back to Seattle, we analyzed our brother's wedding over plastic cups of white wine.

I said, "That was a beautiful wedding gown Debi was wearing." Sip.

"Yes, it was gorgeous. Debi seems like a nice girl." Patty held up her plastic glass. "This is pretty good wine for airline service."

Sip. "How would you know? This is your first glass of wine on a plane, and mine too."

Patty answered, "It's an educated guess." Sip.

"Oh. Well, you're right. Debi seems sweet." Sip. "But she sure is a giggler."

Mom asked, "You mean Debi? Well, I think she was just nervous."

"No, I don't think so. Billy…I mean Bill…said she giggles at everything. That's probably why she had laryngitis."

"I'm just glad the storm didn't damper their plans but that's life in Oklahoma. I sure didn't like having the T.V. on in the backroom giving storm updates. That made me nervous. And poor Billy, I thought he was going to faint when it came his turn to say the vows."

I corrected, "Mom, it's *Bill*, remember? Now that he's married, he wants to be called Bill."

"Kids grow up too fast. Besides, Billy will always be Billy, even when he's sixty."

Patty said, "I'm just glad I had a simple wedding in the backyard."

The flight attendant (not Travis) passed with the beverage cart and Mom ordered three more chardonnays, paying with cash. She opened her bottle and poured only half. "Wasn't that something the twins did with all that rice? Debi looked shocked when it came pouring out of Billy's car and buried her new shoes."

"That was Tara and Sara's idea. Boy, they sure haven't changed very much."

Lois frowned. "Honestly, I've never seen two sisters bicker so much. If I was Kay, I would have disowned them by now."

Patty said, "Well, I think the competition between the twins is an act. They're just attention whores."

Lois sniffed, "Whatever, God wasted His energy making those two annoying girls so pretty because the only thing you notice is how insufferable they are." Lois sighed. "I'm lucky to have such good girls who would never act so foolishly. And I know my granddaughter will never behave like that, either."

Patty smiled and pulled out her wallet with the picture of her kids. She kissed each picture. "I miss them."

I leaned over. "Brianna is the most adorable baby I've ever seen. Look at those dimples.

"Yep, she got those from Tom, except his dimples are hidden under his beard."

Mom said, "Everyone on the Adamsons' side of the family has dimples. Bob's mother had the deepest set of dimples I've ever seen."

Patty sighed, "I've always wanted dimples. Maybe we should invent a machine that gives you dimples? I bet we'd get rich."

"I'd rather invent a machine that allows you to travel clear across the country in a split second without having to worry about it crashing or getting hijacked or losing cabin pressure."

My mother groaned. "Nancy, you are the biggest worrywart." She finished her wine, turned in her seat, and was soon fast asleep. Shortly thereafter, the conversation turned catty in the manner of contemporary sisters on their second glass of wine.

I whispered, "Debi's pretty hippy. She'd better watch her eating habits."

"I know! She certainly doesn't have to worry about dying of that disease Karen Carpenter had. What was that called?"

"Anorexia nervosa. There was a girl at Central who had it bad. She always ate alone in the cafeteria and piled her tray with a ton of junk food but then picked at it and dumped it all in the garbage. Anyway, her name was Lorna and she weighed like seventy pounds." I shook my head. "Did you know anorexia is a psychological disorder? People who suffer from it really think they're fat when the look in the mirror, even if they weigh only seventy pounds."

"That was so sad about Karen."

"Tell me about it. I called in sick the day after she died." I sat back in my seat. "We had a bond, Karen and me. She's my favorite singer. Well, right after Cher."

Patty said, "Maybe we have that disease Karen had? We both always think we're fat."

I turned to my sister. "Well, Patty, you *were* pudgy during your pregnancy but now you're so skinny your hip bones enter the room before you do!" I was proud the same applied to me. "So, what did you think of Debi's little sister Denise? She sure had a mouth on her, and an attitude!"

Patty lowered her voice and leaned over. "Debi said Denise has a drug problem and has already been pregnant once but had a miscarriage."

"You're kidding? Denise is only fourteen! That's Angie's age! I guess I shouldn't complain Angie never wants to leave the house."

"Angie will grow out of being shy." Patty finished her wine and yawned. "I think I'll try to nap."

"Okay, me, too." But I couldn't relax at 30,000 feet and leaned back into my seat and instead thought about the peculiarities of the Dudley family of Tulsa, Oklahoma. I nudged my sister's arm. "Do you think they're talking about us, Patty?"

"Who?" Patty opened one eye.

"The Dudleys. Debi's mom and stepdad looked at me funny when I told them we don't step on spiders. And Denise kept rolling her eyes at everything I said. Maybe they didn't get our sense of humor?"

Patty readjusted herself in her seat under a navy blanket and let out a big yawn. "You have to remember most people are afraid of spiders. We're weird for liking them."

"I know."

"Do you know what my biggest fear is? Besides getting fat?"

"Ghosts?"

"Well, yeah, but besides ghosts. It's a fear of jumping. You know how people say they are afraid of heights or falling? Well, I'm afraid I will jump off something tall, like a bridge. I can't explain it, but I have this overwhelming urge to jump whenever I'm up on something high."

I didn't know if my sister was kidding or not, but I began laughing. "I've never in my life heard of such a fear before. It's kind of funny, in a macabre way."

"Another girl at work as the same fear." Patty yawned again and sat up. "You aren't going to let me sleep, are you?"

"No. If I can't sleep, you can't. Besides, talking gets my mind off the fact we are flying." I paused, letting my mind fill with racing thoughts I could share with my sleepy sister. " Hey, did you know there's another eating disorder called bulimia? Nobody spells it right. I'll bet you can't spell it. I've seen it in books spelled wrong. Anyway, bulimia is like tendinitis. Nobody spells *that* right either. Both have an "i" not an "o." This new transcriptionist at work named Harriett started screaming at me when I told her she misspelled tendinitis and that it doesn't have an 'o'. Honestly, Harriett shouldn't be working as an M.T. because the other thing about her is that she guesses if she doesn't know what the doctor is saying, even though we told her over and over, you *never* guess. That's the hallmark of a good transcriptionist, you know. If in doubt, leave a blank but never guess. That's our motto: Never Guess." I straightened, feeling proud that I never guessed.

Patty managed, "Oh."

I took the utterance as a signal to continue. "Once, Harriett hid cassettes into her drawer because she didn't want to transcribe them because it was Dr. Levinson, who I admit isn't a great dictator but we all have to share in doing the bad and the good doctors, and when I told Harriett that, she *accidentally* spilled her cup of tea on her typewriter and shorted it out. What a mess but—"

"Nancy!" Mom rolled over. "Do you realize you're jabbering? The whole plane knows your life story."

Patty agreed. "You're babbling more than Brianna does!" She turned and faced the other way in her seat. "Try to sleep."

The plane hit some turbulence and I squirmed, looking around. Half the passengers, maybe even more, were napping, some snoring. How could people sleep on planes? I couldn't even sleep in a moving car. Nevertheless, I closed my eyes and immediately thought of Tim. I was relieved his name had not come up even once during the trip because whenever it did, I could see the disappointment in my mother's face. Part of the problem, in my opinion, was Mom's unrealistically high expectations of her eldest daughter. Had I been the baby of the family, or Sue, I might have been dating a cross-dressing polygamist with a pierced tongue without raising eyebrows, but no! Perfect me was living with someone who was *different* and everyone made a big deal of it. Not talking about Tim was the best solution I had come up with so far.

I picked up a magazine and waited for the plane to begin its descent.

Chapter Thirty-Five

They say there is a fine line between love and hate, and that was certainly the case with Tim and me. Our fine line was also drawn in quicksand and at the mercy of a steady current of wildly fluctuating moods and behaviors. When things were good between us, our days were filled with laughter and planning the future.

When things were bad, simple disagreements, sometimes spurred by a single careless remark, escalated into screaming matches and hurling of insults, or objects. I was unable to control myself, and rather than allow a calmer mind to prevail I hurled toward my boiling point just as Tim was reaching his own. Just minutes before, we might have been tearing up the sheets in a wild frenzy, or discussing whether we wanted to barbecue steak or chicken.

We both knew we would make up; it was only a matter of who caved in first, which was almost always me. In the meantime, I sulked, usually in a hot bath with the door locked, while Tim paced, smoked, and drank. Sometimes I used the "down" time to reevaluate the strengths and weaknesses of our disparate relationship:

In the positive category, I believed Tim was highly intelligent (though not in a book-smart way) and was a fascinating conversationalist *if* one could keep up with his sententious, racing manner of speech. Often I was left to nod woodenly or agree ignorantly because I was lost at "I was thinking, hon." Nevertheless, all things considered, it was an attribute I found more positive than negative.

Also in the plus column was Tim's ability to repair anything, and the fact he was a creative and fearless chef who possessed an exultant Mr. Happy (who was always in the mood but especially when I *wasn't* in the mood, which left me feeling like a sexual prop rather than a partner). In any case, a girl could do worse, unless I considered the negatives:

Tim's intolerance for opinions he deemed stupid or unworthy, and his annoying habit of analyzing everything. His personality was the strangest of combinations: Buoyant, good-natured clown on the outside but a fanatical, obsessive thinker on the inside. Unlike a carnival, Tim never shut down.

And then there was Tim's drinking, which had unpredictable results. Sometimes he was a mean drunk and knocked me around, but not always. No, that would be too easy and would mean I could actually *plan* around Tim's binges, see them coming and take the necessary measures. Instead, I never knew what to expect and felt like I was perpetually walking on eggshells.

Tim, of course, did not think he had a drinking problem. "*I drink, no problem!*" was his standard lame response when the subject arose, or "*Everyone drinks, including you!*"

Furthermore, he would compare his drinking to his buddies' similar habits: "*Tom was the one who stole the motorbike from the tavern. I just helped him get it home.*" Or: "*It was Dylan's idea to go to Woodland Park Zoo and steal a monkey. You'd be surprised how easy it was, even after three pitchers of beer....*"

On and on, Tim would proudly recount his finest drunken moments. He also adhered to a finely crafted booze schedule: Beer after work to wind down, whiskey and 7-Up on weekends when he didn't have to go to work, Bloody Marys for hangovers, Irish Coffee for fishing and major holidays (when beer seemed inappropriate at dawn), and whatever else he could find when inventory on the above-mentioned selections has fallen short.

I had tried everything to get him to stop drinking, or at least curtail his intake, including bribery, trickery, seduction (which always worked but the distraction proved only temporary), alternating with withholding of sex (which never worked), and deception (hiding or destroying his bottles of booze). I ordered water or iced tea for myself at restaurants as a hint, but the fox could not be outwitted. Tim was too sly, too thirsty.

By this point in our relationship, six years together, I thought fleetingly about leaving Tim, but even as I promised myself I would walk out if he ever hit me again, I felt he had an inexplicable, almost magnetic-like hold on me. Surely this meant he had some purpose for being in my life, or maybe it was vulnerable Angie I could not leave? It didn't matter. I had made my bed, as messed up as it was, and I would lie in it.

So I trudged through the days, waiting for Sunday—the soberest day of all, unless it was football season. From September to January, Sunday was just another party day spent watching the Seahawks with all of Tim's buddies and their wives, but for the rest of the year, Sunday was *60 Minutes* and *Murder She Wrote*. Sunday was a homecooked meal with milk, not booze, to ease the hangovers from Friday and Saturday. Angie's homework was done by Sunday (now that I had taken control of this aspect of family life). She took her bubble baths on Sundays, and I sometimes joined her, after which I read her a bedtime story or two.

Sundays were Fun-Days in the Joseph household, and on this Sunday, a warm afternoon in June of 1984, I was relaxing on a lounge chair on the front deck, reading Sidney Sheldon's newest trashy novel, while inside, I thought Tim was unclogging the toilet. Suddenly, Rod Stewart began asking huskily, "Do You Think I'm Sexy?" from the stereo in the living room (at full blast), and I looked up as Tim walked out. He was smoking, and he went to stand at the railing of the deck, his butt moving to the rhythm of his favorite song. Then he began to pace. The pacing was alarming but I didn't worry. It was Sunday after all. I put my nose to my book.

Mere seconds passed before Tim said over his shoulder, "I've been thinking." He took a long draw on his cigarette and exhaled a series of smoke rings.

Now I was nervous. "Oh?" I looked up. Tim was barefoot and tanned, wearing tight cutoffs that showed off muscular legs. These facts were the good things; the bad thing was Tim was *thinking*, which meant he was probably about to break the Sunday Rule. Still, I did not ask for details as I was still holding out hope the day would be uneventful, even while I knew that Tim's synapses were programmed at birth (based on the stories I had heard from his father and sister) to continually search his cerebral cortex for a file called "Mischievous Things to Do." His sister recalled that even the nuns at his Catholic grade school were afraid of Tim, who had an affinity for pranks. Among them, property misdirection had been a favorite.

I raised my voice to compete with Rod's own loud rasp, "Remember, tonight *Murder She Wrote* is on, and it's not a repeat. Plus, I'm going to make Beef Stroganoff and Parmesan Garlic Bread!" Pollyanna herself could not have sounded more positive.

Tim walked inside and turned the volume down on the stereo. When he came back out, he said, "I've been thinking about that blueberry bush across the street." He pointed with his cigarette. "That would look perfect in our yard."

Billy Joel was now singing "Uptown Girl," one of my favorite songs. I tried to lose myself in the upbeat melody but it was no use. I asked warily, "Isn't that blueberry bush in the Duncans' yard?"

"Technically, yes."

I shook my head. *Why can't I be an Uptown Girl whose boyfriend does not have a problem recognizing the rights of ownership?* As patiently as I could, I asked, "But won't Burly notice?"

Tim shrugged. "Nah, Burly's denser than a rain forest." Last month, Tim claimed Burly wasn't the sharpest knife in the drawer. Tim was always overusing metaphors, though he didn't know it.

I closed *Master of the Game.* There would be no time for reading today. "I have a better idea, let's go take a nap." I stood up, showed a peek of breast, and winked suggestively. In my favor, "Baker Street" began playing. It was our song.

"Maybe later."

It suddenly dawned on me that Tim might be playing a joke on me. A Sunday joke, how clever! But then he walked around to the back of the house towards the shed and returned with a straight shovel, which he set on the porch. He began drawing schematics on a legal pad that had materialized out of nowhere.

At his side, I inhaled the unmistakable sweet odor of marijuana. I glanced down at the drawing. "Tim, you can't dig that blueberry bush up. It's in the Duncans' yard. It's not yours to dig up."

"Come on. Have you seen Burly's yard? It's a junkyard. He could lose his old lady out there and not notice for a month." He looked towards the street and grinned. "How's that for timing? Now I have just the person to help me."

I turned to see Melanie "Mel" Dickerson, a blowsy woman in her mid-thirties, approach our porch barefoot and wearing a yellow tube-top over large breasts, along with elastic-banded terrycloth shorts. There was no doubt in my mind she shopped the Blue Light Specials at K-Mart. Though it was not yet noon, Mel was drinking red wine from a plastic cup. Her bottle-blond shag was purposefully messy and she looked three sheets to the wind.

"Sounds fun!" Mel said after Tim explained his plan. "But I'll need more wine!" She turned her plastic cup upside down to prove it. "Be back in a jiff."

I watched Mel traipse home on plastic flip-flops. She couldn't have looked more white trash tacky if she tried. Tim had dated her briefly and I sometimes wondered if there was still an attraction. The fact Mel was married to a man named Ray didn't mean it wasn't possible.

"Are you in?" Tim asked me.

I pulled on a cover-up. "No, Tim. I'd love to help but I promised Angie I would take her to the mall." Thank God I had a good excuse! Who knew what Burley might do if he came home and found two of his neighbors drunk and tearing up his yard?

Tim shrugged. "We can handle it without you. Get me some smokes while you're out, and a half rack of Rainier."

After we went shopping, Angie and I went to the movies to see *Star Wars: The Jedi*. We had already seen it but I hoped if we are gone long enough, whatever bad—and no plan of Tim's was without complications—that had occurred during the course of the misdemeanor would have been played out and over when they get home. Better yet, maybe he and Melanie got so wasted they forgot all about the Duncan's blueberry bush?

I pulled into our driveway at 5:15 p.m. and there was indeed a colossal blueberry bush transplanted directly under Angie's bedroom window. Dropped blueberries and leaves are scattered everywhere, including a trail of evidence leading from the Duncan's yard across newly paved Stewart Street to our yard. The perpetrators are nowhere in sight.

Standing next to the bush, Angie asked, "Why'd dad put the blueberry bush under *my* window?"

"I don't have a clue but that's one big blueberry bush." The ground around the blueberry bush was wet and there was a container of Miracle Grow lying empty in the lawn. At least Tim had the good sense to do the job right.

Angie shrugged. "I guess it looks okay there. Maybe you can make some blueberry pancakes some time?"

"Sure." I walked around the back to make sure Tim and Melanie weren't passed out (or screwing) behind the shed and while the shed door is open, it's empty of bodies. Suddenly, Melanie's distinctive I'm-one-of-the-guys guffaw pierced the air followed in short order by Tim's own rowdy banter, and we knew they were at the Dickerson's house.

Angie looked over. "Why does my Dad and Mel do stuff like this?"

"I don't know. I truly don't."

"Are they gonna be arrested?"

I put my arm around Angie's shoulders. "Not today, Ang. Come on, let's go make dinner."

Slicing lean beef into thin pieces, I wondered how come homely Melanie Dickerson intimidated me so much. Why was it she with the dimpled thighs who was living the American Dream (house, husband, new van, high-paying salary as a financial analyst) with her I-don't-give-a-shit attitude and tacky wardrobe? The woman refused to shave her legs and sometimes her underarms, was callously indifferent towards her kids, dismissive of her sporadically employed husband (yet attentive to Tim's every word), and glib about her deconditioned body. About the only indulgence she had were manicures, no doubt in case they were needed to claw the eyes out of anyone who crossed her.

"That was fun today," Angie took a peek inside the paper bag of mushrooms. "But you sure took a long time picking mushrooms at the store."

"Well, fresh mushrooms are important." I had benefited greatly from a year's worth of gourmet cooking lessons (a birthday gift from Tim) and knew fresh mushrooms were white and their caps firmly attached to their stems. Melanie probably wouldn't know the first thing about fresh mushrooms. Her poor family endured night after night of Hamburger Helper, which she bought by the case.

I began dipping flank steak slices into a paper bag of flour and then dropped them into a pan of sizzling butter, olive oil and minced garlic. Angie watched my every move.

"Now what, Mom?"

"We make the sauce." I mixed extra dry sherry, milk, butter, and cornstarch to make the sauce and added it to the cooked meat. I lowered the heat to simmer and put a cover on the pan. "After this simmers until the meat is tender, we add the mushrooms." Hamburger Helper might be easier and cheaper, but that wasn't my style. Proper nutrition was a priority.

I removed my apron, under which I had a halter-top and white shorts, and poured myself a glass of wine when Ray Dickerson appeared at the screen door.

"Ray?"

"Hi, can I come in? Whatever you're cooking, I can smell it from my house and it smells wonderful. What is it?"

"Beef Stroganoff with Mushrooms."

Ray stepped in and inhaled. "I'd forgotten what real food smells like." He leaned into me and took a whiff. "You smell pretty good too."

"Thanks." The perfume was new from Revlon called Enjoli. I had bought the scent after seeing the commercial where a pretty woman in a stylish dress holds a frying pan singing, "*I can bring home the bacon, cook it up in a pan, and never forget you're a man because I'm a W-O-M-A-N!*" It was my favorite fragrance, and I loved the catchy tune because it was one I could actually sing on key, though I resisted a demonstration for Ray. Instead, I offered him a beer, which he happily accepted.

After taking a long pull from the bottle, Ray said, "So, I guess you know what our significant others did today."

I nodded. "Yes. Angie and I were gone, but we know what happened. I wonder how Burly will take it?"

"I just talked to him. He came out and looked at the hole and said he didn't even know that had been a blueberry bush, thought it was huckleberries." Ray shook his head. "He's not exactly the sharpest knife in the drawer."

Angie giggled. "You sound just like my Dad."

"Speaking of your dad, do you know where he is?"

I answered. "They went down to the Duvall Tavern, no doubt to brag." I paused. "Can you believe I got eighty-sixed from the tavern? Bricks has never liked me and was looking for a way to kick me out."

"Well, Bricks doesn't like petite blonds with all their teeth." He took another swallow and wiped his mouth. "In her defense, you really shouldn't put any beverage on the surface of a pool table. That's not ordinary felt, you know. Liquid can completely destroy it."

I raised an eyebrow. "I know that *now*, but Bricks overreacted. I think she's grouchy because she hasn't been laid in a while."

Ray chuckled. "Bricks is coyote-ugly but she has a good heart. Just don't mess with her pool tables. By the way, you sure look pretty. I wish Melanie wore makeup once in a while." Ray shook a head of permed curls and replied sarcastically, "Mel's a women's libber. She thinks women like you are blonde bimbos who are helpless without a man."

"I know." I wasn't offended and never proclaimed to be a women's libber. In fact, I was all about pleasing men, especially my own, which was one reason Melanie and I would never be friends. "I'm different, I guess."

"That's an understatement." Ray finished his beer. "Does it bother you that Melanie has Tim's initials tattooed on her ankle as much as it bothers me?"

"It's a little weird, I guess."

"Sometimes, I wonder, you know, about Tim and Melanie. They certainly seem close." Ray was staring at me. "It doesn't make sense when he comes home to a girl like you."

"Like me?" I could see in his eyes that Ray was smitten with me, and I was flattered, but wished it were Tim who felt this way. I was also grateful Angie was now in the den watching T.V.

Ray couldn't or wouldn't take his eyes off me. He said, "You're a walking, talking Barbie doll who's smart, even though you have the dumb-blonde act down pat. I've seen through that farce from day one."

Modestly I asked, "Really?"

Ray nodded. "You shouldn't be ashamed that you're smart. It's actually a turn-on."

"Oh, I'm not ashamed, it's just that I've always found it is better to *act* dumber than I am, so I'm always underestimated. It's far better than the converse."

Ray tipped his head and peered through his wire-rimmed glasses. "That's a big word, converse."

"Yes, and I'm sure you know what I mean: The real fools are the ones who act smarter than they really are." I dipped my head as I sipped my wine. Flirting came of habit.

Ray chuckled. "I agree." He dropped his beer in the recycle can just as Tim walked in. He was barefoot and wearing only his shorts, and was highly intoxicated.

I smiled pleasantly despite the knots in my stomach. "Hi, hon. Dinner's almost ready."

"Whatever." Tim crouched and reached for a six-pack from the fridge, talking over his shoulder, "Hey, did you check out my fuckin' blueberry bush? I told you we could do it and Burly don't give a shit. Now he has more room for hubcaps and car parts." Standing with the beer tucked under an arm, he acknowledged Ray. "Hey bud, you heading home?"

Ray leaned into the counter, arms crossed. "In a minute. So, what are you guys doing?"

"We're getting in the hot tub and then we're watching *60 Minutes.* Come on, guys, let's party!"

My face fell. *But that's our show.* I forced a smile. "But what about dinner? I made Beef Stroganoff, remember?" I pointed to the stove. "With fresh mushrooms."

"Ain't hungry." Tim stood from his haunches and turned unsteadily holding a six-pack. Then he passed by the living room window in a shirtless blur.

I shook my head, called for Angie, and reached for three plates. "So, Ray, how would you like to stay for dinner?"

Chapter Thirty-Six

Stephen Brodie was among Tim's wealthiest and most successful friends. He worked as regional Vice President for a chain of convenience stores and he and his wife, Natalie, lived relatively simply in a contemporary tri-level with a view of Lake Washington. They were Tim's age and had no children but did own a black Labrador named Oscar and a cabin on Lake Chelan. They could easily have been snooty but instead were a fun-loving and generous couple, and I was honored to be among the guests invited to their New Year's Eve Party.

To properly toast in 1985, I bought a new outfit, choosing a pair of navy stirrup pants, matching pumps, and a ruffle-collared white blouse with linebacker-sized shoulder pads. My newly permed hair was pulled up at the sides and over my ears, held in place with metal combs to show off oversized navy-and-white earrings shaped like elongated triangles. I curled my bangs with a jumbo iron and hair-sprayed them into a large wave that jumped off my forehead. Everything I was wearing was big and flashy, but I wouldn't be alone. In 1985, *everything* was big and flashy.

On the drive to the Brodies' house in Issaquah, Tim, who was dressed in a tan blazer with large suede elbow patches and Levi's, explained what I might expect at the party. "The Brodies throw un-fuckin-believable parties. Natalie will go balls to the walls with appetizers but I don't why she is bothering 'cause no one will eat." He paused to drink from the bottle of beer tucked between his thighs. "Guess what? For helping Steve fix the hot tub tonight, he's paying me in coke. If you're good, I'll share."

"Coke? Really?" I asked looking into a compact as I reapplied another layer of shimmering pink lipstick. "That seems very generous." I had never done cocaine before, but knew it was expensive. I also wasn't sure if I would try it, but I had lots of time to make up my mind because Tim was going exactly the speed limit to overcompensate for drinking while driving.

Forty-five minutes later, we pulled up the steep driveway to the enormous cedar-sided house in the woods. Inside, Natalie Brodie pointed to their black fridge. "We have beer, wine, and mixed drinks. Help yourselves. I need to get ready."

Did she ever, I thought. Natalie's spiral perm resembled corkscrew pasta, and was the same color, and she had no makeup on. I wouldn't be caught dead without makeup.

Tim selected a Rainier. "What's your pleasure, hon?"

I glanced at the Brodies' brass clock, which read 7:00 p.m. Since the night ahead promised to be long, I decided to go slow. "I don't know. Maybe a Diet Pepsi or coffee?"

Tim ignored my request and reached for an open bottle of champagne. "Trust me, you don't want any caffeine." He poured some bubbly into a flute, handed it to me, and motioned to follow him to the bathroom off the kitchen. After locking the door, Tim opened the top drawer of the vanity. "Steve told me where to find it."

"It" was a folded piece of white paper under a box of Tampax. Tim set the paper down and gathered up the drawer's other contents, including a small square mirror, a regular razor blade, and a plastic straw. Slowly and carefully, he opened the folded piece of paper, revealing a small mound of white powder.

"That's cocaine?"

"No, it's baby powder." Tim bent and expertly used the razor blade to chop the cocaine into a fine powder, creating two thin lines and two fat lines directly onto the mirror. It was a meticulous process. "Of course, it's coke. Premium coke. Nothing but the best for you, babe."

I laughed nervously while I admired the Brodies' bathroom, whose décor was a jungle theme with leopard-print wallpaper and towels, matching shower curtain, and black and gold toilet accessories. I took a quick peek behind the silk shower curtain at a black tub with brass fixtures. The whole bathroom was classy, and I wished we had a jungle-themed bathroom rather than one with no theme and a used washer and dryer along one wall.

"Hey, Tim? Let's do our bathroom in a jungle theme."

"Sure." Tim leaned over and snorted one of the thick lines in one flawless move. When he looked up, his face was pinched. "Shit that burns!" He shuddered and shook his head like a wet dog, then put the straw up his other nostril and did the other line. When he was done, he slid the mirror towards me and handed the straw to me. "Your turn, and don't worry, I didn't give you that much." He was rubbing his nostrils and looking pained.

"Does it hurt?" I looked down at the mirror and instinctively rubbed my throat, as Tim was doing. "And are you sure this won't make me do something stupid? I don't want to overdose or anything."

"It burns a bit, but don't worry, that goes away. Hurry up, Steve's waiting."

I was unconvinced. "But how will it make me feel? I mean, look what happened to John Belushi."

"Stop worrying! Belushi was free-basing. Trust me, coke is harmless. You'll see. Plus, there's only enough there to give you a slight buzz."

I asked uneasily, "Free-basing?"

"Injecting heroin and cocaine. Now hurry, you're holding me up."

I replied, "Okay, already." I held my hair out of the way and reluctantly bent over. As ladylike as I could, I put the straw up my nose. I inhaled half the line before abruptly stopping. "Ewww!" The cocaine burned like fire at the back of my throat.

"Hurry, do the other half."

"Okay, okay. Jeez, why the big rush?" I bent down and bravely did the other half. I straightened and lied, "That wasn't bad." It was worse than bad; it was like pouring Drano down my throat and following it with antifreeze.

"Told you. Come on, Steve's waiting."

I followed Tim to the kitchen, where he left through a side door and I found Natalie, now changed into a loose-fitting Oriental-style pantsuit, methodically stuffing mushrooms at the kitchen island. For the task, she used a tiny silver spoon to fill each buttered mushroom cap and afterwards, placed them gingerly into a ceramic dish.

"Those look good," I lied. In fact, the sight of the mushrooms was nauseating. Famished when we arrived, I was now not the least bit hungry and the pain in my throat was replaced with a numb feeling. Sipping champagne I couldn't taste from a black leather and chrome barstool, I asked, "So, what are you stuffing those with?" The mushrooms may not have looked appetizing, but I felt like talking, and stuffed mushrooms seemed as good a topic as any.

"Crab meat, cream cheese, lemon juice, bread crumbs, Dijon mustard, tarragon, and Cognac." Natalie sprinkled the mushrooms with freshly grated Parmesan cheese and a dash of fresh pepper. "I'm also doing mini-quiches."

"Sounds delicious." I swallowed, trying to get the acrid taste from my throat. I looked down and noticed my crossed leg was bobbing up and down, and my heart was racing. I steadied my bouncing leg as I studied Natalie, whose idea of getting ready did not include taming the frizz or applying makeup. Nevertheless, she was attractive in an Earth Mother/Joan Baez sort of way.

"Golly, Natalie. Thanks for inviting us to your great party." *Golly? Did I just say golly? And how can the party be great when it hasn't even started?*

Natalie shrugged. "No problem. Steve's happy that Tim's helping him."

"Yeah, Tim's pretty handy around the house. I call him Mr. Fixer-Upper."

"That's nice." Natalie reached to open an oak cupboard.

"Yeah, but did you know Tim is also an excellent cook? He cooks Angie and me all sorts of exotic dishes, like chicken curry and beef and radishes, which sounds weird but really it's delicious, especially with couscous. Angie loves it, even though she's very picky and won't let her food groups touch. That's funny, huh? Anyway, I didn't even know how to boil water before I met Tim but now that I've had cooking lessons, well, I'm pretty good."

Natalie set a bowl on the counter and blinked. "Uh huh."

I was wondering if Natalie was a Stepford Wife and continued, "I even know how to make his mother's kidney and mushroom pie. Tim said it tasted exactly like his mother's. That's quite a compliment because she's dead, Tim's mother that is. Breast cancer. It was awful." I paused to reflect and suck in some air. If I was prattling like a senile old woman, Natalie wasn't going to point it out.

"So," I peered intently at my nearly empty crystal flute, "what kind of champagne is this? I'll bet it's imported. All good champagnes come from France. My friend Moira drinks champagne like its water and it has to be expensive, but that's just Moira. You should see her collection of—"

Natalie interrupted, "It's Freixenet from QFC, six dollars a bottle." She turned to retrieve several packages from a black refrigerator, including a package of fresh spinach, a wedge of Gruyere cheese, and some ham, which she began chopping on a marble cutting board with amazing speed.

I turned to look out the window and saw Tim's back. He said something to Steve, who began laughing, before turning to pee into the ferns. Peeing outdoors when functioning and clean facilities were nearby was a strictly male custom and something I would never understand. I reached for more champagne and settled back in a barstool I had claimed as my own.

An hour or so later, the party was in full swing and the Brodies' house was buzzing with salvos of conversation. Everyone seemed to be talking at once, so all I could pick out were bits and pieces: "Michael Johnson's Thriller concert was fuckin' unreal…Chuck Knox finally got the Seahawks where they should be…we were at this new disco downtown…invade Beirut…those poor American hostages…fat vagina."

I straightened. *Fat vagina? Did someone actually say fat vagina or was I now hallucinating?* I whipped around. A tall man was talking to a large girl. She had plump cheeks and a double chin and her arm flab swung when she took a drink. It was very possible she had a fat vagina. I reached for the

185

bottle of champagne, wondering if the cocaine was not as harmless as Tim said. After all, this was a man who wasn't exactly upfront when it came to illegal pharmaceuticals. Last New Year's Eve, which we had spent at the Gitche Gumme Motel in Ocean Shores in the midst of a rare snowstorm, Tim slipped LSD into my drink and for nearly two hours—maybe more—I jumped nonstop wearing nothing but tall vinyl boots on the flimsy motel bed singing out of tune and watching the snow fall like white bugs from a psychedelic sky. My worst fear was that the drug would never wear off and I would keep jumping naked long past the time I looked good doing so. I still freak out when I hear the name Gitche Gumee.

"Nancy, hor d'ourves?" It was Natalie asking, holding a black-lacquer serving tray containing dainty quiches and stuffed baked mushrooms.

"No, thanks. Champagne is just fine for now." Oddly, the alcohol was not making me the least bit tipsy despite the empty stomach, though I was antsy and constantly watched the door on the lookout for the arrival of a familiar face. When that happened, I nearly became lightheaded.

The familiar face belonged to Dylan Kuper, Tim's best friend.

Dylan was the kind of man every woman wanted: Intelligent, polite, softspoken, funny, hardworking, and so good-looking a single smile weakened my knees. No man had ever made me feel so inadequate or tongue-tied than Dylan, who was married to a ball-busting beauty named Corinne.

I nervously waved to the impossibly handsome couple, taking in the sensuous blend of cologne and perfume that followed. I gushed, "Corinne! I love your outfit!" As usual, Corinne Kuper was dressed to the nines in glued-on black leather pants over slim hips. She wore red stilettos and a tight red sweater that showed plenty of cleavage. She would be taller than Dylan even if her permed, henna'd hair wasn't teased a mile high.

Corinne barely parted her thin red lips. "Thanks." She then reached into her leather bag and pulled out a bottle of Visine, and tipped her head back. She put two drops in each eye, blinked a couple times, and tossed the Visine back into her purse. Corinne carried Visine everywhere, like I did with hand lotion.

Dylan asked, "Hey, where's Tim?"

I pointed towards the hot tub. "Helping Steve, last time I checked. So, how are you?" My heart was beating madly and I was gulping nervous energy. "We haven't seen you since the football game."

Corinne snapped, "He's fine and he's going to make me a Tequila Sunrise, right Dylan?"

At the mini-bar, Dylan began mixing, while I surreptitiously took measure of Corinne. She was a stunningly attractive, taut-bodied woman in her mid-thirties but she had a few flaws, the overbaked skin being the most glaring. Corinne had better rein in the thrice-weekly tanning sessions or she risked developing malignant melanoma by fifty. Conversely, Dylan's olive skin was naturally dark and came from a Mediterranean heritage.

Holding her Sunrise, a double, of course, Corinne grabbed Dylan by the arm. "Dylan, let's go see Steve and Nat's new aquarium."

"Now? We just got here."

"So? Come on." Corinne pushed Dylan up the switchback staircase. "Now!"

I watched Corinne corral Dylan up the stairs thinking his wife was almost as bad as Tim's other friend's wife, Molly Williamson, and I vowed to always stay a girlfriend; girlfriends weren't nearly as cranky and insecure as wives.

Much later, I wandered upstairs to the Brodies' game room, where I found Dylan engaged (Corinne-less!) in a conversation with a shapely woman in pencil pants and taupe pumps. Not wanting to appear too interested, I sat on a stool and looked up at the T.V. perched high in a corner of the room, where M.T.V. was featuring Boy George's latest video. Boy George was an interesting character and made a beautiful girl, or *queer* if you asked my father, but it was Dylan Kuper who begged my attention, leaned up against the custom oak bar with one leg draped over the other like the Marlboro Man. Besides the tight Levis, he was wearing a baby-blue V-necked sweater with the sleeves pushed up over well-muscled forearms. The confident posture was enormously sexy. I glanced around for Corinne, hoping she left the party to make a Visine run.

Pencil-Pants Girl left the room and I walked up to Dylan, drink in hand, and asked coyly, "So, was the aquarium all you guys thought it would be?" I ventured a sip and slowly licked my lips. Dylan was way out of my league, in almost all respects, so if it was the cocaine making me feel so alluring and bold, I was hooked.

Dylan smiled and my heart did flip-flops. He shrugged, "It's a tank full of water. If you've seen one, you've seen them all."

I giggled, unable to take my eyes off Dylan's dark, chiseled features. In addition to brown eyes and straight white teeth, his thick black hair hung in waves beyond the neckline of his blue sweater. He was hotter than Don Johnson on *Miama Vice*. In fact, Dylan Kuper was gorgeous, and he knew it. He took a slow pull from his bottle of dark beer and added, "Corinne wants to get one for our den, but I'm not sold on the idea."

"Aquariums are fun, but a lot of trouble and expense. A couple months ago, I bought a sucking fish to clean off the algae on the inside of our tank. He was the size of my fist and cost twenty-five dollars, but Stanley died two weeks later. I'm not sure why; he got enough to eat."

"A sucking fish named Stanley?" Dylan picked up a pool cue and began stroking its glossy wood shaft.

"Oh yes, Stanley Wilbur Joseph. We had a funeral and buried poor Stanley in Tupperware under the Monkey Tree in the alley. Angie picked the spot but I delivered the eulogy."

Dylan grinned and asked, "How about a game of pool?" His voice resonated as soft and smooth as a satin pillow.

"Sure, I'm in." Thanks to boyfriend Bill's patient lessons while we were in college, I was a fair pool player. I picked out a pool stick and rolled it across the table to make sure it was straight. "And don't worry, I'll be gentle on your balls."

Dylan's eyes widened as he pinched his nostrils. For once, the smooth-talker was speechless, if only for a second. "That's good. I like gentle."

I tipped my head demurely, reveling in the building sexual tension. Dylan's suave personality was the polar opposite of Tim's, and I had the overwhelming desire to seduce him right there on the pool table, a gutsy, impudent move that would have catastrophic results, most notably at the hands of Corinne. I settled for brushing my hand across his crotch as I passed. He didn't flinch despite there being an almost palpable sexual surge between us. I swallowed hard and tried to catch my breath. I had never experienced such wanton desire. I managed to say hoarsely, "Shall I break or do you want to?"

Dylan's gaze was unwavering, the corner of his mouth barely upturned in a captivating smile. "Ladies first."

I bent to break, my imagination filled with things I was willing to try with a naked Dylan (and a can of whipped cream) but this quickly was replaced with a more vivid image of what Corinne and Tim would do if they caught us. Still, I couldn't concentrate knowing Dylan was behind me and watching. I turned and without thinking, kissed Dylan fully on the lips, very slowly. The kiss was magical and time seemed suspended. I couldn't even tell you if there were other people in the room, nor did I care.

Dylan stepped back. "Wow."

I purred, "There's more where that came from." I turned and broke the balls, just as Corinne stormed in, preceded by the telltale squeak of tight leather pants. She whined, "Dylan! Why did you disappear?" Her tone was shrill. "I've been waiting downstairs for an hour!"

"An hour? I don't think so. Besides, you knew where I was."

Corinne said accusingly, "You said you were coming downstairs."

Dylan sighed, accustomed to the brow-beatings. "I know, but I decided to play pool."

"With her?" Corinne narrowed her eyes at me.

Smiling sweetly, I asked Corinne, "Would you like to play instead?" I knew Corinne hated pool. "I don't mind. I was just passing the time since my date seems to have disappeared."

"Tim's out on the deck getting drunk and being obnoxious." She turned to her husband. "Dylan, come downstairs now. Steve wants to talk to you and I want another line." She grabbed Dylan's arm and shuffled him away like a bad puppy. He risked a quick peek over his shoulder, one full of promise.

After they left, I played a game of pool by myself. I aimed the white ball towards the 7 ball but it hit the 2 ball with a loud crack. Both balls jumped the table and hit the carpeted floor with a double thud. Ordinarily such a foul would carry a steep fine, but no one in the room even noticed. I scooped all the balls into pockets, placed the cue stick in its cherry holder on the wall, and struck up a conversation with a couple I'd never met. When midnight was five minutes away, I followed everyone downstairs, where Tim was in the hot tub with what seemed a dozen or more other people. Under the porch light, I could see most were naked, at least from the waist up, including Natalie and Steve.

At the stroke of twelve, everyone blew paper whistles and shouted "Happy New Year!" I raised my glass and was soon being kissed by strangers.

Chapter Thirty-Seven

Considering I brought in the New Year by flirting blazenly with a married man and snorting cocaine, it would not be a surprise my life would get crazy. For example, how many people do you know whose home has been burglarized in broad daylight by a deaf boy? In this case, a deaf 12-year-old boy named Donny, who found out the hard way it is not a good idea to turn to a life as a cat burglar when you can't hear because then you can't hear when the people whose house you are ransacking walk up behind you and knock you over the head with a brass bookend. The police found ladies' panties in Donny's pockets and little else, but he was charged nevertheless, mostly to teach him a lesson. The home invasion creeped me out, and it would be months before the paranoia of entering our empty house would go away, and even longer before I didn't first examine the hallway for deaf burglars. Maybe this was due to the cocaine, maybe not.

Then I got arrested, and that definitely had something to do with cocaine. It was March of 1986, and Tim was driving his refurbished Bronco north on Highway 203 towards Monroe while next to him I sat with my head in my lap, hyperventilating. As we passed Evergreen Fairgrounds and approached the Courthouse, my heart began racing out of control. I ventured a look up. "Tim, I cannot do this! Really, I can't go in there." I choked back tears and fought welling panic. "I just can't believe this is happening!" I put my head back into my hands, all hope lost that we would get into an accident and be excused from court because now Tim was parking, and acting typically unruffled in the face of disaster.

From the backseat, Ray said, "I can't either. I mean, I could have understood if we got tagged for fishing in the off-season or fishing without a license, but *poaching*? That game warden just needed to get his quota in for the month." Ray groaned in disgust. "And pulling his weapon on us was all show for you, Nancy."

"I don't think so. If Tim hadn't gotten any more cocky, he would have shot us."

"Shit, no," Tim threw his cigarette out the window, "he knew I was just having some fun."

I shook my head. "You have a real problem with authority, Tim."

"Yeah, so sue me. Anyway, once we explain what happened, that we really didn't know lake trout season hadn't started yet, the judge will let us off. Besides, we had two lousy trout in the boat that wouldn't have fed a parakeet. Stop worrying."

"Stop worrying? How can I stop worrying?" I checked my reflection in the mirror. Mascara dotted my cheeks and I wiped it away. "The only thing that will make me stop worrying is if the judge gets the flu and clears his docket for the day because I will *not* look good in a baggy orange jumper."

"Relax, woman! The worst that will probably happen to us is community service, or a fine."

Ray droned cynically, "Yeah, maybe we'll get to count roller skaters at Marymoor Park as our community service. I still can't believe that was your sentence for third-degree assault."

Tim grinned. "I know how to work the system. Besides, I only shoved that old man and he started it. Just ask Nancy. She was a witness."

Not exactly, but I hadn't wanted Tim arrested in front of his own daughter, and the old man *had* overreacted, screaming that we were trespassing when in fact we only cut across a corner of his property to access a public trail leading to the Snoqualmie River, directly behind a trailer park. It was eighty degrees and the beach was packed by the time we arrived so Tim parked on the street and the three of them ran across the old man's property holding their beach towels. That's when he came out with fists raised, understandably angry that his country getaway was now a hundred yards away from the most popular beach in Duvall. He had lurched on scrawny legs towards Tim, but what happened after that I have no idea. Angie and I were already running down the trail to the river.

I squirmed in the Bronco's bucket seat. It was going to be a miracle if I didn't barf in the courtroom, or pass out, especially if I couldn't prove I was absolutely *not* fishing but had only been in the aluminum boat as a spectator. My proof was my adorable, decidedly un-fishing-like outfit for the day: Tight pink jeans with ankle slits, matching pink parka, and white canvas shoes. I was also carrying our Minolta X-370 manual-focus camera at the ready for nature shots. Clearly the game warden ignored all the clues that pointed towards my innocence.

I opened the Bronco door and got out. Nearby, Highway 2 was busy and I thought about making a mad dash into traffic so I wouldn't have to face the judge. I'd never in my life been arrested, and wasn't poaching what men do in Africa when they kill endangered elephants just for their tusks and end up in *National Geographic?* I would never do such a thing; I love elephants!

An hour later, I was nervously explaining to the judge my side of the story, leaving out the part where the three of us did a few lines of coke before we took the boat out. The judge glanced down at the photos I had taken that day to prove my intentions, held up with shaky hands. I was aware I had used the wrong type of film for outdoors, and the wrong aperture, but my photography skills were rusty and the camera was complicated, unwieldy, and heavy, especially with all the fancy lenses and electronic flash attached. I was sure the judge noticed the inferiority of my work. "I'm so sorry, Your Honor."

I was excused, and next called to the stand was Tim, followed by Ray. Both confirmed they hadn't actually checked the fishing season schedule but were pretty sure Flowing Lake was still open for trout. At the time, they were stoned and they were wrong. Go figure.

The judge lowered his gavel and fined us each seventy-five dollars, but ordered no community service. He lectured, "I hope you've all learned your lesson." His eyes were strangely on the only innocent one in the room.

I answered dutifully, "Yes, Your Honor! I can guarantee I will never be caught dead in a fishing boat. Did you know I don't even eat trout? It's just such a gross—"

"Case dismissed!"

In the Bronco heading home, I was grateful I wasn't in shackles, thinking there was no way Dylan would have screwed up opening day of fishing.

Chapter Thirty-Eight

My memory might be a sieve but my mind is like a trap,
and once a good idea gets in there, I can't let it go.
—Timothy Joseph

All I want is to be loved. I deserve that, right?
—Nancy Anne Nash

I just wish everyone got along and stopped fighting and partying.
—Angela Marie Joseph

Tim once joked that if you remembered the sixties, you weren't doing enough drugs. The same could apply to the eighties, where it was cocaine that was often the main and only course of dinner parties. Sure, there were other drugs around, but my favorite was cocaine, an appetite-zapping drug that made it all the easier for me to maintain my anorectic weight of ninety-five pounds. At five feet three inches tall, I wasn't Ethiopian thin, but it was a goal.

What else I liked about cocaine was that it stripped away all the stresses of my day and replaced them with a high sense of superiority, like I was

The Shit even in a room of big-busted, opinionated, tobacco-addicted wives. Coke allowed me to fit into Tim's crowd, plus it increased my I.Q. and dulled a lifelong habit of playing the Dumb Blonde. (Of note, this was a self-perception, not actually confirmed by any reliable standard).

About the only subjects I didn't dare tackle even during a coke high were mathematics, finance, and politics, but this still left medical transcription and it was not uncommon for me to offer diagnosis and prognosis free of charge. Skin disorders were my forte.

Skin is the largest organ on the human body, I'd remind Tim's close clique of childhood friends, pointing out nevi on exposed arms and necks, explaining the difference between solar keratosis (a pre-cancerous form) and the more serious basal cell carcinomas or melanomas. Corinne was my primary concern but she didn't take too kindly to unsolicited medical advice, even when I was quick to agree that an examination by a qualified physician was always wise.

No one asked, so I didn't explain that my skin fascination was my mother's fault. When we were kids, Mom displayed an irrational interest in our dermatological health, insisting on Skin Check Night once a month. Skin Check Night required a magnifying glass and was embarrassing in its diligence, but it did teach me that skin was not only the largest organ but the most sensitive, especially when slathered with cocoa butter and allowed to bake under a sizzling August sun. The worst sunburn of my life had been the summer I met Tim, when I went topless while river rafting on the Snoqualmie River, greased up like a holiday turkey with baby oil with an SPF of zero. The resulting burn to my breasts was so severe I had to soak in a vinegar baths and couldn't wear a bra for a week.

Tim never talked about skin while he was high on coke, preferring conscience-raising topics, usually involving military strategy and war. He'd pace and theorize with bizarre rhetoric spewing forth with volcanic intensity, losing its luster only when the coke wore off, but that was the case with everyone.

Our parties revolved around drinking and smoking pot and snorting cocaine, so it was hard to truly separate what effect was being caused by which chemical, or whose drink belonged to who, but did it really matter?

This was one big, happy family of friends trying to change the world with the help of co-kane.

One of those friends was hunky Dylan Kuper, who was coming around our house a lot more since the Brodies' New Year's Eve party, and it wasn't long before me and Dylan were locking lust-filled eyes across a smoky room. Strangely, coke heightened my senses but convinced me that it dulled the senses of others, so I didn't fear the knowing glances, stolen kisses, and brief caresses would ever be noticed.

Dylan was forbidden territory and I had never wanted anybody more. I knew such thoughts were a certain precursor to disaster, but it didn't matter. If I was spiraling toward self-destruction (and the signs were all there), I might as well do it the bronzed arms of a Greek God with free drugs.

Our first rendezvous alone occurred in Dylan's Firebird on a back road that used to lead to the dump but now lead to a brand-new residential development called Pine Hills. Tim had taken me to that very landfill to do some rat-hunting, shotgun in hand. It was fun for about three minutes because I hated rats almost as much as I did snakes. I remember he had called it a date because afterwards, we went out for dinner.

I followed Dylan's car to a predesignated spot near the old landfill and parked off the road under a spread of cedars. I ran over and got into Dylan's car, which still smelled new, and immediately he reached to kiss me, his taut body covering mine. When the kiss ended, he said huskily, "I would have stolen a car to see you tonight, if I had to." His voice was sexier than it had a right to be and my heart was afire. Other parts were burning, too.

"Really?"

"Really. The attraction between us is driving me nuts, especially not being able to do anything about it."

"Well, now we can." I snuggled under Dylan's arm and for a long time we remained in this position. I had fantasized about having sex with Dylan ever since New Year's Eve but now what seemed important was his comforting, safe embrace. Naturally, I hated that he was married. I added, "Corinne would kill us if she found out, you know."

Dylan released his arm and sat up. "Probably. Want a line?"

I nodded and brought my thumb and forefinger up, spaced just a bit. "Okay, but just a teensy one since I have to work tomorrow." I sat back demurely as if I had just ordered tea and crumpets, and waited patiently for my line. Meanwhile, I wondered if Tim really bought my story that I was going grocery shopping, which in retrospect had been stupid because now I was going to have actually *go* grocery shopping. Damn! Cheating was going to take practice.

Dylan snorted his line and handed over the mirror and straw. He pinched his nostrils before saying, "Nancy, I have to know something. What are you doing with Tim? I like the guy, have known him since junior high, but he's not your type. When we first met you, Corinne and I bet you'd last less than a month with Tim."

I bent to snort the line as ladylike as I could, and sat back up. "I'm not sure. He was so fun loving at first and I felt sorry for him, you know? He had all that bad luck with women. He has his moments, and then there's Angie. I can't walk out on her." I handed the mirror and straw over. "Thank you, Dylan."

"You're welcome." Dylan gathered the drug paraphernalia and put it in the glove box. "Do you love him?"

I thought carefully before I answered. "Well, I love many *qualities* about Tim, but then again, there are lots of things I hate about him. He's gotten physical."

"He's hit you?" Dylan pulled me close to his chest and kissed my forehead. "I'm sorry to hear that."

"I haven't told anyone. I guess I'm embarrassed." A strange melancholy came over me while talking about Tim. I rarely said anything bad about him behind his back, other than a couple times to Ray Dickerson, who was at our house constantly complaining about his own unhappy marriage. Why did so many people end up with the wrong mate, I wondered?

I asked Dylan, "Why is everything so complicated? Why is *love* so complicated?"

"Don't ask me. Corinne and I have split up more times than I can count. We can't agree to disagree."

I wanted to ask if he loved Corinne but when Dylan tightened his embrace, I was sure he didn't. This wasn't going to be an affair. This was the real thing. I could feel it in my heart, which was beating rapidly, only partly due to the coke.

Dylan said, "You know what I like about you? You're not uptight like my old lady, even around someone like Tim. You're always smiling."

I replied, "That's because I'm a better actress than Corinne. Plus, I have an unnaturally high tolerance for chaos."

Dylan murmured, "You know, I think about you all the time."

"All the time?" *Even when making love to Corinne?* "That's so sweet."

Dylan whispered, "I know it's probably hard to believe but I love you."

I knew it! "I love you, too. You're so different from Tim."

Dylan laughed. "There ain't no cat like Tim. He was the school clown who still managed to sleep with the cheerleaders."

I nodded. "He does have an odd charm."

For two hours, we sat looking up at the stars and talking mostly about how miserable our primary relationships were. Eventually, it was time to go home.

"Bye, Princess," Dylan said as we departed. "I'll see you when you get back from California."

I kissed him softly. "I'll be thinking of you the entire time I'm at my brother's wedding."

Chapter Thirty-Nine

My brother Mark married a California girl named Darla, in a gazebo outside her parent's home in Bellflower. For their wedding, Angie went with me, along with Mom and Sue. It was a great time. Darla and her family were great. The wedding and weather and wine and food and motel were great. Everything was great, and all I could think about was Dylan. A week later, nothing was great.

Seated across from Tim, exhausted and struggling to understand what he was talking about, I repeated, "What? Molly and Jim Williamson want us to start a drycleaner and Laundromat with them? You're kidding, right?" We were in a Sea Galley Restaurant so I kept my voice down despite the anxieties building inside. I had known Tim long enough and well enough to know if he wanted this to happen, it would happen.

By way of answer, Tim, who was using a plastic straw to stir his bourbon and seven, pointed his finger at me. "That new outfit you're wearing, I'll bet it has to be drycleaned."

I smoothed first the front of my ivory silk blouse, then the sides of my crisp linen skirt. "Yes, but the outfit isn't new." How does one explain to a man who wore four-year-old flannel shirts that two weeks old was not technically new?

"It still needs to be drycleaned and that's my point. See, Molly was laid off and needs work and says the drycleaning business can make a ton of money. She used to work for her uncle, who owns a drycleaning business in Bellevue. He has a yacht and a mansion on the lake."

I nodded lamely, still waiting for the "why" in this newest scheme. His last one was moving to Saudi Arabia to work in a hospital and earn a "handsome income that was not taxed," according to the recruiters. Tim actually applied for both of us to work overseas, and we no doubt would have been accepted had we been married in accordance with Saudi law.

I replied, "Go on." *Either that, or shoot me now.*

Tim blew smoke and said, "We'd make a killing because Duvall doesn't have a drycleaner and just one run-down filthy Laundromat I wouldn't wash a dog's bed in. It's all about supply and demand."

"Supply and demand?" I was so tired mentally, emotionally, and physically. Pretending things were peachy keen with Tim was taking a lot of energy, as was my affair-of-the-heart with Dylan, which had still not progressed beyond heavy petting. Sure, cocaine was a vasoconstrictor, but it never seemed to constrict Tim.

I swallowed and tried to be open-minded. "Well, it certainly sounds interesting."

"It's more than interesting. It will be a goldmine. Molly knows what the hell she's talking about."

I inwardly groaned. Molly was a sourpuss. A few months ago, her and I had a rather uncomfortable encounter that had begun (like many events at the time) with spiked beverages and a couple of snorts, followed inevitably by jumping into the Dickerson's hot tub. Soon it was just the husbands in the hot tub (where the wives were, I don't recall), including an uncharacteristically jolly Jim Williamson, as well as Dylan, Ray, a neighbor named Mike Strange, and one lone twenty-something girl.

In hindsight, jumping into a tub full of partially clothed men could have incited a number of raunchy and lascivious behaviors but these were not professional athletes, these were my friends! Besides, I was fully clothed in an orange string bikini, and trusted every single husband. Really, the whole incident had gotten blown completely out of proportion but Tim insisted, as he nursed his own hangover with an extra-spicy jumbo Bloody Mary, that I apologize to all the wives, so I apologized, first to Molly, who was quiet for so long after that I thought she had hung up. Finally she said, "Fine. Apology accepted but don't ever do such a thing again, at least not with my husband."

Middle-aged women were such insecure bitches, and now I might be partners with one? My life was definitely getting much too complicated.

Across from me in the Sea Galley, Tim was jabbering nonstop as he usually did when latched onto a plan to get rich so he could retire early. "Don't worry! Everything will all fall into place. Besides, if Danny and Rhonda Rucker can run a pizza place and make money, we can run our own successful business." He motioned for the waitress and ordered another drink. He turned back to me. "You look like shit."

"I have a throbbing headache, and I'm tired from my trip." I reached for my purse and a bottle of Tylenol. I took two tablets and downed them with water. "Where's the money to start the business going to come from?"

Tim snapped his fingers, proud that he has done his homework. "I already talked to the bank while you were gone. Jim and me are both going to get home-equity lines of credit. We already found a space to lease in the new strip mall in between the drug store and the Mexican restaurant. It's a prime location."

And prime rent. "But, won't—"

"Trust me on this one, Nance. Plus, we can hire Angie so she can get some job training."

"Great," I answered sarcastically, "I am sure she will be thrilled."

Three months later, in the late fall of 1985, Valley Drycleaners & Laundromat opened its doors. Three weeks after that, following a highly advertised Grand Opening offering 50% off on all drycleaning (except leather, furs, and wedding gowns), plus coupons for free Fluff & Folds, Jim and Molly split up. It was a nasty breakup that involved the police, which meant our shop had nobody to run it.

At the Mexican restaurant next door, the remaining partners discussed strategy. Jim dejectedly picked up a chip and scooped some salsa. "Well, Molly filed for divorce. We've been having problems but I thought having this business might give her something to do, you know, keep her mind busy."

I gritted my teeth, resisting the urge to suffocate Jim with the large red sombrero on the wall behind us. "I wish you had told us how bad things were. Maybe we wouldn't have agreed to go into business with you guys."

"I know, I'm sorry. Molly's got some issues."

"Don't we all." Tim tilted his chair back and began puffing away, deep in thought. Finally, he let the rattan chair connect with the tile floor and said, "We could hire someone but then that cuts into our profit margin. I think one of us should quit our job and run the shop." Tim was looking directly at me as he stubbed out his cigarette and reached for another.

I yelped in disbelief he would even suggest such a thing. "Forget it! I am not giving up my well-paying job as a medical transcriptionist to handle dirty clothes!"

Tim disagreed. "I'm closer to retirement and have better benefits. Plus, you're cuter. We need someone cute working the counter." He winked,"You'll get free drycleaning, Nancy, remember?"

I lifted a thin eyebrow, "What on earth will I need drycleaning for if I am working in a Laundromat?"

Jim reached for an Ixtapa matchbook and lit a Camel, blowing the smoke up and away from the table with lopsided lips. "Sorry," he said through the haze, "but there's no way I can quit my job at Microsoft."

"I can't afford to quit my job either," Tim said as he blew his own smoke. "I'm the one with a 401-K."

I slurped my Margarita Gold, watching Tim and Jim smoke in a choreographed rhythm, each blowing smoke up and away, but in opposite directions with that peculiar head tilt and pursed lips that smokers had. Even the way they held their cigarettes was similar. I didn't smoke but if there was ever a time to begin, now seemed ideal. I eyed Tim's pack of smokes, unfiltered Merits.

"Well, hon?" Tim said, "we can't throw in the towel now. We have too much to lose." He paused. "Come on, it'll be a change of pace from your job and it's only temporary. Besides, I'll help out when I got off work."

Jim said, "And I'll come down and close the shop and do the books."

"See? Everything's going to be fine."

I stared dejectedly at Jim and Tim. *Dylan would never propose such a ridiculous idea* "Oh, all right, for thirty days on a *trial* basis. I'll see if Rick will let me take a leave-of-absence."

Tim beamed at the victory. "This calls for another round!"

The next day, when Dylan called me at work, I told him about the newest crisis in my life. He was sympathetic but not surprised.

"That's too bad, but I'm not surprised about Molly and Jim. They've been together since junior high and have split up more times than me and Corinne. They used to go to a marriage counselor. Anyway, there's a good side to you working at the shop."

"Really? Please tell, because all I see is the end of my social life."

Dylan cooed, "It'll give me a legit excuse to see you when I drop off Corinne's drycleaning. I'll tell her you're giving us a discount and she'll drop Redmond Cleaners in a New York second."

Chapter Forty

As owners of Valley Drycleaners & Laundromat, we tried all the usual gimmicks to drum up business: Balloons, promotional coupons, local advertising, free coffee and donuts, flyers, and even briefly offered tuxedo rentals. The tuxedo-rental business, however, turned into a major hassle, especially the measuring part, so that side venture lasted less than three months. Not surprisingly, many of the clever ideas came from Jill and her husband Big John, whose own business enterprise was a convenience market and attached restaurant called the Happy Clown, located near Fish Lake a few miles east side of Stevens Pass. The only problem was the store was convenient only to others. For Big John and Jill, it was a never-ending nightmare fraught with sticky-fingered and unreliable employees, shoplifters, spring floods, and cash-flow problems. If anybody could relate to the dilemma and Tim and I had found ourselves in, it was my stepsister and her husband.

At Jill's suggestion, we hired a florist named Sharon, who sold her freshly made flower arrangements and gifts from a cooler display in the lobby of the drycleaners and split the profits 80/20 with VDL. This was only moderately successful, though it did make the lobby smell fresh as a daisy.

Because Valley Drycleaners & Laundromat was a "drop shop," this meant the actual drycleaning services were not done on-site but contracted out to another establishment with those facilities, thus saving on equipment costs and electric bills, and it worked like this: Tim dropped the "dirty" clothes off at Simon & Son's Fine Cleaning in nearby Woodinville on his way to work, and then he picked up the finished product, drycleaned and on hangers, on his way home from work. Once at the shop, a routine followed: I bagged each and every garment individually and affixed the invoice that matched the numbers on the tag. The bagged items were then hung alphabetically by the customer's last name on an oval-shaped bar that hung from the ceiling in the back of the shop, out of view of the customers. With a click of a foot-operated button, the electrical rack rotated.

Tim was responsible for maintenance, including equipment repairs, and cleaning and waxing the linoleum floor. Jim was in charge of "closing" the shop and performing bookkeeping duties and making banking deposits.

I worked the counter and collected quarters from the washers and dryers into a big coffee can every night. Then I counted and rolled the coins into paper sleeves. The quarters were essential to a smooth operation but I soon grew to hate quarters, especially their metallic smell and filthiness. It was a tedious, unglamorous business and the only thing keeping me going was Dylan.

The holidays came and went and my thirty-day trial entered its fifth month. On Saint Patrick's Day, a busy Friday, especially in the Laundromat, I barely sat all day and was relieved when four o'clock arrived and Jim took over. I was even more pleased Tim told me the big man himself, Simon of Simon & Son, had invited us to join him at his hangout, Creekside Grill, to celebrate the Irish holiday and discuss business. I was hoping for a miracle; maybe Simon wanted to buy us out?

At the restaurant, the 54-year-old Dutchman with a thick accent leaned over and asked, "Hey, Nancy, da ya know why da Irish celebrate St. Patrick's Day?"

"They like green beer?" I joked, knowing there was a story to follow.

Simon lit up a cigar. "Actually, Patrick was a very smart fella and one Monday in March centuries ago, he charmed all da snakes from Ireland into da sea, where dey drowned. For dis, all da Irish women fell in love with Patrick and made him a Saint. That's why dere's St. Patrick's Day."

"Really? A land with no snakes!" I turned to Tim. "Let's move to Ireland."

Tim laughed. "Maybe next year, if we ever make some money." He reached for the pack of cigarettes in his shirt pocket, not bothering to offer me one, because no matter how much I tried, I looked ridiculous smoking. I knew this because each time I began smoking, people told me, "You look ridiculous." Why no one else looked ridiculous smoking was unclear, and neither could one offer a specific reason as to why *I* looked so ridiculous smoking. I asked the appropriate question, of course: "Why do I look ridiculous smoking?" The answer was always the same. "I don't know, but you look ridiculous smoking."

It was another of life's great mysteries.

Simon said, "Speaking of money. I've been thinking."

I put my wine glass down, full of hope. "Yes?" I flashed him a wide smile and wished I had cleavage. "About what?"

"Well, I know your business is floundering, but I have a proposal. How 'bout if you turn your drycleaners into anodda Simon & Son's franchise?"

It wasn't exactly the news I wanted. I wanted him to take the damn business off our hands, and throw in a Caribbean cruise for our troubles. I finished my wine. "Sure, Simon, but can our franchise be in Ireland?"

By midsummer of that same year, my love affair with Dylan was blossoming, to the point I was promising to leave Tim and he was promising to divorce Corinne (*again*, rumor had it, but I didn't delve). It was not sex that formed this relationship but escapism from controlling partners, and our decision was made after sharing a French kiss, two fat lines, and a bottle of Moen champagne, while stretched on a blanket near the Snoqualmie River. We had both left work early and met at the end of an abandoned farming road, where we parked our cars and walked, holding hands, through the woods to the riverside.

On the blanket, I told Dylan, "I can't wait for us to be together like a couple without hiding." I reached for Dylan's pack of cigarettes. "May I?"

"Sure, but you look ridiculous when you smoke." Dylan was lying prone on my belly and looked up. "I want to be together too, but Corinne just started a new job and I need to ease her into the whole thing. I don't want to hurt her, or Kendra. "

"I know." I ran my fingers through Dylan's thick dark hair. "It'll all work out, don't worry." His daughter, who was Angie's age, would hate me forever, but I wasn't thinking about Kendra.

Dylan sat up and reached for my hands with his. He said, "We'll ease them into the news. We can both move out and get our own places, maybe by August? I want to do this right." He lifted one hand and softly caressed my cheek, his eyes boring into my own with a look beyond lust, almost gratitude.

I nodded. "Yes, I agree." It was June and I was exhilarated and uneasy at the same time. It wasn't impossible to predict how Tim and Corinne would handle our announcement that we were in love: They'd hunt us down like animals and if we were caught, they'd torture us. It was overwhelming to think about that, so I changed the subject. "Okay, Dylan, I have to ask. Why do I look so ridiculous smoking?"

Dylan layed back down and fingered his mustache, looking up at the blue sky. He said, "Well, first of all, you hold the cigarette like it's going to bite you, and then you blow the smoke out real fast without inhaling, and your face gets this pinched look like you've been sucking on lemons. Really, the whole thing is embarrassing to watch and quite ridiculous."

"Oh."

He turned to look at me. "But you're beautiful."

I giggled and turned on my belly next to Dylan. "So are you."

When the sun began setting, we parted ways with plans to meet the following day at The Keg in the U-District near my work. It would be our first venture out in public, but the U-District was a long way from Duvall, where Corinne worked at the newly opened aerobics studio.

"If anybody asks, we bumped into each other. It's not that implausible considering we both work in Seattle."

"Yeah. Besides, so what if we decided to have a few drinks? We're just friends, right?" I winked. I'd do anything to be with Dylan, whose vocabulary was far more impressive than Tim's, even if his libido was not.

The next day, Ray Dickerson was at our house listening to the heated one-way conversation Tim was having. He witnessed Tim's face turn red, watched his temporal veins gyrate and his jaw contract. He knew something was very, very wrong. He asked, "Tim? What's wrong?"

Tim said into the phone, "Don't worry, Corinne, I'll take care of everything." He hung up and Ray watched him walk calmly to the hall closet, where he got out his shotgun and a case of shells.

Ray put up a hand, "Whoa, buddy, what the hell are you doing?"

Tim ignored Ray, loaded the gun, made a phone call, and said, simply, "Bingo."

Ray hurried across the street to his own house and called 9-1-1.

Chapter Forty-One

Patty handed me their phone and said, "Nancy, it's Tim again. He *really* wants to talk to you. He said it's important."

"It always is." I reluctantly took the cordless phone and went onto my sister's back porch, out of earshot of her family, especially her two young children, and tried to sound calm. "Hello?"

Ice clank before Tim spoke. "Nance? Don't hang up. I was just calling to see how you were doing."

"Fine," I lied. How could I be fine? I was living out of a suitcase with my sister and her family after fleeing Tim's nearly murderous rampage. I counted the seconds before he mentioned Dylan. One, two...

"Nancy? I know you only slept with Dylan because of the drugs. It hurt, I won't lie, but well, drugs can fuck you up, I know." He swallowed and said, "I just wanted to say I forgive you."

How very noble. And by the way, Dylan and I never slept together, at least not in the way you mean. "Is that why you called, to talk about Dylan?"

Tim answered, "Yes. I mean, no. Well, maybe. Sorry, I guess I'm nervous talking to you."

I rolled my eyes. "I've never seen you nervous in your entire life."

Tim laughed. "Look, will you please come over for dinner for your birthday? I was thinking of cooking lobster."

He almost had me with lobster but I gathered my strength. "No." I put my hand to my chest, feeling my heart pounding, and inhaled. "Tim, I'm getting an apartment with Moira. I need time to sort through things. Everything is so mixed up. You threatened to kill me, remember?" And Ray Dickerson undoubtedly saved two lives.

Ice rattled as Tim's sunny disposition darkened into a thundercloud. "Do you blame me? You slept with my best friend!"

"And *you* slept with Fern Templeton. Dylan told me all about that affair." Fern, an attractive administrator at the hospital, had recently bought a turn-of-the-century home in Kirkland that needed constant repairs, which handyman Tim performed without compensation and with an eagerness that immediately raised suspicion. I eventually questioned Tim about his relationship with Fern and he denied it, but Dylan, now in my court, had confirmed it was true. He said Tim bragged he and Fern had sex on her kitchen floor after he re-plumbed her dishwasher. I wondered what else he re-plumbed.

Tim retorted, "That meant nothing. Besides, Dylan was using you and believe me, you weren't his first fling. What he did was chickenshit, but Dylan's conquests are notorious. I'll bet you didn't know about him and Rhonda, did you?"

"Rhonda Rucker?"

Tim repeated, "Yeah, Rhonda Rucker. She told me a long time ago about their one-night stand."

I answered, "I don't care. That's over, let it be." I closed my eyes and relived the frightening day we got caught. Dylan and I had been at the Rucker's rural mobile home, one of our favorite hideaways (ironic in the face of what Tim had just told me), when we learned from Ray Dickerson that Corinne had found out about our affair from a friend who had been at the Keg the same night as us. Dylan and I looked at each other. Suddenly, his brown eyes went flat and cold, and he muttered just one word, *bitch*. I was not at all sure to whom he was referring. Me? Corinne? Rhonda? Or maybe it was Teresa?

Teresa was the Rucker's four-year-old daughter who had, minutes before the alarm sounded, been playing mummy, her favorite game. From head to toe, she was wrapped in duct tape with only her face uncovered. She was propped up against the sofa like an ironing board without saying a word and everyone thought it was hilarious. After the phone call, I didn't think Teresa duct-taped was hilarious at all. In a crisis, my instincts took over and I knew it was wrong for parents to duct-tape their toddlers like mummies, even when requested.

After Ray called and warned us, Dylan and I escaped to a safehouse in Green Lake, owned by a friend of Dylan's. We stayed there an entire week, hoping it was enough time for tempers to cool, while the magic of our whirlwind romance evaporated in the bleak face of discovery, and drugs. Dylan and I both agreed to part ways, but I was still upset that he went back to Corinne, and more surprised she took him back. Despite all of this, I still had strong feelings for Dylan, or at least my idealized version of him.

Ice rattled as Tim asked, "Then why can't we just work this out? I love you."

"You have a funny way of showing it. Look, we've had problems for a long time, Tim. It wasn't just the drugs."

"Yeah, it *was* the drugs. I don't know about you, but I haven't touched the white stuff since you left."

I said truthfully, "Me, neither."

"Good. Anyway, listen. Every relationship has problems but the answer is not to walk away. You don't want to throw away seven years, do you?"

Only seven years? It seemed a short time to be so crazy already.

Tim added, "Hon, you know I put you on a pedestal."

That was true. Tim put me on a pedestal but both of us knew he could knock me off at any time, at his discretion. He had hit me three times now, each time with more force. The degrading shame that followed was far worse than the marks that he left. But the most degrading moment was the time (after being hit across the windpipe), I threatened an overdose that had been meant to be a wakeup call to Tim that the abuse was taking its toll, not a reason to be humiliated by a mental health evaluation and coerced into signing a no-harm contract. I could hear the nurses telling Tim to "keep an eye on your girlfriend" and "make sure she makes a followup appointment with behavioral health."

I had watched dejectedly as Tim nodded with great concern: *Yes doctor, of course.* He had a knack for turning my weaknesses into his strengths, and I was so distraught and embarrassed by the whole experience, all I could do was hang my head down. I didn't have the guts to tell the nurse that Tim—a popular employee at the very hospital—had hit me, nor the energy to explain to the intake counselor that I had never intended to kill myself. That was an act of selfishness I could never commit. When we got home, I crawled into bed ashamed while the real whacko quaffed Jack Daniels in the den.

I inhaled and spoke firmly into the phone, "Look, Tim, I don't trust you and I'm afraid of you. How can a relationship like that work?"

Tim hissed, "*You* don't trust *me*? That's hilarious coming from you. I'll tell you what: Just come get your shit before I throw it all on the fuckin' lawn."

With that, he slammed the phone down.

The next day, I went to get my *shit* while Tim was at work. It wasn't on the front lawn, probably because it wasn't raining. See, that's key when you throw someone's *shit* on the lawn: It has to be raining and it is preferable to have the entire neighborhood watching. My mother once threw my dad's *shit* on the front porch and her timing was perfect, Halloween Eve of 1971. And Melanie did the same thing to Ray's stuff, not once but twice, and both times the rain was coming down sideways. One had to admire such audacity.

After loading my car with shit, I wrote Angie a good-bye note, telling her how sorry I was for everything, and while backing out of the driveway, wondered if I would ever be on the good end of throwing shit onto the lawn rather than picking it up because it was mine.

Chapter Forty-Two

Rick and Moira's breakup came as no surprise, at least not to their employees. Rick, who possessed a law degree, was a methodical, practical, erudite man who did nothing impulsively, while Moira Batista teetered gloriously and glamorously on the edge. They were fire and ice, like Tim and me.

Now that we were single at the same time, it was Moira who suggested we get an apartment together. After looking for an entire weekend, we settled on a two-bedroom, two-bath condominium overlooking Volunteer Park on Seattle's Capitol Hill. It was October fourth, my thirtieth birthday, the day we moved in, and as soon as we were settled I called my mother with my new phone number and address.

Mom sounded sympathetic but it was mixed with joy. "Oh, honey! I know this is difficult but it's for the best, really. Tim isn't right for you, you'll see, and you and Moira, well, you two single gals will have such a good time!"

My voice cracked. "Sure. The apartment's really nice. You and Bob will have to visit."

She replied, "Absolutely, maybe after the holidays? Anyway, Happy Birthday, honey."

I hung up knowing my mother and Bob would be celebrating the news and turned to watch Moira, who was pouring champagne into flutes with sapphire globe bases. She handed one to me.

"Happy Birthday, girlfriend."

"Thanks, but this isn't exactly how I envisioned spending my thirtieth birthday." I followed Moira to our living room, where we settled into opposite ends of Moira's antique davenport behind a glass coffee table piled with CDs. Against a wall and ready to hook up was a top-of-the-line T.V. and stereo/CD system. I told Moira, "You have a lot of expensive stuff."

Moira lit up a Newport. "I like expensive stuff." She exhaled through bright red lips. "So, I know one of the bouquets you got today was from Tim the Meddler, but who was the other one from?"

I chuckled as I sipped my bubbly. *Tim the Meddler.* Boy, ain't that the truth! He's always trying to solve everyone's problems but his own. Anyway, the flowers were from Ray Dickerson. He's the neighbor who called the police after Tim found out about me and Dylan."

"Is that the neighbor who was always at your house complaining about his wife?"

"Yeah. Ray thinks Melanie's having an affair with her boss, plus she's a slob."

"Oh." Moira shook her lacquered head of black hair. Not many women would get away with such a severe hairstyle, but it showed off her high cheekbones and swan neck. She leaned back and drew her knees up to her chest. "Guess what? I have a date on Friday."

"Already?"

"Yep." Moira leaned over to put her cigarette out. "Rick can kiss my ass."

I nodded. "So, is this one English-speaking?"

Moira narrowed her charcoal-lined eyes. "Who?"

"Your date."

"Yes. Why?"

"Well, it seems you go for the foreigners, except for Rick. Remember when I met you? You were dating that Pakistani guy, the one with the sticky fingers, and then there was the Russian exchange student who you said had the biggest shlong you'd ever seen, but the worst breath, too."

Moira reached for the bottle and refilled our glasses. "Omigod, Nancy, I thought Vladimir was going to perforate my uterus! One night I measured his erect penis and it was ten and a half inches! Not that I complained, that is, until he opened his mouth."

I joked, "Size isn't all that matters."

Moira groaned as she stood and stretched. She was wearing black cotton stirrup pants and an extra-large "Thriller" T-shirt from a Michael Jackson concert. "Yeah, right, and diamonds aren't a girl's best friend. I'm going to get us some appetizers."

From the kitchen, Moira said, "Speaking of diamonds, Omar only *borrowed* that necklace. He told his boss he was going to put it back in the vault after the opera."

"Moira, I don't know. Given our track record, maybe we should try being lesbians?"

Moira returned with a china plate of cracked pepper crackers, smoked salmon dip, slices of Havarti, and a tub of caviar, all purchased at the nearby QFC hours earlier. She set the tray on the coffee table before going to the glass stereo cabinet and retrieving a leather-bound black journal. "This is my Big Black Book. I keep track of every person I've been with." Moira flipped through the pages. "Oh yeah, here she is, Danica. She was a freak. Trust me, men are better."

I replied, "I was only kidding, and I trust you." I ventured a peeked at the Big Black Book, curious how many entries there were, but Moira snapped it shut. I said, "So, tell me about this date of yours."

"His name is Dean McMahon." Moira grabbed a cracker and covered it with salmon spread and caviar. She took a bite and swallowed. "God this is orgasmic! Anyway, I met Dean at the park. He's over six feet tall, dark-blond, owns a Mercedes, and is taking me to Palisades for dinner."

"Wow."

"Yeah, Dean's an investment banker." Moira might have been a girl raised on a pig farm in Iowa, but grown up she was sophisticated and stuck close to the city. Her potential suitors were wealthy and always white-collar, and whether English was their first or second language didn't mean much; Moira spoke three languages fluently, including Russian, and could wing the rest.

I droned, "Well, if you bring the banker home, please be quiet. My earplugs will only block out so much!" I didn't need to ask if Dean McMahon would end up the next entry in her Big Black Book.

Chapter Forty-Three

Professional Dictation, in the very beginning, was an all-female workforce, owned by a savvy businesswoman named Lillian Byrnes before it was sold to Rick Greene. Without exception, its receptionists were young and female, usually students attending the University looking for part-time, nearby jobs. That changed in 1986, when P.D. hired its first male transcriptionist, followed in short order by its very first male receptionist.

The former, Donald, was married. The latter, Carson, was gay. This was not speculation but fact, as Carson, who paired cashmere scarves with pastel-colored jackets and skintight jeans, spoke openly about his "life partner" Bryce. At first, this was awkward, especially for me, as I had never seen a real gay person up close, at least not that I knew of. Whenever Carson came to my desk to deliver a message or supplies, I smiled and was very polite because Carson was an extremely attractive homosexual with salon-styled beige-blond hair with bleached tips, but I was careful not to get too close.

Within weeks, however, Carson was everyone's best friend and was especially helpful in dispensing fashion advice. He told me I was the best-dressed person in the office, but that I should dare to wear red more often. Flattered beyond belief, the next day I brought Carson ("and Bryce" the card said) a big batch of white-chocolate-chip cookies with pecans, because gay people love nuts. At least that's what Tim said, and he turned out to be right because Carson giddily clapped his hands before he carefully peeled back the plastic on the plate and when he took a bite of cookie, his eyes rolled back and he fanned his face with a hairless and pampered hand. After work that day, I bought two red sweaters and a pair of dark-red slacks from The Limited, size two.

After Donald and Carson, P.D. hired another man, Tom, who was straight in every way one can be straight, including being nearly 6 feet 5 inches tall and as thin as a ruler. Tom had a great sense of humor and an impressive knowledge of the shortcuts and back roads through the maze of Seattle and the surrounding suburbs that made him the ideal courier for their fast-growing business, one dependent on deadlines and getting work to and from the office in a timely fashion.

The men were a welcome addition to the estrogen-laden office but much to the staff's dismay, Carson Gilbert's tenure was cut short when four months into the job, he was snatched by a client named Pamela McKnight, a C.P.A. who came in with a rush job and was so impressed with P.D.'s receptionist's professionalism (and no doubt his taut derriere), she hired him for double the pay. Carson's loss was unfortunate for the company but most distressing to me, who had never met someone so helpful and informative about creating style through use of texture and color. Many of Carson's tips I instantly applied, including accessorizing with bright scarves left untied and draped oh-so-casually over a fitted blazer.

Carson's replacement was a man named Gavin Catalina, who was most definitely heterosexual, something I discovered after Moira set us up because she said we'd make a cute couple and the office needed a romance. On one point, Moira was right: We did make a cute couple.

Gavin was taut-bodied and good-looking, though a bit self-conscious about his premature balding. In his late twenties at the time and a recent graduate in Political Science from the University, Gavin aspired to be elected to public office one day, but he turned out to be far too pragmatic for me. After all, I wasn't even registered to vote. When I let this fact slip, Gavin spit his micro-beer clear across the table. In a voice filled with disdain, he asked, "Why do you live in America if you don't exercise your right to vote?"

I shrank back in embarrassment and promised to register to vote ASAP (while simultaneously wondering what one wore to register). I was in a vulnerable state and eager to please, even a man with whom I had nothing in common. Honestly, discussing politics with Gavin was the last thing I wanted to do and I found myself thinking constantly about Carson: *I wonder what Carson would think about the red crepe pantsuit I just bought. The buttons are brass and bring out the golden highlights in my hair but were they too big and distracting? Maybe I should have bought the red parachute pants with the straw belt?*

Gavin would be talking about political agendas, the Iran-Contra Conflict, or any number of world events, while I was obsessed about my wardrobe (superficial only to the fashion impaired). Really, the only political statement I made with any degree of confidence and accuracy was that President Reagan was cool for proclaiming there to be a National Medical Transcriptionist Week every third week in May. Because of this, I told Gavin I was really glad our President didn't die after John Hinckley shot him, and I'd probably vote Republican. That is, just as soon as I registered.

A few weeks later, expressing regret he probably didn't feel, Gavin broke up with me. He said he was most sorry because of his timing, right before Christmas.

"I'm sorry, you know, it being almost Christmas, but—"

"That's okay, I understand, really." I was so relieved he was the one who broke it off. As far as it being the holidays, that didn't really matter. I expected bad things around Christmas, and if it were up to me, Christmas would be canceled permanently and replaced with an extra Halloween.

"I just don't think we have enough in common, but you're a nice girl." Gavin reached over and patted my hand. "You sure you're okay?"

I tried to look sad, lest I hurt Gavin's feelings. "I'll be fine, and I wish you luck finding someone who is into, you know, voting and all that."

"Well, it's not that simple. You don't really get *into* voting, Nancy." Gavin sighed loudly. "Never mind. I'll see you in the office on Monday."

After shaking hands and promising to remain friends, I got out of Gavin's car and entered through the security doors of my apartment building. On the third floor, I reluctantly unlocked my apartment door, and walked into Holiday Hell.

Chapter Forty-Four

Moira Batista cherished Christmas—it was her favorite time of year—and she embraced the magic of the holidays I didn't get by spending large amounts of her disposable income on expensive decorations and gifts, and festive outfits. She had twenty or more boxes marked "Christmas" in our storage unit and most of their contents had been purchased at Hallmark Stores after the holidays, when the discounts were heavy. Her Department 56 Christmas village houses collection alone was worth a bundle and covered every flat surface in our apartment.

Moira also collected reindeers and snowmen and antique Santa Clauses and glass angels. She decorated with rugs and towels printed with mistletoe and holly. Our apartment looked like a Macy's display and smelled like pine and cinnamon, and would have made an elf proud. It was very heartwarming, *if* you loved Christmas.

I loathed Christmas, but I didn't let on. I participated gamely in gift-exchanges and office parties, secretly abhorring all things Christmas. The most stressful part of going along with the holidays to me was the chore of properly decorating the tree, which had to be perfectly shaped and costly. Cheap Charlie Brown trees would not do. For reasons unclear, I was driven by an intense need to have the most beautiful and perfectly decorated tree in the neighborhood.

I knew Christmas trees were commercial exploitation at its worst, but it was a trap I could not avoid. I was obsessed with meticulous, symmetrical detail while choosing and hanging ornaments. God save the person who tried to help me, like Tim, whose taste in tree decorating was garish at best. I had spent three Christmas Days with Patty and her family in the past five years, all because of a fight over the Christmas tree. Once, Tim wanted to decorate our six-foot Grand Fir with panty and bra sets (mine to be exact), but with a young child living in the household, I nixed that idea in favor of a country theme with red apples, plaid bows, and wooden replicas of rocking chairs. I had none of these items packed away and thus, it was necessary to spend a hundred bucks on top of the fifty we had spent for the tree. When I was done, however, I hated the look and was contemplating redoing it in a Victorian theme like the gorgeous thirty-foot tree displayed outside the Nordstrom's at the mall. How lovely those intricately detailed ornaments were of miniature pink and ivory replicas of women's boots and shoes and lace fans!

Quickly, I began undecorating the tree of its corny country knickknacks so I could run to the mall and buy the Victorian ones, when Tim walked in and demanded I put all the ornaments back up and stop obsessing about how the tree looked because, who cared? He said it was a tree that would be lying brittle by the curb for the Boy Scouts in a month.

He had a point but we still fought about it. Looking back, the only good Christmas me and Tim had spent together so far was the year before, when I decided to make a home movie for Dad and Kay using Tim's dad's brand-new VCR, "the greatest invention ever," according to Tim. With the VCR in hand, Tim filmed our rambler, our X-Mas tree decorated in a nautical theme complete with a fishing-net tree skirt, and a brief shot of Angie riding her bike before she ditched the bike and ducked behind a tree. Later, he filmed me parading around in several lascivious costumes from Frederick's of Hollywood before the camera ran out of film and we had to buy more film for the *real* purpose for borrowing the VCR in the first place, which was to make a family holiday video: G-Rated, I was quick to point out.

Fresh film installed, we drove to my sister Sue's house in Renton, which she now shared with her new husband, Steve, whom she had met at church. There, Tim captured on film now-redheaded Sue with her two sons, Anthony and baby Andrew. Steve Wolf worked long hours for his father's construction company, and ironically had little time for his own home repairs. Chagrined, Sue pointed out the broken fence that blew over in a storm two years prior, a shed with a leaking roof, and the bathroom door Anthony kicked in during a typical four-year-old tantrum. It was early afternoon and Sue was drinking vodka and orange juice, and joked the one in her glass was the only screwdriver we'd find around their house.

Next was a stop at Bill and Debi's mobile home nearby, where we were introduced to Mork and Mindy, two barrel-shaped Chows that growled through the wire fence with bared ugly teeth. The home movie concluded with shots of Patty teaching almost four-year-old Brianna how to make divinity and Tom playing ball with six-and-a-half-year-old Robbie. The only ones missing in the video were Mark and his wife Darla. Mark was in the navy stationed in San Diego and couldn't take leave, even for a family Christmas video.

When Dad received the video, he called and said it was the best Christmas present he had ever got. Hearing this made me cry, but if I *wasn't* crying in December, something was wrong.

That first Christmas living with Moira, I began obsessing about Tim and Angie. I wondered what they were doing for the holidays, and what was on their Christmas lists? Did they get a real tree and if so, what kind? The tree Moira and Dean picked out was a seven-foot Noble fir, which Moira decorated with gold-plated musical instrument replicas. Under the tree was a red velvet skirt that Moira and on top was a shimmering gold star.

Twinkling strings of gold lights lined the apartment windows, and a nativity set made of porcelain sat regally on the center of a table. Festive towels and placemats and rugs decorated every inch of the apartment.

On Christmas Eve, Moira invited all her chorus friends over to gather around the piano so they could sing holiday songs. I dreaded the evening. I couldn't sing on tune, even the basic lyrics to traditional Christmas carols, yet I had nowhere to go. In the end, I plastered a smile to my face, simply mouthed the words, sipped my eggnog, and wished Jesus had been born in August, when at least the sun would be shining and I could ignore all the silliness of Christmas by sitting poolside somewhere sipping foo-foo drinks and wearing a bikini with matching sarong.

Instead, I was wearing new cream-colored cuffed trousers and a sequined ivory sweater, standing across from Moira's ebony Yamaha upright—a piece that undoubtedly cost more than my Ford Mustang. Under the soft glow of dual Tiffany lamps, I observed Moira's guests dressed in sparkling red and green outfits singing unabashedly with perfect pitch, daring not admit to anyone in the room I hated Christmas, the most celebrated of holidays. Inside, I promised myself next year I would completely ignore the month of December.

Screw my sister's birthday, screw Bob's birthday, screw Jesus! Next December was simply going to be the last month of the year, a dismal month sure to be more wet than white.

Chapter Forty-Five

Steve Wolf was only twenty-two years old when he was diagnosed with the rarest and deadliest form of thyroid cancer, and his son Andrew a mere six weeks old. The symptoms had begun as a nagging cough that turned to hoarseness and difficulty swallowing. Sue finally convinced him to see a doctor, who initially diagnosed a sinus infection. He was put on antibiotics but when his symptoms worsened and Steve lost a lot of weight, Sue called me and asked if knew of any good doctors.

I did, and Steve ended up going to see an ENT (head/neck/throat) specialist at Swedish Hospital with whom I was familiar during the course of my work. The surgeon, Harold Novack, had recommended a lymph node biopsy, and a week later, he told the stunned couple that Steve had an aggressive tumor called anaplastic thyroid carcinoma.

Sue called me again. "Steve has cancer, Nancy, *cancer*! And his chest x-ray showed some funny spots and Dr. Novack acted real worried and wants Steve to have more tests." Sue's speech was pressured, nearly manic. "Thyroid cancer can't spread to the lungs, can it?"

Of course it can. Cancer can put up shop anywhere it wants in the human body. No organ is immune. As soothingly as I could, I said, "Don't worry, Sue. What kind of tests?"

Sue replied uneasily, "I don't know, a CAT scan, I think. But he's only twenty-two, and I'm so scared! I don't want Andrew to grow up without his daddy!"

I reassured my sister, who I was sure was overreacting. "Sue, just calm down. Let's wait to see what the tests show."

Two weeks later, Steve was in the hospital for major surgery, and there was no more unwelcome coincidence than me ending up transcribing the dictation of that very surgery, performed by Harold Novack, M.D. I knew there was a conflict of interest at play but there was no one else who could transcribe the tape as productively. Swedish was an important longstanding client and my account. So, I put on my headsets, took a deep breath, and began transcribing the details of Steven L. Wolf's total thyroidectomy and median sternotomy, an operation that opened up the chest cavity for exploratory purposes. Five pages later, I ended the report with a signature line, printed it out, and handed it, along with the others I had typed, to the office proofreader, shaking like a leaf. My brother-in-law's thyroid tumor was so extensive it had distorted the anatomy of his neck and was wrapped around his vocal cords, his larynx, even a pulmonary vein and artery. If that weren't bad enough, his lungs were peppered with metastatic nodules that were deemed unresectable.

Steve's disease was advanced and incurable, yet I could not tell my sister—*not anyone*—because I had signed a Confidentiality Agreement as part of my employment requirements, and it might as well have been signed in blood.

That night, I sat anxiously by the phone and when Sue called to "break" the news that Steve's cancer had spread to his lungs and he would need radiation treatments, I broke down. "I'm so, so sorry."

I was crying but Sue's voice was eerily, uncharacteristically calm. "Nancy, the Lord will get us through this. We must believe in His strength and His will. Tonight, our church will be doing a prayer chain for Steve. Could you call everyone in the family and ask them to join us?"

Steve needs more than a prayer chain. "Of course." I hung up feeling miserable, wondering what if Tim got cancer while we were separated and I wasn't there to support him? What would happen to Angie? If Tim died, Angie would be completely alone.

Steve's grave condition had me questioning my motives for the separation. Had I acted too prematurely? I wasn't perfect, why should I expect Tim to be? Many times, especially during the retched holidays, I picked up the phone to call Tim but hung up before I dialed. Now I was using the phone to dial Patty and the rest of my family to tell them about the prayer chain for Steve.

By February of 1987, my insecurities about the breakup had mounted to almost unbearable levels, despite Ray's insistence I was doing the right thing staying away from Tim. He had made it clear he thought I could do better than Tim, but I remained as confused as ever, especially after Ray and I ended up in a Bellevue hotel for the sole purpose of a one-night stand, no strings attached. I was so ashamed, I cried for a week and told Ray it would never happen again.

There was a bright spot in my life, however, and that was *L.A. Law*, which Moira and I watched without fail, filling the commercials with gossip about Susan Dey (cute hair!), Harry Hamlin (dreamy dimples!) or Jimmy Smits (hot in every way!). Afterwards, however, I felt empty and counted the hours until another Friday, and the next drama-filled episode of *L.A. Law*.

In March, on a very cold Wednesday, while Moira was at the movies with Dean, Tim surprised me with a phone call. It had been months since we spoke and hearing his upbeat voice was like having a severed limb suddenly grow back. "Hi, Tim. How are you?" I settled in on Moira's sofa, hoping for a pleasant conversation with a man who always made me laugh.

"Well, I'm calling because I was wondering if you could switch nights at the shop with me? I want to take Angie and some friends to the movies on Friday, but that's my night to close. They want to see *Pretty in Pink* with that redhead who looks like Angie."

"Molly Ringwald."

"Yes, that's her. Anyway, I'll work for you tomorrow night if you can work for me Friday."

"Well, *L.A. Law* is on, but if I close on time, I can be back here by nine."

"Great show. I'm kind of hooked myself." Tim paused before joking, "My Fridays aren't exactly filled with excitement, unless you count taxiing teenaged girls around."

I grinned, feeling the same way. "So, what's up?"

Ice clinked and Tim's voice cracked when he spoke. "I've been thinking a lot about you. I miss your cooking."

"Really?" I asked. "It wasn't that long ago you said I couldn't boil water."

"That was then. Now you could be a chef. You're really amazing in the kitchen."

I laughed, allowing the pile of bad memories blow away like leaves in a fall storm. There was a pause before Tim spoke, voice cracking. "Nancy? I miss you more than anything."

My heart went into my throat.

He continued, "I worship you. I would get down on my hands and knees and kiss the ground you walk on just to hold you one more time. I know it's not original, but it's true."

I closed my eyes and was silent for what seemed a long time. I asked, "Really?"

"Really. I'll even go into treatment and get clean and sober if that means saving us. These past months have been hell. I know I've been an asshole and I need help. But I need you to get through this. I can't do it alone."

"Treatment?" I nearly dropped the phone and any resolve I might have had vanished with that one word. "Seriously?"

"Yeah. Can you believe it? I'm fuckin' forty and it's taken this long to want to straighten up my act."

"I don't know what to say." I wanted more than ever to believe Tim. "You mean, no more booze forever?"

"Yes," Tim answered. He cleared his throat and said, "By the way, hon, I didn't burn your box of pictures and letters, or your scrapbooks. I just said that because I was hurt. Everything's here waiting. Nance? I love you more than anything on earth. Please, please come back home. I'm nothing without you."

I'm nothing without you. The significance of that statement to an insecure, self-doubting woman like me could not be measured. Tim needed me to be complete, and for that I could not walk away. I told him I would give him a second chance, and then I tearfully told him about Steve.

Moira took the news well because Dean moved in right after I moved out. Back at Tim and Angie's house (*my* house, I was reminded) in Duvall, I was greeted with a handmade sign on the front door: "Welcome home, Nancy!"

Inside, I soaked up the familiarity. Most of my belongings had been put into storage since Moira had everything imaginable to furnish an apartment, and together, Tim, Angie, and I cleaned out my storage unit and took everything back to Duvall, "where it belonged." While Tim was cooking, Angie helped me unpacked. Together we opened boxes and put things back where they had been eight months prior. I unwrapped a favorite photograph of us at the Woodland Park Zoo and handed it to Angie. "Let's put this on the hall stand."

"Okay." She studied the picture. "You have such pretty hair. I wish I was blond."

"What are you talking about, Angie? Your hair is naturally gorgeous!" It was true. Angie had a thick mane of hair the color of pennies bathed in sunlight. I leaned into my "daughter" and lowered my voice. "But, if you want, maybe I'll take you to Gene Juarez for a style and cut?"

"Cool!" Sixteen-year-old Angie giddily opened another box and retrieved an item wrapped in newspaper. When it was unwrapped, she held it up. "Oh, I remember this." It was a muted pastel swirled-glass candleholder. Next, Angie opened a matching pair of champagne flutes and placed them on the buffet. "Aren't these from your mom?"

"Yes. They're hand-painted Rueven glass. Mom said the Leavenworth store where she bought these pieces went out of business."

Tim was in the doorway to the kitchen drinking Mountain Dew from a can, and I could see the remorse in his eyes. There used to be *four* glasses and a matching bowl with scalloped edges, all broken when he flung them into a wall in an intoxicated rage. I watched the muscles in his jaw tighten. I could feel his unbearable shame.

The odor of Indian curry filled the air and my stomach growled. "So, honey, how's that chicken curry coming along? It smells delicious!"

I was thinking that if Tim truly got sober, I *must* make things right this time.

It was my duty.

Chapter Forty-Six

Tim entered an inpatient alcohol dependency program in March of 1987, and for this I was incredibly proud of his courage and commitment. After all, the most important step to beating booze was *admitting* one had a problem. At least that's what I'd read. By this time, I had gone to a few Al-Anon meetings and learned a lot about the disease of alcoholism. I also found out I was codependent and an enabler. No big surprise there. I thrived on being needed, and probably should have been a nurse.

Right after Tim got admitted to the rehab center, I stumbled across something that astonished me. I was at work thumbing through my favorite reference book, Vera Pyle's *Current Medical Terminology* (known in my profession as the "Silver Book"), and there I was, listed in the Fifth Edition: "Blue Angel Syndrome: A pathological infatuation in which partners in a relationship sacrifice themselves and their own best interests."

In other words, the Nancy Anne Nash Syndrome, but I had a better definition: Being unselfish and making sure everyone around me was happy, no matter how miserable I had to make things to get them there. I didn't think being Blue Angel was something to be ashamed of, and it was better than a Red Devil, which is sometimes what I thought Tim was.

The first time Angie and me visited Tim at the drug and alcohol rehab facility of St. Peter's Hospital in Olympia, I was taken aback at how withdrawn he was, and how much grayer he was at the temples. I don't know why, but I expected him to be in high spirits that he was saving our relationship *and* his liver, but he looked depressed. After a brief hug and hello, we were asked to attend a family members' meeting, held in a room appointed like a den. There, people gathered awkwardly in a circle and began talking about their significant other's "drug of choice."

A plain young woman spoke first, wringing her hands, eyes downcast. "Lester's drug of choice is marijuana. It's destroying our marriage."

There were murmurs of understanding before the woman next to her began, "Well, my husband Bernie's drug of choice is scotch. Once he starts, he can't stop. I told the kids their father was sick; now I know he really is."

Listening to this, I squeezed Angie's hand. It was my turn and I wanted to say *everything* was Tim's drug of choice—beer, whiskey, pot, cocaine, LSD—but I could not bring myself to speak to a group of complete strangers. I passed with a red face.

After several more sad stories, the last to speak was an elderly man, whose hands were tremulous. Crying softly, he admitted to the group that his wife of 38 years was an alcoholic. "It would kill our grandchildren if they knew. We have six grandkids, all so special." He struggled for composure. "I've done everything to help Shirley. Everything. I love her, but her drinking is ruining our lives." He wiped his eyes and looked around. It was a room filled with the sounds of people sniffling and blowing their noses.

After the meeting, Angie and I met with Tim and his addiction counselor, a former alcoholic named Alice. The counselor asked us to get comfortable and began, "Nancy, let's start with you. Would you please share how Tim's drinking has affected your life?"

I squirmed, hating to be in the spotlight. "Well, um, Tim can be sort of like Dr. Jekyll and Mr. Hyde when he drinks. Plus, I worry about his liver. I don't want him to die of cirrhosis." I glanced at Angie for support, but she was staring straight ahead, arms crossed. I continued, "I guess I don't understand why Tim can't drink like a normal person."

Alice questioned, "A normal person, like you?"

I squirmed, wondering if Tim had shared all our dirty little secrets, including our experimentation with cocaine. I looked towards Tim for a clue but he remained stone-faced. "Well, my personality doesn't change when I drink. I don't get nasty and mean." *I'm not the one in rehab.* "I know I've drank too much before and—"

Tim interjected, "Nancy's absolutely right. I have to take responsibility for my addiction. She isn't the alcoholic, I am."

My eyes went wide and my jaw dropped. Man, this place was good! I looked directly into Tim's sad green eyes and smiled, full of love. "But don't worry, you'll get better. We love you." I had the urge to jump across the room and into Tim's lap, when Alice cleared her throat loudly.

"Tim, can you share with Nancy and your daughter how you feel about your recovery thus far?"

Tim deadpanned, "I feel like I need a cigarette." He was hunched forward and working his jaw muscles to get out the words. He said to the floor, "I guess I've learned I haven't been very honest because of my drinking and that it has hurt those I love." Briefly, he looked up at his only daughter. "Squirt, I'm so sorry."

Angie fidgeted uncomfortably and murmured, "I know."

Alice asked, "Is that all?"

Tim finally looked at me. "I just want to start over with a clean slate." His voice cracked, "I want to make you both proud. I want to be a good man."

Angie straightened. "Really, Dad?" Her green eyes were suddenly alert.

"Really. No more fighting and loud parties and drugs." He got up and walked to his "girls," and he knelt at our feet. We then shared a group hug, crying joyfully, thankful Tim had been cured. Honestly, that's what I thought. Thirty days in rehab and Tim would be a changed, cured man who would never crave alcohol again.

I picked Tim up by myself on the day of his discharge from rehab, when Alice reminded us that Tim had a disease and that sobriety needed to be approached one day at a time.

Tim repeated with a wink, "Yep, one day at a time; that's the AA motto." On the walk to the car, he immediately lit up a cigarette and handed me a large manila folder. "Here. This is all the paperwork and shit from treatment. You wouldn't believe the tests we had to take."

"What kind of tests?"

"I don't know. Personality ones to see if you're crazy or not." He pointed to the folder. "You can either file it or burn it, I don't care."

The drive home was awkward and I wished Angie was with us, but she was with her grandparents. It felt like Tim and I were starting over from scratch, so I compensated with light chatter, updating him on the happenings at my office. "Moira broke up with Dean. She said he was a mama's boy, but I could have told her that. He might have had money, but he was way too prissy. She's dating a surgical resident now."

Tim reached for his crotch. "I have a boner."

I glanced over and down. "Yes, I see."

"Hon, that was the longest fuckin' thirty days in my life. I can't wait to get home and get you into bed."

Afterwards, Tim rolled over and immediately began snoring, and I decided to file his treatment paperwork. First, I looked for the tests he had been talking about. There it was, an M.M.P.I., or Minnesota Multiphasic Personality Inventory. I was familiar with the test but couldn't make any sense out of Tim's M.M.P.I. score, which used a combination of letters, numbers, and symbols. What I did understand was another report with a "Summary Section" typed in a Times New Roman size 12 font: "Tim Joseph is a 40-year-old single white male who has a strong need to compartmentalize his feelings. He tends toward antisocial behavior, but this appears more for "shock value" than a true disregard for social norms. He likes to be in control and believes his beliefs and values are superior to others."

Another test concluded, "Tim Joseph displays deep-seated, unresolved issues with women."

Duh! I could have saved the psychologists a lot of time. When I was done snooping, I replaced the contents of the folder and placed the file in the filing cabinet under the tab, "Tim's Sobriety." The evidence was damaging and I would probably destroy it.

Someday.

Chapter Forty-Seven

Now that Tim had sobered up, the major business remodel that had been put on hold resumed, and soon Valley Drycleaners & Laundromat became a Simon & Son's Fine Drycleaning store with a classy new look: Dark-green marble countertops and tile entryway with forest-green carpeting and gold accents, including a gold shepherd's hook for the clothes that were picked up by our customers. A privacy wall was built to separate the back processing area, where all the grunt work was done, from the lobby. Live Boston ferns hung from brass-plated pots and a Washingtonian palm sat in the corner to created ambience.

The Laundromat portion, which Simon & Son's had nothing to do with, was accessible by a swinging door, separated by a large counter, under which were baggies of soap for sale, which we bagged ourselves from bulk detergent bought at Costco. For a small fee, we offered "fluff and fold," a service where we transferred loads from washers to dryers so customers didn't need to hang around. For a bigger feeds, we also offered drop-off service, where we did it all.

By then, I had become an expert in the business of drycleaning, or more specifically Stain Identification. This was critical because, depending on the stain, it was pretreated differently. The only time I didn't press for details on a stain's origin was when it was crunchy.

Crunchy stains gave me the creeps and these items got thrown into the bag marked "extra care."

Because of our affiliation with upscale Simon & Son's, our prices went up and our new customer base was more finicky and demanding that we were accustomed to. They wanted medium-heavy starch, light starch, or no-starch-or-my-husband-will-kill-me. They expected next-day service and lemon drops on the counter. We aimed to please, but the complaints increased:

Four bucks to clean linen pants? That's outrageous! And this pleat is pressed crooked.

This skirt shrunk, I'm telling you! I could wear this last week and now I can't even get the second button snapped.

When I brought these in, they were blue and now they're green.

The buttons are missing.

The zipper is broken.

This isn't mine.

You can still see the red wine spill on this white silk blouse and I paid extra for pretreatment!

I felt sorry for this latter customer, a teenaged girl who was frantic because the white blouse and the wine both belonged to her mother. I tried to explain that red wine on white silk was a horrible combination, perhaps the nastiest in the drycleaning business. Upon hearing this, the young girl burst into tears and I let her have the blouse without charging her for the cleaning.

There were good days and bad days, typical when one works in retail, but after a long, strife-filled *year* into my "ninety-day trial period" at our shop, I finally called it quits and announced I was going back to the far better-compensated chaos at P.D. Unfortunately, hiring my replacement would solve one problem while it created a dozen more. By then, Jim had dropped out of the business to spend more time with his new girlfriend and thus, it was left up to me and Tim. Up went the "Help Wanted" signs, and the parade of losers began.

First in the door was Jody, who was hired without a resume because she could start immediately. Unfortunately, 18-year-old Jody, who was tall, lithe, and model-pretty, ended up stealing clothes *after* they were drycleaned and was caught because she left a trail of evidence as wide as the street: It was always her initials on every receipt of missing items, and not coincidentally, the items in question were always womens' clothing, in her size, including a bikini.

Claudia was next. She was not a thief but was chronically late, or sick, and moved like molasses, which sorely tested my patience. Zombies did not get dozens of pieces of drycleaning bagged and tagged by 4:00 p.m. *as guaranteed,* so I ended up helping Claudia, who was getting paid minimum wage, plus tips and free laundry services.

One Saturday afternoon, as we often did, Tim and I dropped by the shop to check on things, particularly Claudia. We were happy the Laundromat was packed with customers and that bags of soap were neatly stacked in a basket on the counter to sell to customers. The machines were wiped down and things looked in order, until we noticed something was missing, and that was Claudia. We looked everywhere, including the bathroom and the mechanical room, to no avail. I was frantic when Claudia walked through the front door holding a Styrofoam takeout box. The shop filled with the scent of Mexican food.

"Oh, hi, guys." Claudia lifted the box. "I was hungry."

I glanced at the cash register, which I could tell was unlocked. I walked over and opened the drawer. It was full of rolls of quarters, cash, and a banded stack of checks. "You left the cash register unattended?"

"Only for a minute. It wasn't busy when I left."

The urge to strangle Claudia was overpowering. I clenched my teeth. "You're fired."

"What?" Claudia burst into tears and customers turned curiously. "But I'm in the middle of doing a fluff-and-fold and the customer has already paid. Please!"

I was insistent. "You left cash and property unattended! Do you not realize how serious that is?"

Claudia's cheeks puffed. "Well, yes, but…I was only going to be gone—"

Suddenly I caught a whiff of something else: Jose Cuervo and strawberries. "Claudia? Did you also have a Margarita?"

"Just one. They're on special."

I threw up my hands and shot daggers at Tim in hopes of spurring him to get involved. Unfortunately, if I was looking for support, I didn't get it. He shrugged, "For godsakes, woman, one Margarita never killed anybody."

That's ironic coming from a recovering alcoholic. I ignored Tim and said, "Sorry, Claudia, I have to let you go."

After Claudia left with her personal items, Tim handed me a plastic laundry basket full of unfolded T-shirts and underwear and gray socks. He read the invoice and said, "You fired the help so you'll have to finish the job, and do a good job. You know how picky Calvin Graham is about his briefs being folded just right."

I smiled as I accepted the basket, refusing to feel sorry for firing Claudia. It was the right thing to do, even if my business partner and boyfriend didn't agree.

"Of course I'll do a good job, Tim. I always do."

Chapter Forty-Eight

Tim's sobriety lasted thirty-six days. During that time, we joined "Club Soda," a group of recovering alcoholics (and their partners) who met for nonalcoholic events such as dining and dancing. Most of the time, they were held in regular restaurants or nightclubs where alcohol was readily available, and *everybody* was smoking. Cigarettes had replaced booze and I seemed to be the only one who was struggling to breathe. In a show of support, I had quit Afrin cold turkey and rarely could breathe through my nose so I tasted nicotine for hours, and the only thing I enjoyed at these events was watching everybody try to dance sober through a blue haze.

Far worse were Al-Anon meetings, which were almost always held in the basement of a church, presumably because no one dared think about drinking in a place of worship. There, I squirmed listening to the pitiful stories of people who were way worse off than me. The women were often downtrodden and dowdy, whose "significant others" were in jail or jobless. I attended the meetings in my Sunday best and when it came my turn to talk, I passed, afraid to share any part of my life with the strangers at the table.

When Tim restarted drinking, it was not full-blown, hard-stuff drinking, but drinking in moderation. He even switched to "light" beer, which I later learned had lesser calories, not lesser alcohol content. This is when Tim shared with me the things he had *really* learned in rehab: 1) Don't hide or make excuses for your addiction, and act contrite because that was the fastest way out the door. 2) It was possible to *control* one's drinking, not give it up. That was, he said, the whole purpose of treatment: To learn how to drink responsibly.

After that, I stopped going to Al-Anon. There seemed no point.

One night of Tim's responsible drinking, a Friday in June, his beverage of choice was cheap bourbon. Sure, he started out with bourbon and 7-Up, but soon it was bourbon and water on the rocks, and then bourbon straight up, and when the bottle was nearly empty, Tim joked it must have evaporated. "How'd that happen?" he asked the bottle before running into the edge of the portable dishwasher on wheels. The dishwasher rolled back into the oak dining room table, where sat a vase of flowers. The vase tipped and sunflowers and water went everywhere, dripping onto the hardwood floors.

This would have been embarrassing to watch, had Angie and me not had an unusual way of handling it: We pretended Tim was invisible, without even first discussing it. We simply ignored him, even after he tripped over the wood-burning stove and fell dangerously close to the aquarium, or when he accused us both of "being on the rag." We totally ignored the puddle on the floor and the wilting sunflowers.

Tim naturally got violently ill that night but no one went to his rescue, though I was relieved when I heard him close our bedroom door. This meant he was alive and had not aspirated on his own vomit and lay unconscious and dying on the bathroom floor, in my mind the worst possible way to expire.

After that, Tim was remorseful and sober for another nine days before his next binge. Pretty soon, there were no more sober days.

At first, it was uncomfortable going out with friends, who knew about Tim's stint in treatment, when he'd ordered a drink and I was sure they were thinking it was somehow my fault he had begun drinking again. After a few rounds, however, Tim was back to being Tim, the life of the party. Eventually his experience with treatment and sobriety was simply another source for stories, and a way for him to vent. Clearly, Tim was angry he had been "forced" to go in treatment.

Oddly enough, these were not horrible times. Tim now accepted *he* had The Problem and how he chose to deal with it was his business, not mine, and because the responsibility had been shifted where it belonged, our fights were less intense. When Tim got really drunk, he left Angie and me alone. It was the best we could hope for.

For my part, I remained supportive and worked not on making Tim better but making myself great. I worked out at the nearby Ladies' Fitness Center, kept the house spotless and updated, and made sure Angie got all the help she needed with her schoolwork. It was all about keeping things orderly in the middle of a battlefield, something my mother had routinely been expected to do, and she taught me well.

Really, things were going pretty well…until the marriage proposal.

Chapter Forty-Nine

I only vaguely remember, but Tim proposed something like this. After making love, we crawled under the covers and began watching a new episode of *Magnum, P.I.* I told Tim he looked just as good in his short tight cutoffs as Tom Selleck (which was true) and he asked me to marry him. My answer was yes, and the details of where and when (and why, in case you're wondering) came later. The first person we told was Angie in a phone call. The next day, my sister Patty called with bad news: Angie had decided she was not coming to our wedding, less than two months away.

I asked in disbelief, "What do you mean, Patty? She *has* to go. Is she there? Can I talk to her?"

Patty replied, "No, her and Brianna walked to the store. Listen, Angie's been through a lot with you and Tim. I mean, the fighting, the breakups, you always coming over here whenever you're mad at him or when he's drinking. Angie isn't the only one who thinks you guys getting married isn't a good idea."

"We're working things out."

"Well, Angie isn't so sure."

"Tell her to please call me, Patty. I need to talk to her."

I hung up, heartbroken, but I knew a rift had developed between Angie and me, one formed from endless lies, hidden report cards, skipping classes, missing homework assignments, and sneaking out to be with a derelict named Lee Mingo. I had worked so hard for Angie's education and she didn't seem at all to appreciate it. It was like I'd been slapped in the face when Angie fell for a dropout who couldn't care less about a proper education, ironic since the reason Angie was living with Patty and Tom was so she could attend a school in a better school and more funded school district. In Woodinville, Angie got one-on-one tutoring and her IEP was followed to the letter. Her grades were up and her attitude was completely turned around. I never thought it might be because she was no longer living with her father and me.

I did the only thing I could think of: I sat down at my portable typewriter and wrote Angie a letter.

June 16, 1987

Dearest Angie:

You have had many "mothers" in your short life, all of whom I am sure loved you very much, and while I may not be your real mother, to me you are my one and only daughter and are very special to me. What has happened between us will never change that. I love you! I hope you are feeling better about school again now that you are in a program that understands your needs. And the best part, you don't have to repeat 10th grade! I also know you hated helping us at the shop and I don't blame you. (Good news: we just hired someone who seems to be working out and so far hasn't stolen anything!) Maybe someday we'll sell that place and the headache will be over! (Just don't tell your dad I said that!).

I guess the real reason I am writing, besides to let you know how much your father and I love you, is to tell you we want you at our wedding. You are part of this family and your father will be so upset if his little girl is not by his side on this special day. So please, please change your mind.

Remember, we love you no matter what.

Love always,
Nancy aka "Mom"

P.S. I am so sorry for slapping you! Please forgive me.
P.S.S. I know you are also mad about your dad and me not allowing you
to see Lee, but I think you will understand when you are older. He is a
bad influence and will bring you down. You deserve better!!

XOXOXO
"Mom"

It was a letter strikingly similar to the letter my own mother wrote to me in 1978. In any case, after begging some more, Angie did attend our wedding, but there were an alarming number of invited guests who didn't because they supposedly had other obligations on August 1, 1987. The list of the missing included Patty and Tom, as well as all of my siblings and stepsiblings. Even Moira gave the excuse she had to work that Saturday. It wasn't out of the realm of possibility but Moira was boss even without the title. She could have easily gotten out of work to attend her good friend's wedding. Then again, I was glad the ceremony was simple, aboard *Sindrome* while moored in Blake Island State Park, and our guest list was short because I wanted to get it over with as quickly as possible.

Tim and I exchanged borrowed rings and afterwards, feasted on alder-smoked salmon and drank champagne. The newlyweds toasted to forever.

"Cheers to happiness forever!" I raised my glass and smiled for our guests, among them Mel and Ray, who didn't look that happy.

Next to me, Tim said dutifully, "Cheers!" He took a sip of his sparkling wine and added his own toast, "To my third old lady. Let's hope three's a charm!"

Everybody laughed, except Ray.

Chapter Fifty

Our two-part honeymoon was a yo-yo of adventure and misery. You would probably think, by now, I'd expect that, but I was still disappointed, especially when part one began magically the morning after the ceremony, when we cruised north on waters as flat and reflective as a mirror under a cloudless blue sky. Hours later, while cruising north through Saratoga Passage off Whidbey Island, we were welcomed by a pod of porpoises, and I made Tim stop the boat so I could snap pictures. The only tense moments were while navigating treacherous Deception Pass at the tip of the island. Tim had studied the tides and currents and was mindful of the shoals that lurked. Nevertheless, the sea was sucked through the cliff-lined channel like a syringe. Below us, the swirling whirlpools galvanized me into a frozen posture, fearing any unplanned or slight movement would send the boat into a vortex and with it, my future. Twenty minutes had seemed much longer but soon we were in the breathtaking San Juan Islands. We celebrated Tim's fortieth birthday two days later in Roche Harbor before heading to the Gulf Coast Islands of Canada. From a sandy beach off the northeastern coast of Vancouver Island, I collected a souvenir—a lovely but quite dead starfish—which began to stink so badly sitting on the bow of the boat, it was tossed into a cove near Pender Harbor. At least I got a photo.

Part two of our honeymoon started on a plane headed for Mazatlan, the "Pearl of The Pacific." Aboard the Boeing 727, all I could think about were my father's vague but ominous references to the "lies in the skies," which were the reasons he refused to fly commercially. He never elaborated on the lies (in retrospect a plus, or I may never have flown), but given he was a pilot and an air-traffic controller, I was sufficiently worried and in-flight remained clutched to the armrests and practicing what I believed to be Lamaze breathing. Next to me, oblivious to our peril, Tim was drinking Bloody Marys and flirting jauntily with the stewardesses. My Mimosa was gone and had done little to steady my nerves.

I knew it was unlikely I'd ever truly get over my fear of flying. Other than flights to both brothers' weddings, the only other plane trip I had ever taken was terrifying, and without the knowledge, or permission, of my mother. I was six and the ride was aboard a tiny prop plane named Big Bee because it was yellow, and Dad was the pilot. The day was rainy and windy, and when the plane hit a thundercloud and lightning struck a wing, I was sure we were going to crash and wet my pants. It was a humiliating way to be introduced to flying.

Our jetliner landed in Mazatlan after what seemed an eternity circling, and I was sure the pilot made a mistake because the Mazatlan Airport was the size of a 7-11 and was being guarded by men with machine guns. We disembarked directly onto the ground outside, not in a terminal, where a Spanish stewardess with a thick black ponytail to her waist chirped in a thick accent, "Enjoy your veesit to Mazatlan!"

I was sweating profusely before we got to our bus. I immediately put my hair into a ponytail and wiped perspiration from my forehead. Breathing the hot thick air was like chugging warm oatmeal. We boarded a rickety (non-air-conditioned) bus that took us to our hotel, The Holiday Inn, where the concierge handed over a set of keys and a box fan.

"You take thees por favor. Air conditioner no work."

I sputtered, "What? You're joking, right?" By then, I was sweating so hard my clothes were soaked. Tucked into cute new sandals, my feet made a squishy sound with each step. My bikini panties were soaked under my skirt.

"No, senora. Por favor, you take thees fan. No charge."

Tim took the fan and promised if hotel maintenance didn't fix the air-conditioning, he would. We took the elevator to the third floor, where our room was like a sauna but had a gorgeous view of the ocean. By then, the sun was setting and we watched as the azure sky was transformed into sinewy ropes of topaz, crimson and amethyst. Below, the surface of the water danced with illuminated light and beckoned a swim. Instead, we had sex on the patio where there was a breeze.

Chapter Fifty-One

On a tour of Old Mazatlan—where the locals lived and shopped—it was clear the city was suffering a construction crisis, either that or building codes were nonexistent. The buildings that might have held promise, or had started with actual blueprints, now were abandoned in various stages of completion, full of gaping holes and jutting re-bar. On the dirty streets, vendors were everywhere, as they were at the beach, including small children selling pieces of gum for a nickel. Old Mazatlan was colorful and interesting, but I was glad to be back at our resort and doing what I most like when I'm at the beach—reading a book and working on my tan— while Tim went marlin fishing. At the lagoon near our hotel, I set up a lounge chair and lathered on suntan lotion with an SPF of eight. I didn't want to get skin cancer, but I also didn't want to look like Casper the Ghost when I got back home. I retrieved my newest hardback, *Windmills of the Gods,* from my mesh beach bag, and leaned blissfully back.

I read for five minutes before I was got too hot and waded into the water, first to my waist, then to my neck. Above me, a female para-sailor in a colorful chute was being drug across the blue sky by a small plane when suddenly she was lowered into the water and dropped like a bug. I watched the girl swim to shore in fascination, wishing I had the guts to do such a thing, but that would require me to get over several pathologic fears, among them fear of heights, fear of small planes, and most of all, fear of spending fifty bucks to plummet into the sea while hordes of strangers gawked. The girl who fell from the sky was greeted by a boy on the beach, and after they hugged she squealed and pointed to the sky. I would be barfing.

In my favor, I was adventurous in other ways, such as agreeing to open-seas boating, once enduring a three-hour crossing of the treacherous Strait of Juan de Fuca aboard *Sindrome*. We had left Port Townsend on the northern Olympic Peninsula bright and early, when the waters were calm, but the trip turned into terror when a heavy fog descended an hour out and we could not see more than a few feet in front of us. The Straits were a major shipping lane between Alaska, Canada, and the Pacific Northwest so every few minutes Tim and I alternated sounding the foghorn. Then, out of nowhere, a huge round light appeared and my heart stopped, sure it was a freightliner ready to plow them into nothing but fiberglass chips, but it turned out to be a channel marker. Eventually, we arrived safely and moored at the public dock in Victoria Harbor directly across from The Empress, a hauntingly beautiful and immense vine-covered brick hotel.

Another August, when Tim and me were crossing the Georgia Strait, having departed from the Port of Nanaimo on the west central side of Vancouver Island, we hit a strong southerly wind sideways and it took us twice as long to cross the water as it should have. By the time we could see land on the other side, *Sindrome* was running on fumes. Fortunately, the compass and navigational charts had served us well and it was the Port of Vancouver, British Columbia, where we ended up as planned, albeit a few hours late.

I walked back to her lounge chair, ordered a wine cooler, and watched the endless onslaught of beach vendors peddling everything from fruit to temporary tattoos to colorful wooden parrots and stuffed iguanas.

I got my hair braided with beads ala Bo Derek, which took an hour and the señorita doing the braiding said nothing until I handed her a five-dollar U.S. bill. Her brown eyes lit up and she began speaking in rapid-fire Spanish. "Gracias gracias gracias!" The girl stuffed the five in her dress pocket and ran down the beach.

Lying under the Mexican sun and playing with the pretty beads at the ends of my braids, I agreed the summer humidity was intolerable, but I could grow accustomed to living a life of perpetual summer in Mazatlan, where I'd have a closet full of bikinis and flip-flops and sleeveless sundresses, and little else. Life would always be perfect if we lived in the Tropic of Cancer and it was this thought, and another wine cooler, that induced a deep sleep on the beach.

"Nancy? Wake up!"

I jerked groggily and beaded braids slapped my neck. When I focused, Tim was standing over me, grinning like a Cheshire cat. He smelled like a brewery, but then again, I probably smelled like strawberries and coconut. "What? What's the matter?"

"Whoa, babe. Look at you!"

I touched my braids. "I haven't seen it. No mirror."

"I was talking about your skin. It's redder than a cherry. Anyway, guess what? I just bought us a timeshare! See, I stopped at this bar on the beach to have a couple cold ones, and there was this guy there selling timeshares real cheap. I got us a steal!"

I sat up, confused. "I thought you went marlin fishing?" I reached for my suntan lotion and reapplied another layer, feeling pleased I could see some color developing on my legs and arms.

Tim answered, "I did. This was after." He removed his sunglasses to expose raccoon's eyes. "All you gotta do is sign the contract and we're in."

I cupped a hand over my eyes to block out the sun. "Contract?"

Tim beckoned with a freckled arm. "Come on. Mitch's going to meet buy us drinks to celebrate."

"Mitch?"

"Hurry. Put on your fancy cover-up and let's go."

At a bar on the beach, which was filled with scantily dressed and sunburned tourists much like myself, Tim made the introductions.

"Mitch Nelson, meet my wife, Nancy."

Mitch held out a tanned hand. "Very pleased to meet you, beautiful lady." He let go and when the drinks appeared, he handed me a Mai Tai before handing another to Tim. He said to me, "You know, this special deal ends tomorrow, so your husband is very lucky we ran into each other earlier."

"Oh." Mitch was obviously Caucasian in ethnicity, with silvery blond hair, but his skin was bronzed as dark as the locals, and weathered. I guessed he was younger than he appeared, but he was still beach boy handsome with a spurious smile and sly gray eyes. He might as well have worn a nametag that said, "Mitch Nelson, Con Artist."

He handed me a brochure. "Please, have a look."

I flipped tentatively through the brochure feeling sick to my stomach. The yo-yo was back in full force and I wondered how we could afford a timeshare? And what were the legalities regarding property ownership in a foreign country? I ventured, "It looks like an ordinary apartment building to me."

Mitch looked offended. "No, no! *La Playa* is one of the better units in all of Mazatlan. You'll love it!"

I nodded wanly as I translated. *"The Beach?* That's not very unique." I looked at Tim. "Are you sure? Won't this cost a lot of money?"

Tim answered, "Only six grand. Plus, we won't get a better souvenir from Mexico than a timeshare!"

I asked, "Even better than the leather lizard I bought you on the beach today?"

Mitch chuckled. "Don't worry. Our financing department can arrange affordable monthly installments."

"Excellent." Tim was mentally living in the timeshare.

The salesman pointed at a picture in the brochure. "This particular unit doesn't have a view, but it's close to the pool, and you can always do some trading, depending on what week you purchase." He next handed over a contract and two pens. "The good thing is the value of timeshares can only go up. Think of this as an investment."

"See, hon, that's what I was trying to tell you! We really can't go wrong." Tim drained his drink and snapped for another. "Senorita, bring us another round on me!"

I examined the contract and eventually signed above the dotted line, right next to my husband's signature.

A big purchase such as this naturally required a fancier celebration than foo-foo drinks in a cabana, and Tim and I ended up at Señor Frog's, which was noisy and smoky. Immediately a camarera in a bright yellow sundress with white ruffle trim appeared at their table.

Tim ordered, "A shot of your finest mescal and a Corona with lime."

Oh great. I was going to be spending the second night of my Mexican honeymoon with Tim *and* tequila. I thought about the perfect T-shirt for him I had seen in a mail-order catalog that proclaimed: "Instant Asshole: Just Add Tequila." Another T-shirt in the same catalog said, "Instant Bitch: Remove Chocolate." I didn't order either T-shirt, but at Senor Frog's, I ordered a tall glass of water. The last thing I needed was more alcohol.

"Water? What's up with that? We're on our honeymoon!"

"Nothing's the matter, water just sounds good. I've had a lot to drink already and need something in my stomach first."

When the drinks came, Tim tipped his head and drained his Corona first. "I'll bet you have sun sickness."

"Sun sickness? What's that?"

"Too much fun-in-the-sun. Have you seen yourself? You're the color of a Mai Tai. And I'll bet you haven't eaten a single thing all day." He did the shot of mescal and wiped his mouth. "So, did you?"

"Did I what?" I drew it out as long as I could. "Oh, look, there's that couple from California we met last night. They were so nice."

Tim craned his neck. "She's good-looking but he was a jerk." He turned. "What'd you eat today?"

"Quesadillas." I embellished the lie. "Our hotel served all its guests brunch on the beach." At the mention of food, I realized I was starving and my mouth watered as I watched the passing trays filled with spicy fried food.

Tim ordered and chugged a second shot of golden amber liquid, and shuddered. "Woo-wee, that's some mean firewater. Hey, remember that kid at the hydroplane races who got dared to drink a whole fuckin' pint of Jose Cuerva and then keeled over? That fucker was dead before they hauled him off in the ambulance."

"Isn't that why it's called ta-kill-ya?" I willed him not to order a third shot.

Tim ignored the comment and lit up a cigarette. "You know why they put a worm in every bottle of mescal?"

"There's a worm infestation in Mexico and that's how they're solving it?" I swiped a hand across my forehead, which felt on fire. A veggie burrito and good night's sleep under crisp cool sheets were all I could think of.

Tim said, "Because they have hallucinogenic powers, the worm that is. Anyway, that's why you see so many crazy drunk Mexicans."

"I see." And I was about to see one crazy Gringo.

Tim scooped up a chip in salsa and pushed the bowl of chips my direction. "You look like shit. Have some chips and you'll feel better. You know what happens when you don't eat. *I* suffer."

"Very funny." I rubbed my throbbing temples. The food arrived and I devoured it. And Tim was right, I felt a lot better, but not good enough for Tim.

"I know just the thing to snap you out of your bad mood. You need a shot of tequila."

I clenched my teeth. "I am not in a bad mood. I'm just tired. Secondly, the only time tequila will go down my throat is if it is poured there after I'm dead."

"Okay then, a Margarita. Have one for me, hon. We're on our fucking honeymoon!"

So I had a Margarita on the rocks, which I puked up on the walk back to our hotel, crouched behind a six-foot windmill palm. At our suite on the second floor, I crawled into bed while my tanked husband weaved his way towards the door. "Well, I'm outta here."

"Where? Maybe you better stay here." I didn't want him to stay but it seemed the appropriately concerned new-wife thing to say.

"Just 'cause you can't handle your liquor doesn't mean I can't have any fun. You can be a real party-pisser, you know." It was the mescal talking now. "It ain't my fuckin' fault you fried yourself in the sun."

"I know." My head spun, my skin sizzled. *Please just go away and leave me alone.* "Whatever Tim. I don't care what you do, just let me sleep." The door slammed and I threw up one more time before falling into a fitful sleep.

Late into the night, I woke to a hand draped across my naked hot belly in a room like a sauna. Behind me, Tim was snoring and blowing fetid breath my direction. Outside our open balcony, Mariachi music and drunken laughter floated up from the beach.

I disentangled myself carefully from Tim's hands and the flimsy sheets, and sat on the balcony, where at least there was a breeze, however balmy. I was pretty sure the timeshare was a scam and yes, I could have and should have refused to sign the contract, but that would have humiliated Tim and put him in a foul mood for the remainder of our honeymoon.

So much for moderating his drinking, though I knew I could hardly call the kettle black considering my current hung-over state. I should have eaten something on the beach yesterday but white bikinis are unforgiving of the tiniest of flaws, particularly in the glaring Mexican sun. I couldn't risk a pouch belly in public.

I closed my eyes and leaned back into the deck chair. In my head, I wasn't hearing snappy Mariachi music now, but Karen Carpenter singing *"We've Only Just Begun,"* but the lyrics were different:

We've only just begun
To unravel
White lies and a time-a-share
A bucket of Coronas for luck, and we're on our way.
And yes, we've just begun
To unravel
Sharing horizons that are unknown to us
Ignoring the red flags along the way
Talking it over in our heads but not to each other
Working together but apart day to day…

I tiptoed to the bathroom, turned on the light and locked the door. After reapplying a special blend of Aloe vera (courtesy of the concierge) to my sunburned skin, I began undoing the cumbersome braids from my long blond hair. When I was done, I examined my pink reflection in the mirror and thought about what my mother was always saying, that character was built on adversity.

If that were true, I was going to have character sprouting from my ya-ya.

Back home, we learned our business survived despite its owners being gone for fourteen days, much to my disappointment. I had been hoping for a major electrical fire that caused no loss of life but destroyed the building, which naturally was heavily insured. Really, the only mishaps were a malfunction of one of the super-capacity industrial washers (in great demand for sleeping bags) and the inexplicable disappearance of a lilac taffeta prom dress. I mean, how could a lilac taffeta prom dress—which according to our manager Ruth was ugly and a size 16 with gaudy ruffles and tacky plastic beads on the bodice—get lost in a sea of mostly men's suits and shirts?

When the parents of the girl whose dress it was threatened to sue us in small claims court for $200, a frantic search ensued. Eventually the lilac getup was discovered in the tagged bag of another customer's large pre-fall cleaning order.

Tim looked at the dress and said, "Ruth, you were right. That is one ugly prom dress."

Ruth nodded. "The girl who brought it in wasn't exactly Cinderella." She turned to me and said, "Some guy stopped in looking for you. Said he was an old friend." Ruth pulled a piece of paper from her apron. "Carl Callahan. Didn't leave a number."

Tim's jaw contracted. "Carl? How'd he know where to find you?"

I knew exactly how, though hadn't bothered to tell Tim, until now. "A couple weeks ago, I guess he called the house and Angie answered and told him I was at work, here. She didn't know not to give out the number because he said he was a friend."

"So, guess this means ole' Carl wants you back?"

"Very funny." Curiosity had the best of me and I asked Ruth, "So, what did he look like?"

Ruth shrugged. "Balding, pudgy, had puppy eyes. He was eating an ice cream cone when he came in, licking the cone like a kid."

Tim asked, "What flavor?"

Ruth's heavy shoulders hitched. "I know because it's my favorite: Pistachio."

"Hey, that's my favorite, too." Tim poked the air with his swivel straw, chewed like a dog bone. "Except it doesn't always agree with my gut."

I nodded and warned Ruth, "Take my advice and avoid being anywhere near Tim when he eats pistachio ice cream." I fanned my face. "He doesn't break wind, he *crushes* it, and it lingers forever."

Ruth shrugged. "Does the same thing to me."

Chapter Fifty-Two

The worst part about getting hit is not the shock, nor is it the humiliation or the betrayal. No, the very worst thing about getting smacked by your own husband is that such as an action requires a *counteraction*, and a ton of energy. I didn't have an ounce of energy, but when Tim wrung my neck and shoved me into the coat closet, where I slumped in pain onto a pile of boots, I wasted no time packing up my car with my belongings and storming out. I warned Tim I was never coming back.

I meant it, too. It was the spring of 1988 and in short order I found an apartment in Kirkland, signed a six-month lease, and told Tim our marriage was over. I had yet to call a lawyer, but no good came of hasty decisions, and money was an issue. On the phone, I told Tim he was a hopeless drunk and he called me a super-psycho-bitch. I kind of liked that, actually. I was *better* than your regular, average bitch. I was a super-psycho-bitch! During that heated exchange, it was hard to tell who slammed the phone down first.

Living in my one-bedroom apartment, I felt a lovely freedom to do whatever I wanted, whenever I wanted, with whomever I wanted. Sometimes that was meeting Ray for therapy and drinks, but most of the time what I did was shop, or dine at restaurants alone while reading a book. Back at home, I'd immediately crawl into bed and fall asleep reading my book, usually before 8 p.m. Books were big in my life, and my favorite author was still J.A. Jance. I loved her character J.P. Beaumont, called Beau, a homicide detective who worked the streets of Seattle and hung out at the Doghouse Tavern (before he had the good sense to quit booze), and many nights I lost myself in the gritty fictional world that J.A. Jance had created, or at least I tried. The apartment was 680 square feet of luxury space but was surrounded by endless noise. At night, it was the neighbor on the other side of my bedroom wall, whose parrots squawked continuously, or the neighbors upstairs, a young couple who did nothing but screw and scream. During the weekends, it was noise from traffic, kids, horns, banging doors, and doorbells. I hadn't lived in an apartment for years and longed for the peace-and-quiet of Duvall, without Tim, of course, and without a business to run, which is the only time we saw each other, when our shifts crossed.

Towards the middle of my six-month lease on a Saturday night, while engrossed in the newest issue of *Cosmo*, especially the article, "Great Orgasms…Solo!" two men knocked loudly and persistently at my front door. It was nearly midnight and I tiptoed to look through the peephole, not recognizing either one. I slipped back into bed but the strangers began kicking at her door, demanding it be opened.

"We know you're in there, Kathy!"

"Open the fuckin" door!"

The banging continued and I was afraid to walk past the door to get to the phone to call the police—let alone inform the intruders I was not Kathy—so I hid in my closet, just feet from the entranceway where the men began arguing.

"Are you sure this is the right fuckin' apartment?"

"Shit, yeah. I've been here a million times." Bang bang. "Bitch! We know you're in there!"

"Why ain't she answering?"

"Fuckin' bitch is probably passed out. Kathy! Kathy!"

There was brief interlude when the kicking and screaming stopped. It was followed by, "Oh shit."

"Shit what?"

"The door. It says 216-C."

"Yeah, so?"

"Kathy lives in 216-**G**."

"Fuckin' moron."

"Don't call me that. You paid her for the rock before we even saw it. That's fuckin' moronic."

The next day, Tim and me had a preplanned meeting at our shop to discuss our upcoming corporate tax filing, during which I told him, without planning to, about what had happened the night before. In the light of day, the whole incident didn't seem that bad, but I dreaded another night in my apartment alone.

Tim wasn't all that concerned. "Yeah, well that's apartment life. Maybe you should get a deadbolt?" Tim was chewing on a plastic stir straw in an attempt to quit smoking and looked like shit, his skin sallow and his pants loose. On his neck, the freckle I admonished him to watch was darker, had developed irregular borders, and looked crusted over.

I peered to get a better look. "The lesion on your neck looks like it's changed. When was the last time you had it examined?"

Tim took the straw out of his mouth and pointed it into the air. "Forget my fuckin' neck. You don't care anyway."

Looking at my husband in his debilitated condition, clearly the result of not having me around, I felt my resolve slipping. On top of that, I was tired of the apartment life I had chosen, tired of being on a budget, and fed up with having my peace disturbed. I guess I was more tired of all that than living with an alcoholic asshole because I willed Tim to promise he'd never hit me again so I could move back home. Stupid as it was, my Blue Angel was in total control and the only way to shut her up was to kill her. As sweetly as I could, I said, "Of course, I care."

"Look, Nancy, it's not working with us. I'm sorry I hit you but nothing's changed. One minute we're in love and the next we're trying to kill each other, and you want to blame everything on my drinking. It's not that simple. There's a helluva lot more to our problems, way more." The bell rung on the front door indicating a customer and Tim rounded the corner to help, leaving me to bite my lip in an effort not to cry.

Scraping across my mind were drug-seeking morons, the cacophony of obnoxious pet birds, the vituperative mother across the hall. In two seconds, I turned 360 degrees and hated Tim all over, glad to let him die of metastatic melanoma or a cirrhotic liver, or just plain loneliness, all of which were distinct possibilities.

And, how dare he say his drinking wasn't the problem! He never got physical or mean when sober. How could he not see that?

Tim returned with an armful of men's shirts and began pinning numbered tags to each shirt, along with another tag indicating the starch requested. "File for divorce if you want. I don't care anymore."

I replied snottily, "Well then, I will. You've given me no choice."

Tim sneered. "That's fuckin' great. So what do you want to do about the shop?" His jaw tightened and his neck veins looked ready to burst. "Or were you just going to walk away from that, too?"

"Of course not. We'll sell the business." Damn! My head was reeling. This wasn't the way it was supposed to work out! Tim was supposed to miss me and repent for his mistakes by crawling back on hands and knees (sober), but here he was smugly chewing on a straw and looking like he was the king of drycleaning, or at least starch. And the odor of beer on his breath was hard to ignore.

He sneered. "Sell a business that's losing money every month? Get real."

"Well then, you can find another partner."

Tim shook his head. "You make it sound so easy but that's your problem. You live in La La Land."

I retorted, "At least I'm not a drunk and a wife-beater. Anyway, I'll call an attorney as soon as I can." I spied a stain on a blue chambray shirt. "That looks like perfume. Don't forget to put a yellow tag to pretreat that stain."

"Like you fuckin' care," Tim muttered angrily before walking away to greet another customer. Seconds later, he was sweet-talking, "Good afternoon, Mrs. Chadwick. How are you this fine today? Looks like you have quite an armful. Here, let me help."

I left through the back door, which I slammed.

Three months after that encounter, I moved back in with Tim. On some levels, I knew I was crazy, but craziness seems less crazy when it's familiar. Living in Duvall with Tim wasn't Disneyland but it was the only real home I knew, and despite it all, I really believed I loved Tim and that he was my soulmate. Why else would we keep ending up back together? It was hard to believe but that April, it would be the ten-year anniversary of our first date.

There was good thrown into the mix of all the turmoil: In May, Angie had married an enlisted man named Jeff Kilroy, who was stationed at Eielson Air Force Base in Fairbanks. We received wedding pictures in the mail, but I didn't meet Jeff until my mom and Bob's own tenth-year anniversary party.

Angie's husband turned out to be soft-spoken and quiet, with perfect military manners. I didn't say it aloud, but I was immensely relieved when it appeared Angie had not married a man like her father.

Chapter Fifty-Three

My brother-in-law Steve didn't die, but he came damn close. Following a nearly eight-hour operation, Sue's husband spent a month in the hospital battling infections and complications, once going into cardiac arrest and another time elapsing into a brief coma. Sue was at Steve's side everyday praying, and holding the baby who may never know his father, as well as trying to explain to five-year-old Anthony what was happening to the only daddy *he* had ever known.

When Mom visited Steve, she told us he looked a bit like Frankenstein with bolts protruding from the sides of his neck and his once-handsome face unrecognizable and bloated from the steroids. When he was finally discharged from Swedish Hospital, he had several drains in his chest and large bandages that had to be changed daily. A stapled incision on his chest resembled the "V" of an autopsy incision.

Get your affairs in order, Mrs. Wolf, the doctor had told my sister the day Steve went home. Sue let the meaning of the doctor's statement's slowly sink in. "Get your affairs in order" was the candy-coated version of "your husband's a goner."

With Steve unable to work, Sue was desperate for money and began her own in-home daycare. She didn't exactly like other people's kids, but it was something she could do from home. As soon as "Susan's Playpen" opened, she was in put in charge of five children, including her own two sons. A month later, Sue was praying for a lot of things, but at the top of her list was asking God to please, please let Steve live so she could quit taking care of other people's noisy, dirty, screaming, whining children, annoying children. She knew God well enough to know this would require a miracle of enormous proportions.

Seemingly overnight, "Susan's Playpen" had become nothing more than a penitentiary temporarily incarcerating three hooligans belonging to a single mother. The Wolf house could not withstand one more broken window or door, the family cat had long disappeared, and Anthony was acting out by beating up on his mother's customer's kids.

Meanwhile, Steve was undergoing both chemotherapy and radiation treatments, which had to be halted when his immune system weakened. Some days he could barely get out of bed, so everything was left to Sue. Not surprisingly, it was during this period when Sue experienced her very first migraine, a Wednesday that had started with spilling her first cup of coffee. She was wearing sweats, having given up on looking nice for evil children, so the stain was hardly noticeable but the burn still stung like hell. She retrieved the first-aid cream and was applying it to her thigh when suddenly she saw flashing bright lights that dropped her to her hands and knees, on which she crawled to their bathroom and vomited. Sue didn't know she was having a migraine; she thought an armadillo had crawled through her ear in the middle of the night and was now using the inside of her skull as a scratching post. Even the dull glare from the cracked bathroom fixture intensified the pain at her temples and she squeezed her eyes shut, slumped at the feet of a porcelain toilet that was cracked and had a tricky handle. She reached for that handle, hoping the toilet didn't clog, while in the so-called "playpen," five children were rioting. Her hair was now a stringy mess and she brushed brown strands from her face when she thought she smelled something frying. It smelled like bacon and this caused another wave of nausea followed by dry heaves.

Her next migraine didn't come on until four months later, and by then Sue felt like she was tumbling towards toddler-induced insanity. All hope seemed lost but then a bonafide miracle did occur: Steve was given the astonishing news that a followup CAT scan of his chest showed dramatic shrinkage of the tumors in his lungs. A few weeks later, the cancer that had widely spread was undetectable. It was a miracle, and with Steve's health restored, he started his own construction company, and Sue's daycare was officially closed for business.

Chapter Fifty-Four

Rick Greene decided to approach one of his most loyal (and emotional) employees with a different tactic. He knew me well enough, and began, "Nancy, think of the computer as a big Victorian house with lots of little rooms. Each room is a directory, and in each directory there are little hatboxes. Inside the hatboxes are files of information, but to get to these files, you have to access a directory, I mean, a *room*, before you can open the hatbox."

"Uh huh." I wanted to cry and find a new job in that order. I was slurping my second Starbucks double nonfat extra-foamy vanilla latte just to get me through the morning hoping Microsoft and Bill Gates and his stupid computers would drop off the face of earth.

Rick picked a small black object made of plastic. "This is called a mouse."

I droned. "Of course it is. And the mouse lives in the house."

Rick cocked his head. I was also his most smart-mouthed employee. "The *mouse* is an electronic accessory that allows you to maneuver through your desktop without using the keyboard. It's really quite amazing."

"Desktop?" My head was swimming and I looked lovingly at my electric typewriter, still with its cover on. There had to be a way to convince Rick I would never understand how to use such a complex and technical piece of equipment as a computer. I grimaced. "Could you back up?" *Again.*

"The desktop is what you see on your screen when you first log on. It contains icons for all the programs and applications that you will be using regularly." Rick began clicking keys in rapid success. On the screen appeared: "C:*.*"

Rick continued, "The living room is the heart of the house. We'll call the living room the "C" or hard drive. The command I just typed is asking the computer to show me what information is inside the hatboxes that are in the living room. By typing "asterisk dot asterisk," I am asking to see *all* the hatboxes in this directory."

"You mean room?"

"Exactly." Rick was an extraordinarily patient man, and I delighted in his analogies. I watched as the black screen filled with a long list of characters mixed with numbers, clearly dates, looking partially like this:

Directory c:\

02/03/88 01:42PM	441 bytes	testreport.doc
02/03/88 02:16PM	1,595 bytes	opreport.doc
02/03/88 03:38 PM	6,879 bytes	consultreport.doc

"See, unlike your typewriter, the computer runs on an operating system known as MS-DOS and has a huge memory. By typing simple commands, you can perform tasks like copy, delete, and move, and in seconds, access a list of all the documents you have created, including important information about each document."

Rick deleted a file in one stroke and then copied another file from one directory to another, again faster than lightning.

Holy cow! I wondered if I was going to be embarrassed about spending the morning in a panic because Rick was making me give up my trusty IBM Selectric to learn the computer. I was the last holdout in the office and had said I didn't see the point of learning something so complicated when I was one of the highest producers in the office using a typewriter.

Rick picked up a floppy disk and inserted into a slot on the front of the computer. "Think of this floppy disk as a visitor to the house who can exchange and keep information from the house and all its rooms. The visitor is known as "A" drive. You must back up all of your important documents onto the floppy disk in case the computer crashes." I watched Rick type "Copy c:*.* a:"

"What's that?"

"I am commanding that everything stored on the hard drive also be copied to the floppy drive. The asterisks mean all files and the back slashes direct where I want to the files to be copied, the so-called target drive. You can also type in "move" or "dir" for directory, even "del" for delete. Those are called commands."

The training went on another two hours, including a mind boggling lesson on creating macros as shortcuts (which seemed anything but), when Rick hit another key and the document on the screen disappeared and was replaced with the setup screen with four choices. "You must properly exit all applications. Here, you will chose option 4, "exit." It is critical that you do this step anytime you leave a document."

"Why? What if I don't?"

Rick stood and said matter-of-factly, "You will risk losing all the information of the document you were working on. In other words, everything you have typed. You'd have to start over."

"Eww."

He nodded. "It's just another reason to learn the computer."

Actually, it was a huge reason! Having to retranscribe a document you had just transcribed, particularly if it had been a "stat," because of faulty ribbons, careless spills, or copiers that ate originals, was a medical transcriptionist's most significant on-the-job hazard second only to carpal tunnel syndrome, and maybe hemorrhoids.

For the first time all afternoon, I smiled. "Thanks for the lessons, but I have one more question."

Rick rubbed his beard thoughtfully. "Yes?"

"Which one of the rooms in this Victorian house has my typewriter?"

A rare, small smile appeared on Rick's pleasant face as he stood up and scurried away to his office. Six weeks later, I was using the computer to transcribe all the accounts to which I was assigned, though a great deal of the time I was just following concise instructions, hitting key strokes in combination and using a cheat sheet to make the computer do what my typewriter wasn't capable of doing. The urge to use Wite-Out on my monitor's screen was, at times, irresistible.

Chapter Fifty-Five

"The Peter Principle: In a hierarchically structured administration, employees tend to be promoted up to their level of incompetence."

Benny Meyer, the engineering department manager at Group Health Cooperative, was a good example of the Peter Principle. He had started out as a maintenance engineer like Tim but was "promoted" to his current position when the old manager abruptly left and no one else wanted the job. The problem was Benny was the only brother of one of the engineers he managed. Tim promptly filed a nepotism complaint with the union and there was a lengthy investigation that led to division among the crew. Eventually, Benny resigned. Tim was only slightly mollified because the bickering and backstabbing only worsened.

I was empathetic with Tim's ongoing job stress and often helped him compose and type letters that were sent off to the union rep and the administration of Group Health. However, as bad as Benny Meyer was as a manager, no one typified the Peter Principle with such cunning clarity as the woman who would become Rick Greene's first wife, and who made Moira's management style seem tame in comparison.

Granted, Moira had mellowed and by this time was married to a Russian exchange student she had met at the University of Washington. Their wedding was an elaborate, traditional Catholic ceremony, with

Moira wearing a stunning medieval-style ivory gown with a tight-fitting bodice and low neck that showed off her ivory skin. I wasn't present for the ceremony since it was held in a cathedral in Leningrad, but I saw the pictures and the wedding was a visual masterpiece. A few weeks later, Moira became pregnant and moved back to the States for what she believed would be better Ob-Gyn care, leaving her husband, Volojov, behind. It was supposed to be a temporary arrangement.

The pregnancy notwithstanding, Moira's job as P.D.'s temporary manager (only until the baby was born, after which she planned to move back to Russia) grew increasingly stressful. We were always short-handed and therefore desperate, so when an attractive Filipina named Trixi Velasco applied for a transcriptionist position (with minimal experience), Moira felt obligated to give the woman—who wore a tailored red suit with stilettos to her interview—a chance.

Over the following weeks, under Moira's guidance, Trixi eventually mastered family practice chart notes, which consisted mostly of pediatric visits for colds and ear infections and the like, but beyond that, her skill level was not up to performing the job of M.T. in the same league as her counterparts, including Moira and me, who had received certification in our field. Eventually, Trixi did transcription part-time and worked the front desk the other half, answering the phones in designer suits and matching shoes. All afternoon, her Asian twitter reverberated throughout the office. No one disliked Trixi, really, though Moira thought she was incredibly superficial and difficult to work with, especially when criticized. But then Trixi started dating Rick and began taking on all sorts of office tasks of her own accord. She began reorganizing files and instituting new policy and procedure. She began a major renovation on company funds of Rick's cramped office.

In the middle of an already hectic week, Rick came to work and noticed there was giraffe topiary in his office, where the day before had been a filing cabinet. In place of a functional (and free) Kinko's Copy calendar was an enormous black-and-gold framed picture of two lions basking in the jungle. Rick was not particularly fond of the jungle and feared his austere and sparsely appointed home, done in neutrals, was also about to get an African makeover, the reason being he had just asked Trixi to marry him. Thus, in an attempt to divert her attentions from interior decorating, Rick promoted her to office manager to replace Moira, who had stepped down as manager at her doctor's orders, and went back to being a transcriptionist.

A few months later, Rick did the unthinkable: He appointed his fiancé president of the company he had built into one of the premier transcription services in Western Washington. Rick explained he had his reason (while being cornered by a handful of feral employees): First, he wanted to focus on developing software for mammography clinicians and hoped to market that in the form of another company all together. The office staff thought there was another reason: Trixi had coerced him into the job because she needed a better income to pay for her rapidly multiplying designer shoe collection, one that was already so expansive (she boasted owning over two hundred pairs of shoes) by the time she and Rick got engaged that Rick had to convert the spare bedroom of his 1940s Craftsman-style house in Ravenna to a *shoe* room.

Trixi's promotion started a rush of two-week notices, and one day I found myself in the undesirable position of proofreader because our usual proofreader walked off the job. At his former desk (above which was a poster that said "It's hard to soar like an eagle when you're surrounded by turkeys") were stacks of nonfinalized documents sitting in the inbox waiting to be corrected and given back to the transcriptionists. One of those transcriptionists, Phyllis, was as passive-aggressive as she was postmenopausal. For this reason, I approached her extra cautiously, wishing I had a plate of brownies laced with hormone replacement therapy to go with the reports.

"Phyllis?" My voice was cheery and I smiled. "Good morning! You're looking lovely today. New perm?" I handed over the stack of reports filled with red marks. "Great job, Phyllis. There were only a few errors." Okay, multiple.

"Errors?" Phyllis was fanning herself despite the air conditioning, and her perm was a gray-brown desiccated frizz ball. She took the reports and pursed her lips. "I made mistakes?"

I smiled. "Well, just some minor ones." I picked up a report and pointed to some red marks. "Um, well, in this report, it should be

'C.A.B.G.' That's an acronym that stands for Coronary Artery Bypass Graft, not "cabbage," even though that was how doctors pronounce it. It's an easy mistake."

I paused and pointed to another report. "Also, I know Dr. Samara is difficult but what he was saying here was 'Vietnamese restaurant', not feet-and-knees restaurant.'" If you'd listen again, I am sure you would agree."

Phyllis removed her glasses, which hung from a chain, and grabbed the stack of reports. "If the doctors would pronunciate more clearly, it certainly would make my job easier."

I smiled encouragingly, "Don't worry, you'll get the hang of it. By the way, the blanks you couldn't hear were 'anal wink' and 'pulmonary toilet.'"

Phyllis's jaw dropped and her sweaty face reddened further. A hand flew to her bosom. "Oh dear, but that sounds obscene! I can't type *that*!"

"For godsakes, Phyllis, it's called medical terminology." Moira waddled past us wearing her uniform of worn black stirrup pants and a baggy T-shirt that did nothing to hide her growing belly. She asked me, "So, what's up with Trixi? She looked like she's been crying." As usual, Moira was nursing a can of Diet Coke.

"I'm not sure. I haven't talked to her. So, how are you feeling?"

Moira groaned. "Me and Volojov got in another fight."

"Oh, I'm sorry." I was probably the only one in the office who knew Volojov—whom I called Blowjob—was living (for economic reasons) with his ex-wife back in Leningrad, in an apartment the size of the average American bathroom.

Moira rubbed her lower back, "He'll get over it. Hey, where's Gary?" She picked up the contents of a manila envelope filled with cassette tapes. "I need to get some more sticky paper."

"He quit."

"Figures. So how many does that—"

"But sweetie! I want a big wedding!"

Trixi's grating shrill pierced from down the hall and the office went quiet so everyone could listen.

"I...know...you...did." Rick's words were spoken carefully, like he was speaking to a toddler. "Under the circumstances, however, I believe a simple ceremony will do. I do not have the time nor do I want to spend the money on some lavish ceremony that will be over in fifteen minutes. We could get married in my backyard and save the money to spend on more important things."

"How can we get married outside? We live in Seattle!"

Rick answered patiently, "The middle of August is a fairly safe time for nice weather in Seattle. Besides, the gazebo is covered and if it rains, we'll go inside and have the ceremony in the living room."

"But your living room is ugly. You don't even have any furniture!"

Moira nodded and whispered to me, "Rick has furniture. It's just very utilitarian."

Trixi whined, "Can we at least have an ice sculpture? And caterers?"

Rick cleared his throat. "Do you not understand the concept of a budget? You have already exceeded the limits for the renovation of your office."

"Well, I want a new dress."

"That's fine. Keep it reasonable."

"Well, I am not buying off the rack." Trixi sniffled.

A phone rang and Rick said, "We can discuss this later, Trixi. I need to answer that and hurry to get downtown for a meeting."

The conversation ended and there was just even enough time for us all to get back to our desks before Trixi walked into the transcription area. By then, her staff was mimicking deep concentration with their earphones on. At my desk, I immediately opened my Dorland's Dictionary, pretending to look up a term. Trixi tapped my shoulder and I jumped in a fake startle. "Oh, you scared me!" I turned around and found that Trixi resembled a bottle of Welch's grape juice, dressed head to toe in copious shades of plum, including open-toed purple pumps with gold heels, and acrylic nails painted the color of a port wine stain.

Trixi asked excitedly, "Ooh, has anyone seen Diane? I must speak with her."

Moira snapped, "She's at that meeting *you* arranged. It seems to me that's all Diane does these days is go to meetings. In fact, shouldn't you be there?"

Trixi shook her head rapidly. "No, no! I am not needed. Diane will report back to me with details."

Diane Winters had begun working as a transcriptionist but was soon promoted to office manager and eventually what Trixi referred to as Human Resources Director, but "Employee Relations Smoother-Over" or "Professional Meeting Moderator" would have been better job descriptions. Once, Diane's job was arranging for weekly in-office manicures for Trixi and her two daughters, who periodically worked the reception desk. When Diane was being tied down by Trixi's personal errands, she was planning her wedding to another Georgia native named Scott.

I answered, "I haven't seen Diane all morning, but I've been busy trying to get this account done by myself." *Hint hint.*

Trixi looked perplexed. "Oh?"

Trish nodded and reminded our boss, "We're swamped because Abby called in sick again."

"Abby?" Trixi perfectly plucked brows knitted in a monumental struggle for understanding.

"Abby Thomsen, the MT you hired a few months ago. She's your height, curly hair." *Swears like a sailor, drives a '87 Buick, always braless.*

Trixi's head bobbed excitedly. "Oh yes! Is she working out?"

"Not if you call calling in sick on a weekly basis working out."

Trixi's Asian features crumbled. "Oh, no! I thought, well, she seemed so nice."

I bit my cheek. "She's *very* nice but we need reliability, and the Smith Gender Reassignment Clinic is supposed to be her account. Now I'm stuck with it on top of Swedish and Seattle Neurosurgical Associates." Actually I liked doing the gender reassignment clinic work, which treated patients of one sex undergoing the psychological and eventual anatomic transition into the opposite sex. In other words, transsexuals, and no one knew transsexuals better than the Smith Clinic, though while typing their reports I didn't always get a good visual, especially when it involved the surgical reconstruction and/or removal of genitalia.

Trixi asked, "Well, maybe Valene can help you?"

"Valene is swamped with Seattle Sleep Disorders Center and Dr. Donovan's polysomnographies."

Trixi turned to Trish. "Trish, maybe you can stay late?"

"Sorry," Trish said, "I have to pick my son up from daycare by five o'clock sharp unless I want to pay Heidi an extra twenty dollars per hour."

Trixi turned next Moira, who put one palm to the air, another to her gravid belly. "Stop! Don't even ask. I've been sicker than a dog with this kid and am on doctor's orders to rest. I only came in to drop off my timecard, and please, Trixi, don't screw up payroll again."

Trixi's eyes went wide and her mouth formed an O. "Oh no! I will be careful! The mistake before, that was not—"

"Whatever." Moira pushed a hand through her grown-out brown hair. She had no time for dye jobs or haircuts and it showed. Her face was pale and makeupless, and a sprinkling of pimples dotted the jaw line of an otherwise unblemished face. Moira was thirty-nine years old and the pregnancy was taking its toll. She yawned. "See you guys tomorrow if I don't explode first."

"Don't worry, Trixi, I'll work overtime to get the work done."

Trixi nodded unenthusiastically. "Thank you, Nancy. I know I can always depend on you." She retrieved her designer handbag and said, "If Diane gets back before I do, tell her I need her to call Aetna about those changes I'm making in the employee health benefits. I was going to do it but I have a migraine and am going home." She pointed towards Rick's office. "He's being so difficult about our wedding."

Before we could ask *what* changes, Trixi was gone.

Chapter Fifty-Six

Right after Rick and Trixi's wedding, Professional Dictation moved to brand-new office space in a brick building a few blocks away. The first thing Trixi did there, as President *and* Mrs. Greene, was to move the employee mini-refrigerator into her own office. She did this in the middle of the night when the office was closed, and the next day, when I went to put my six-pack of Lemon Diet Pepsi (the sustenance of my day) into the fridge, I thought the place had been robbed. That is, until I noticed nothing else was gone, including a room full of brand-new IBM computers. I sent Trixi a scathing letter, choosing this relatively minor clash as a major crusade. I won and the fridge was put back.

Next, Trixi installed a deluxe manicure station in her office to accommodate her weekly nail sessions, and after that, it was one selfish act after another, all at the expense of employee raises and benefits.

In short order, Trixi went through six personal assistants, three receptionists, two office assistants, and one vice-president, an effeminate man named Lyle who was brought in to fill the void while Trixi concentrated on marketing.

In the new office, where bedlam continued amidst far nicer surroundings, P.D. did somehow manage to hire several talented and lovely ladies, one of whom was named Donna Presley, a dogmatic woman with an eye for detail, a penchant for politics, and a razor-sharp tongue. Also brought on board were Carla, Sandy, and Lynnette, hard workers who formed their own clique. Bonding us all was our unified belief that Trixi Greene's management style was based on one simple philosophy: "One must delegate so as to have more time to manipulate."

After Trixi was put in charge, I realized how much I missed working for Rick Greene. While it was true he was referred to as "Wooden Man" because he displayed so little emotion, he was also unpretentious and honest, and how he fell for someone like Trixi was the subject of ongoing gossip:

Trixi must be good in bed.
She must be great in bed and pay Rick for sex.
She must pay Rick period.
Maybe she's blackmailing Rick?
Maybe Rick finally knocked her up even with an incompetent cervix?

These theories aside, one thing was clear: The woman was a neurotic egomaniac who boasted without shame. Five minutes in a room with Trixi was like a crash course in how to drop labels: *Do you like my new suit? It is Armani, custom-tailored, and my shoes they are Via Spaga and I love them so much I have this exact pair in six colors! This handbag is Gucci and matches my briefcase where I keep my bottle of Opium by Yves Saint Laurent but only when I am not in the mood for Chanel No.5, and my nail polish is a limited-edition Christian Dior—expensive but so worth it—and well, my hair is styled exclusively by Jasmine in Belltown, but don't bother trying to get in because she isn't taking any new clients. Oh dear, I just noticed here in my Day Planner that today I must take the Mercedes in for an oil change!*

Meetings with Trixi were astounding in their capacity to disarm with such arrant conceit and dreaded by her staff because they were rarely unavoidable. One did not tell Trixi no, unless standing in the unemployment line sounded like a great way to pass the time, and besides, there was no other company in the city that paid its transcriptionists as well as P.D.

Trixi's first December as President, she handed out Christmas bonuses based not on any formula of seniority or production but whether the employee was in her good graces or not. To go along with the so-called bonuses, Trixi ordered pizza as a "gesture of her appreciation" and it ended up being just she and her daughters Malani and Katana eating limp and tasteless Little Caesar's Pizza because the real worker bees—the ones who generated the profits—had cleared out to go spend their pittance on drinks and appetizers and to gossip about Trixi Greene.

In a matter of a year, my once-ideal job had become as strife-filled as my home life, especially now that Tim was back to drinking regularly and heavily. Some days I would find myself stuck in late-afternoon traffic on the 520 Bridge over Lake Washington and actually enjoyed the idle time because either way I was headed, I didn't want to go. In fact, it was hard to tell who was causing more trouble in my life: Trixi or Tim.

The previous March, while dining out, I had confronted Tim about a receipt I had found in one of his coat pockets that was on its way to our drycleaners. The purchase was from Victoria's Secret dated a week before Valentine's Day of a black-mesh bustier (size 36C) with matching garter and panties (medium), items I had not received and wouldn't fit into unless I gained twenty pounds and had a boob job. Tim claimed it wasn't his receipt but

I knew better. I waited until the waitress had dropped off our drinks and taken our order, and said in hushed tones, "The receipt had our account number on it, Tim. Stop lying."

Tim took a sip of his bourbon and seven. "Okay, look, I'm sorry. It was a mistake but it happened months ago and was a one-night stand. There's nothing more to it."

I nearly choked on my wine. "What? You *slept* with Jessica?"

"Once, okay? It was a mistake. Don't make this into more than it is."

I was so humiliated, I was seeing stars. "Are we talking about Jessica Wright, the same nurse we just had dinner with because you just set Danny Rucker up on a doubledate?"

"Yeah," Tim had shrugged "So?"

"So?!" I looked around me. The restaurant was filled with people we knew, some business acquaintances, and was the one place where Tim knew I would never make a scene. I lowered my voice to a hiss. "That's un-fucking-believable. What did you guys do? Play footsies under the table when me and Danny weren't looking?" I threw my napkin on my plate and stood up. Without raising my voice, I said, "You're an asshole, you know that?"

I left the restaurant and went to the privacy of our parked car and began to sob. The maze of marital betrayal never ended and deep down, I knew Tim's affair (maybe affairs?) was the price I was being forced to pay for my indiscretion with Dylan. He called it the Dylan Fiasco, though strangely never blamed Dylan. No, *that* whole situation was my fault. Because of this, the Dylan Fiasco chained me to a thick post of self-serving guilt.

While I feeling sorry for myself in the car, I was praying that some scientist or inventor would discover a drug or procedure that would make men like Tim give up their boozy, womanizing ways. I didn't care if the cure was induced chemically, surgically, or illegally. I just wanted a nice, normal husband. It was a recurring fantasy, and it got better: Because this was a permanent change through the miracles of medicine (and covered by insurance), Tim and I would grow old together and laugh about the crazy old days, Tim sitting in a wheelchair on oxygen, befuddled on account of the government-backed Personality Rearrangement Trial Protocol on top of cirrhosis and emphysema; me next to him in my own rocker, sipping tea and looking younger than my stated age. I'd reach over and pat his liver-spotted hand:

We've sure had some rough times, old man, but we got through them, didn't we? Remember the time in 1978 in Tri-Cities for the hydroboat races when that hippie on a Harley grabbed me and you chased him down? Or the time we started that Laundromat and drycleaner? Boy, that sure was crazy, and such a headache! And then there was that time you invited those two young girls from Medical Records on our vacation to Orcas Island? Goodness sakes, was I surprised when they showed up on the dock in bikinis and holding duffle bags!

I wouldn't even mention Fern or Jessica or Dylan, but recall the good times: The many boating vacations; the summer with Mark when they cruised the southern Puget Sound waters and moored in Poulsbo, where the boys swam with jellyfish; Angie's Sweet Sixteen birthday dinner at Snoqualmie Falls Lodge, which set us back a couple hundred dollars, but the view of the raging falls and seeing Angie so grownup in a new dress had been worth it.

You sure raised some eyebrows with your shenanigans, but look at us now!

Tim would be harmless and his weathered face would wrinkle as he turned his vacant eyes my direction. *Yep*—cough sputter cough sputter—*yep, yep, yep.*

The fantasy abruptly ended when Tim appeared at the driver's door, fumbling with his keys and looking looped.

Like an idiot, I unlocked the door.

Chapter Fifty-Seven

In the summer of 1990, Melanie Dickerson and I embarked on a road trip together. We had long ago put aside our differences and became unlikely friends, and our destination was Mesa, Arizona, where Melanie was moving because she and Ray were splitting up. The purpose of the trip was to find an apartment before she and her daughters moved there. Along the way, Mel thought it would be fun to visit Las Vegas *and* the Grand Canyon.

In Bakersfield, California, after Melanie pulled into a convenience store for a six-pack of Diet Tab, she shared some shocking news. "I think Ray's having an affair."

"What?" I almost chocked on my own Diet Dr. Pepper. "You're kidding, right?"

Melanie reached for her pack of cigarettes and lit up. "Nope. Ain't that the shit? He's such a hypocrite, always accusing me of cheating and now he's screwing some skinny bitch from Ferndale." Melanie exhaled and her Mazda filled with smoke. I cranked my window down further.

"I just can't believe that."

"Believe it."

I asked, "Why would he do that after all you've been through?"

"Why? He's an asshole." She took a drag and said through the smoke. "It's probably because I'm fat."

Melanie wasn't fat, just unconditioned and overnourished. I said sincerely, "I'm so sorry. I guess you know I've been there, so I know how you feel." After the Jessica blow-up, Tim agreed he needed to work on our relationship, and for the time being, things were going well between us. He had cut back on his drinking and regularly brought me flowers and cards. He hadn't raised his hand in anger in almost a year.

Melanie extinguished her cigarette and lit up another one. "Besides battling my weight, I'm totally depressed in this dreary, gray climate. Even Prozac isn't helping." Her voice began to crack and I wondered if she was on the verge of crying, something I had never seen her do. A brief silence passed before she said, "At least I'll be suffering in the Arizona sunshine."

I giggled and glanced over at Melanie. I realized she was as full of fear and hope and dreams as any other woman. She was like *me*, but with a different shell. Like always, she was driving barefoot and her toenails were freshly painted blood red from a recent pedicure. Strangely, perfect nails were as vain as Melanie got. She never wore makeup, which would have softened her strong features, and sported oversized dark plastic frames on her prescription glasses. Really, Melanie would be attractive if she lost some weight and grew out the chopped layers of drab-brown hair and got some highlights. She also needed a decent support bra, an eyebrow/underarm wax, and her tacky wardrobe needed an overhaul.

Okay, so Melanie needed a major makeover but deep, deep down was a beautiful woman.

I said, "I knew you guys were having trouble, but I can't believe Ray is cheating. He was always so big on trust."

"Trust is a one-way street with Ray. He also said he wouldn't get physical but he has. When I think about it, Ray is all talk, and his promises are made of water. It all goes back to his father. He told me he never wanted to be like his old man, but he's *just* like him."

After a stop to visit the Grand Canyon, which was far more spectacular in person than in postcards, Melanie and I toured Mesa apartments before she decided on a two-bedroom apartment that opened onto a palm-lined courtyard and, beyond that, a kidney-shaped pool. The next day, we floated down a nearby river, which was really a manmade irrigation ditch, but in the brutal Arizona sun it hardly mattered.

A week later, I was back home and played down how much fun I had with Melanie, though I did tell Tim about Ray's affair. I expected Jessica's name to come up but it didn't.

Tim hugged me tightly. "You look great tanned." He kissed my head. "I missed you."

I looked up. "I missed you, too."

Tim grabbed my hands and held them to his chest. "While you were gone, I was thinking."

"Yeah? About me?" I was close enough to know Tim's breath did not smell like booze and I relaxed into his chest, glad to be home. When he was sober, my husband was a nice guy.

Tim murmured, "Yes, and something else. I'll tell you in the bedroom."

There, I forgot all about Melanie and Ray's problems. Instead, I began daydreaming about Tim's newest plan: Buying a new house.

Chapter Fifty-Eight

In the winter of 1991, the Pacific Northwest real estate market was termed a "seller's market." Our neighbors were selling their homes for close to thirty thousand more than they paid for them just ten years before. Some ended up with so many offers, there were bidding wars. This included the home Samantha Strange lived in, alone.

The previous August, her husband Mike had lost his battle with leukemia, dying (seven months after his wedding) of pneumonia while in the hospital and awaiting a bone marrow transplant. As I had been at Mary-Jane's funeral, I was overwrought with emotion at Mike's memorial service, especially when Sam got up to eulogize her late husband and sang the Bette Midler tearjerker, "The Wind Beneath My Wings."

When Sam put the house up for sale, Tim and I didn't hesitate making an offer on Mike's customized rambler with numerous bay windows and elegant French doors, plus a built-in brick BBQ pit and paved-stone patio. Unfortunately, a brother and sister who worked for Microsoft outbid us and offered to pay cash. Our rambler wasn't even on the market yet, so Sam had to turn us down.

It took months but our "cute starter home" (as it was being marketed) finally sold and we began a frantic search for another house. On our respective "wish" lists, Tim wanted a two-car garage and some acreage, and I wanted a brand-new house with a front porch and a country kitchen with an island. I loved the idea of buying a *new* house. What better way to get rid of a lot of bad memories and start afresh?

We settled on a cedar-sided builder's home near Lake Joy, fifteen miles outside of Duvall so it was still close to our shop. The house sat on one-and-a-half acres, had a two-car garage, a large oak kitchen (no island, but a huge pantry), and a finished basement.

We moved in on Tim's forty-fourth birthday in early August of 1991, and the first thing Tim did was rent a backhoe so he could begin clearing our raw property. He was thinking of building a pond, or maybe a pool. He really didn't have a plan, and acted like a kid on a toy, tearing through trees and flattening hills. He started a huge fire to burn the trees and debris he had cleared, and nearly lit the neighbor's fence on fire. This was, of course, because he was smashed.

While Tim was doing this, I was thinking about an A.A. saying I heard: *Craziness is doing the exact same thing over and over, and expecting different results.*

I was that kind of crazy and so was my marriage, but it no longer mattered. I had detached, just like the books on codependents had advised me to do. Really, I should have gotten an A+ in Detachment, watching like an apparition as Tim ruined our new house, tracking muddied shoes across our slate-blue carpeting (despite my sign that asked guests to remove their shoes), denting walls, breaking water lines. Every night he drank until he was drunk and then expected gratuitous sex. He treated me like a pornographic accessory, and I knew it was the price I was paying for falling in love with Dylan. Five years had done little to diminish the pain for either of us.

The first couple of weeks of living in the cedar house, I busied myself by going through the motions of unpacking and getting the house in order. This included reorganizing our pantry, where I found a great deal of satisfaction in stacking the shelves with neat rows of canned foods and bulk dry items. One day, I was reorganizing the kitchen cupboards yet again, when I heard a loud thump that rattled the walls. From the balcony off the kitchen, I saw that Tim had rammed the corner of the house with the tractor and a piece of cedar siding swung precariously. He looked up and I shook my head, then closed the sliding door and looked around.

The house had an odd floor plan, and I didn't like that there was a bathroom right off the living room, not even down a hallway. What was the builder thinking? There was also no formal dining room, just an area for a table directly behind the front door, which had no foyer.

I hated the cedar house, but I loved the master bath, and despite it being 74 degrees outside according to our thermometer, I craved a long, hot bath. I filled the tub with water and soap, undressed, and slipped into the master suite's sauna-tub below a skylight. I eased further and further under the bubbles, thinking how easy it would be to sink my head underwater until my lungs filled with nothing but jasmine-scented water. It wouldn't be suicide; it would be salvation.

Of course, I had no intention of killing myself, and soaked languidly until the bath water grew tepid. I stepped out of the tub and released the stopper to the drain, just as Tim came stumbling around the corner mumbling. I quickly grabbed my bathrobe and wrapped it around my waist, cinching it tightly. I felt so vulnerable in the midst of the man who was my husband and with a voice that was wooden, I said, "Hi."

Tim leaned into the doorframe with one hand above his head. "What are you doing in the bathtub on such a nice summer day?" He tipped his bottle of beer with his other hand but missed his mouth and beer dribbled onto the plush blue carpet. He was drunk but he didn't slur his words. "Get dressed and come to the backyard. I want to show you something."

I looked down at the beer spill and my heart began beating wildly and my chest flushed, sure signs I was nervous, though why I was unsure of. We had certainly played out this weary scene more than once. My hair was up and I let it fall loose and picked up my brush. For one brief moment, I had an overwhelming desire to throw the brush directly into Tim's drunken face, but that would be unwise and probably land me in the hospital. I said simply, "I know why you're doing this."

Tim's features twisted in drunken confusion. "Doing what?"

"Staying a drunk. Ruining our house. Making me miserable." I began brushing my hair, looking into the sad face in the mirror. "It's because of Dylan." I turned. "Are you ever going to stop punishing me for that?"

Tim's confusion turned to disgust. "That's old news. You screwed up.

End of story. Besides, me and Dylan worked that mess out. We're buddies."

The latter was semi-true; Dylan and Tim and reached some sort of treaty, but I had been excluded, left to fend for myself and hide my discomfort when Dylan stopped by to visit and we all pretended things were back to normal. My heart still pounded when Dylan was around and sometimes I simply left the room. I couldn't tell you if it was love or hate I was feeling.

I replied, "Well, something's wrong. We can't go on like this."

"Forget it. I'm going outside. I have better things to do than argue." Tim turned to leave but stopped and turned back around. "Just for the record, how many more of my friends have you fucked?" His tone was contemptuous. "Or will I have to find out the hard way?"

"You just proved I'm right, you know." In that moment, I realized that even if Tim got sober and stayed that way, which was unlikely, our marriage was over. I was trying to stay calm but nervously sputtered, "I'm done. We're done. This marriage is over."

The beer bottle, now empty, dropped from Tim's hand and he kicked it into the wall, where it landed with a thud. "Then why the fuck did we buy this house?"

I screamed, my anger seething out of control. "Because I thought it would be a new start! Because I wanted us to be happy! Can't you see I have sacrificed everything out of guilt to make up for what I've done in the past? But it isn't worth it anymore! You're a nasty drunk who will never change!"

"Bitch!" Tim raised his fist. "I oughta—"

"What? Smack me? Go ahead Tim, prove you are a man!" I looked directly into my husband's clouded eyes, the eyes of a stranger, and challenged, "So, hitting me will solve everything, won't it? Just beat the old lady up, smack her around a couple times to put her in her place. It certainly wouldn't be the first time." Tim's hand remained raised but I forced myself not to flinch to preserve some dignity, even if I was about to get the shit kicked out of me.

Tim lowered his arm. "Fuck you, slut. You aren't even worth smacking."

I remained still, emotionless, filled with a hatred I didn't know was possible. *Not this time anyway.*

Tim said, "Get out." He walked out of the bathroom and minutes later, when I could see through the living room window that he was in the back of our property near the burn pile, I quickly pulled on a pair of jeans and jacket, grabbed my purse with my car keys, and was soon backing my Mercury Cougar out of a not yet familiar driveway. I nearly went into the ditch but by gunning the gas pedal, the car pealed back, spitting up gravel. I put the car in forward just as Tim rounded the corner near the garage. He shouted, "Don't ever come back, bitch!" and pitched a beer can towards my car. The can missed because I was already gone.

I didn't cry as I headed for the city and an affordable hotel. Along the way I decided with a clear head that I was filing for divorce ASAP, not caring we had been in our new house a mere twenty-one days. In fact, I was willing to *give* Tim the strange cedar house with the stupid floor plan and the timeshare, which we had used exactly twice. I was ready to give it all up to be free and happy.

I checked into the Silver Cloud Inn, paying with a credit card, feeling hopeful that happiness was sure to come my way with crazy Tim out of my way.

And that might have happened, if I hadn't ended up replacing crazy Tim with someone even crazier.

Chapter Fifty-Nine

For the first few weeks after I filed for divorce, I was aware there were at least a dozen people who were thinking "I told you so," but only three actually said it out loud: My Mother, Patty, and Moira. But I had supporters, including Bob and Gwendolyn, who sadly had been diagnosed with salivary gland cancer a few months before. Gwen had begun chemotherapy and rather than mourn the gradual, unsightly loss of her waist-length hair, she cut it short and sassy and let it go gray. This was one tough broad, and I loved her dearly. Breaking the news about the divorce to my in-laws was extremely difficult, and I hoped we could somehow remain friends.

Suddenly without a roof over my head, Trish kindly offered to let me temporarily live in her finished basement for cheap rent, and I was overjoyed by her generosity and welcomed her company. She was recently divorced and living with her toddler son, Thomas, and their split-level was far from Duvall, so it was a perfect place for me to sort out the mess I had made of my life. And it was getting messier by the minute because thrown into the mix was my budding and highly complicated relationship with Ray Dickerson.

It had all started, not so innocently, when Ray called me at work and invited me for coffee after he heard the news that I had left Tim. I accepted, and Ray showed up at the café with a bouquet of flowers and a card that said, "Hang in There," picturing a photograph of a frenzied cat hanging from a branch with one paw. Inside it read, "Thinking of you, Ray." He told me over Margaritas that the split-up was not my fault. He began lavishing me with cards and gifts, and before I knew it, we were having an affair. Trish knew it, too, but never said anything and I was relieved; I was completely unprepared to discuss what was happening with married Ray when Tim wasn't yet out of the picture, at least not on paper. All I knew was a pattern had emerged, and as much as I tried to fight it, it was real and it was strong: I gravitated towards married men.

Why Trish didn't hate me for what I was doing with Ray, I didn't know, but she certainly could have; her ex-husband had an affair and the aftermath was devastating. Instead, she was the ideal roommate—patient, nonjudgmental, and levelheaded (traits I did not possess)—and I hoped by living with Trish, these things would rub off. I especially hoped so when I made the appointment with the same divorce attorney she had used, Arabella Sanchez.

Seated in an office with a view of the Space Needle, I kept my hands folded in my lap to prevent biting nails that were already down to the quick. Across from me was divorce attorney Arabella Sanchez. She opened a yellow legal pad and asked, "Do you wish to file for a Legal Separation or Dissolution of Marriage?"

A thumbnail shot to my mouth. "I'm not sure. I walked out on my husband and our new house. We were there only three weeks."

Ms. Sanchez nodded. "Is there a chance of a reconciliation?"

"No." *Not unless Tim changes.*

"Then I would advise a Dissolution of Marriage. A divorce."

I swallowed. "Yes, a divorce." *God I hate Tim for making me go through this!*

Ms. Sanchez asked, "Are there children involved?" She was very pretty, and her dark hair was cut in a stylish bob. She could have walked off the set of *L.A. Law*, and I was disappointed by her looks; I wanted a barracuda for a lawyer, not a babe with a glamorous name. I wanted an attorney named Brutus.

I blurted, "No. I mean, yes. Well, kind of."

Behind a pair of tortoise-shell frames, Ms. Sanchez' eyes were kind and forgiving. "So there will be custody issues?"

I now understood. "No. My husband has children from prior relationships, but we have no children together." *Thank God.*

"Okay, how about assets? House, boat, vehicles, retirement accounts, stocks, bonds. And has your husband hired his own attorney?"

"I don't know if Tim has gotten an attorney yet. As far as assets, we own and run a business together. It's a drycleaners and Laundromat. We also have the new house, plus a timeshare in Mazatlan." My head was spinning and my stomach burned. "Oh, and a boat, but that's really Tim's." I didn't want anything except for my troubles to go away. "I didn't think this was going to be complicated."

Ms. Sanchez pulled some papers from a briefcase. "Divorce is never simple, nor is its aftermath. I will be representing you and promise to get you the best settlement I can."

I nervously laughed. "I don't want anything, just the divorce."

The attorney dipped her head and peered over her glasses. "You said you and Tim have been married for five years and lived together for seven prior to that?"

Ashamed it had finally failed after such a long period, I gulped, "Yes."

"Was he unfaithful during that time? It could be used as grounds."

I answered honestly, "Yes, but infedility is the least of our problems, and that's not why I want the divorce. Just put 'irreconcilable differences.' Isn't that what everyone says when there are a lot of reasons?"

Ms. Sanchez nodded as she poised a pen over her yellow legal pad. "In the State of Washington, you are entitled to a fair settlement; half the assets and property you acquired as a couple for the entire relationship."

You don't understand. I am consumed with guilt about the new house and marrying Tim when I knew it was a monumental mistake marrying an alcoholic and if I cross Tim now, he'll make my life a living hell! He'll stalk me and harass me and our divorce will be worse than our marriage!

I said softly, "I just want out, Ms. Sanchez."

"Please, call me Arabella." She put her pen down and picked up an embossed briefcase. "I'll let you think about that some more, maybe discuss it with your family? You and your husband will need to come up with a business plan, as well. In the meantime, I will require a retainer so I can prepare the legal documents. As soon as the Dissolution is filed, and providing that your husband does not contest, your divorce will be final in ninety days."

"Sure, great." I reached for my checkbook and handed over a check to Dover Smith Sanchez & Corbett for five hundred dollars as a retainer. Leaving Downtown Seattle, I was as depressed as ever and there was no doubt in my mind Tim would contest.

The ink wasn't even dry on the check when Ray Dickerson swept in on the fair-haired neighbor he had coveted for so long. I didn't resist; when you're in pieces, you need a broom.

The following April, after I signed a quit deed on the house (and after we formulated a business plan, i.e., a schedule of who worked when at our joint business), the Dissolution of Marriage in the case of Nancy A. Joseph, Petitioner, vs. Timothy Joseph Joseph, Respondent, was finalized. I celebrated by going to dinner alone and ordering lobster, as well as giving two weeks' notice to Trixi Greene. I already had a new job lined up at Evergreen Hospital Medical Center in Kirkland. Trixi attempted to entice me to stay in the form of a "quality bonus," which I declined. The check, I knew, was made of rubber.

Tim celebrated our divorce by helping his girlfriend, Janine, move in with him. When Janine was settled, he surprised her with a wardrobe of practically new dresses and skirts, all size two, including his now-ex-wife's favorite red wool jacket, a butter-yellow suit-dress, and a dove-gray cashmere sweater, all items I was told had been mistakenly donated to the Salvation Army.

I wasn't that upset. A wardrobe can be replaced and it seemed a fair trade for escape from Tim's abusive, booze-saturated grip.

Chapter Sixty

Angie's high-school years were no easier than her grade school years had been, even with the Individualized Educational Program, remedial classes, and a dedicated math and English tutor. Constantly, Angie talked of dropping out for various reasons, but the truth was that many of Angie's woes were directly linked to her volatile relationship with Lee Mingo, a boyfriend who ended up dropping out after getting suspended multiple times for various offences ranging from throwing a rock through the window in Science class, and smoking marijuana on school property.

Lee Mingo was a boy prone to setting low personal standards that he consistently failed to achieve. And that name! *Lee Gary Mingo* sounded like some sort of tropical parasite you'd pick up from bad mangoes in Costa Rica that caused profuse diarrhea and hallucinations.

Unfortunately, our efforts at getting Angie to break up with Lee always backfired. The more we put Lee Mingo down, the more 17-year-old Angie had gravitated toward the wayward youngest son of trailer-park transients. Much to our regret, Angie did drop out of high school but also dumped Lee after she spent a summer living with he and his mother in a trailer park.

Angie went on to get her driver's license and her G.E.D., and eventually married levelheaded Jeff. Everyone hoped they would live happily ever after. When she told me about the divorce, I didn't pry for details. She moved back to Washington State from Fairbanks, got a full-time job at a grocery outlet in Carnation, and began living with her father. Two months later, she was moving into my recently purchased townhouse. It wasn't until we were unpacking Angie's belongings that I asked what happened at her Dad's. I'd get to the reasons for her breakup with Jeff later.

Angie shrugged and said with characteristic understatement, "Dad drinks and fights with Janine. I got tired of the yelling." She paused to put toiletries on the dresser. "Nancy? I just don't understand why people who say they love each other can't get along, like me and Jeff."

I hung another sweater and answered, "Me, neither." I was among that group. Ray and I were seeing each other and supposedly in love, but all we did was fight, mostly about when he was going to divorce Melanie. He had already talked to an attorney but was struggling with the decision because of his two young daughters.

Angie opened another box, which my kitten, Lily, immediately climbed into. "Dad told Janine he still loves you and that you guys would still be together if you didn't sleep with all his friends." She lifted Lily from the box and held her to her chest. "I'm not judging, Mom. That's just what Dad said. When he gets drunk, he says all sorts of crazy things, but you already know that."

Lily leapt from Angie's arms and attacked the leg of my pants. She was six months old and I loved her unconditionally.

I said to Angie, "I can't change the way your father thinks." The last thing I wanted to do was bad-mouth Tim in front of his daughter, further adding fuel to the fire. "I just hope you find someone special who treats you right. In my Divorce Lifeline support group, I can't believe how many women are trying to leave abusive relationships. It makes me feel better I'm not alone, but it also scares me because of your own upbringing." I was fishing and Angie took the bait.

"Don't worry. Jeff didn't abuse me. He never even yelled at me, but, I don't know, I guess I was just bored." Angie sat on the edge of the bed holding a blouse. "After Lee, I guess I wanted somebody nice and sweet, and Jeff was, but, well...I don't know. It's hard to explain."

I sat down next to my stepdaughter, thinking about the "Blue Angel" reference I found all those years ago. "There's no need for an explanation, Ang. I completely understand. You go for the bad boys, like me. Men who seem exciting but are not exactly nice, and your mission is to try to fix them or save them. Of course, it never works."

"I know!" Angie slumped on the bed, sweater in hand. "I hate that."

"Me, too," I answered uneasily. Already I knew Ray needed fixing and saving. Every part of me knew that wasn't my obligation and that I should walk away and put my needs first, even as he professed that I was his true love and soulmate, but I couldn't. Now the guilt that came with being involved with yet another married man was nearly incapacitating. At the back of my mind was Melanie, who had forsaken her seasonal affective disorder and left sunny Mesa to try another reconciliation with Ray. When I entered the picture, I sabotaged all chances of that.

Looking at my stepdaughter, I changed the subject. "So, Angie, when was the last time you had Beef and Radishes?"

Angie's eyes widened. "Years. Is that what you're making for dinner?"

I put an arm around her and gave her a squeeze. "I'm making anything you want."

She grinned. "Hot fudge sundaes with maraschinos?"

Chapter Sixty-One

Five years later, June 1996.

From my vantage point—the screened-in back patio of a rambler in Montrose, Colorado—I could view the jagged silhouette of the majestic San Juan mountain range, and parts of the surrounding Uncompahgre Valley. Alas, the breathtaking views and cloudless day did nothing to lift my spirits because that summer afternoon I was feeling deserted and depressed, and could practically hear the devil sneering atop my shoulder:

Well, Stupid, this is what you get when during your own painful, bitter divorce you get involved with another tormented man going through his own painful, bitter divorce: An instant replay of marriage number one. Here, take my pitchfork and stab yourself in the heart!

There were other days when I felt conflicted about whether I was lonely or nuts, and that's when I heard my inner Blue Angel:

You must make things work with Ray. He left his wife and kids for you! Try harder, Nancy, harder! Fix Ray and make him the happiest he has ever been, and it will be a feather in your cap.

Then there was my mother's voice: *What on earth are you doing living a thousand miles from home in a desert when you could be in lush, green Washington near your loving family? You can't possibly be happy with the likes of Ray Dickerson, especially when the highlight of your day is watching pigs roll around in the mud.*

Actually, the highlight of my day was trying to concoct another clever recipe using tomatoes. It was astonishing to me how much fruit four plants could bear in a single season. Every afternoon, I was out with my bucket plucking tomatoes before they rotted, and then spent hours poring over recipes that would use up fifty tomatoes of three varieties. I learned to can and prepare homemade tomato sauce, but this left more tomatoes, some of which I ended up tossing into the compost pile for lack of motivation. Really, taking care of tomatoes could have been a full-time job, but at least it was one where I picked the hours and worked independently, and most importantly never had to fire anyone. In melancholy moods, which were frequent, I thought about the drycleaner and Laundromat Tim and I had owned and sold. At the time, I would have singled out only one positive experience the whole time we owned the place, and that was doing the laundry service for a movie crew that was filming in an old farmhouse just up the road. The made-for-T.V. mystery movie was called *Hit and Run* and starred Jimmy Smits and Judith Light, and on the first day we drove to the site for a pickup, I was surprised at how tiny Judith Light was, but not at how gorgeous Jimmy Smits was in person. By the time the movie was released in 1987, its title had been changed to *Stamp of a Killer*, but it was the same movie with the same stars, and I didn't even have autographs as a memento.

Looking back, handling silk blouses and linen trousers was amusing compared to what I was doing now, which was living with Ray in a rural farming community in Western Colorado. I hadn't been forced to move here, but I had been given an ultimatum, and looking back, my choice should have been a no-brainer. *No, Ray, I am not moving to Montrose even if it means we have to break up because you can't handle a long-distance relationship. Besides, you're still married, remember? And your kids hate me. And I'm miserable. Let's cut our losses while we can. Oh, by the way, have a good life; send me a postcard.*

Ray did eventually divorce Melanie (who promptly returned to Mesa), and I moved to Montrose, and it was hard to tell who was more miserable. A definite pattern had emerged and I wondered if I had inadvertently placed an ad in the personals that read "Unstable woman with low self-esteem seeks needy, sex-obsessed, overly jealous man with anger management issues for long-term abusive relationship. Addictions preferred. Married okay. Nice and normal need not apply." On top of that, I was now labeled the one thing I promised myself I would never become after what happened with Dylan (who was none of the above), and that was "homewrecker."

Truthfully, I did not feel *entirely* at fault for Ray's divorce. I'd been witness for twelve years to a marriage fraught with problems, and far from perfect. What Melanie didn't know was that I felt ingratiated to Ray for many reasons, and it felt natural for me to fall into the open arms of someone who already loved me. I guess you could say I fell in love with Ray because of our friendship, and because an instant relationship was all I had the energy for after being married to high-strung, alcohol-dependent Tim. Unfortunately, Ray had his own set of issues and was prone to debilitating depression and self-loathing. When that passed, he was pompous and gregarious.

Summed up, Ray, as a boyfriend, sucked compared to what he was like as a married lover. Then again, his own wife, Melanie, had warned me of Ray's dark side on our trip to Arizona, but it was a side I never saw. Back in Duvall, whenever neighbor Ray was around me he was pleasant. Now, he told me he was so in love with me, it hurt. He declared the Garth Brooks' mega hit "Shameless" was our song. Having a song, however, couldn't overcome my inability to communicate honestly if it would hurt others' feelings, or Ray's deep-seated insecurities and mistrusting nature, which led to a jealous-streak wider than the Colorado River. Ray believed there was not a penis for miles—young, old, black, white, even ones attracted to other penises—which was not at any given flaccid or rigid moment seeking to move in on *his* Nancy.

Flattering, but not true.

No, the waiter was not checking me out under the table. I dropped my napkin! And so what if the cashier checked out my ass? It doesn't mean I want to jump in the sack with him.

No, Dylan is not still interested in me. He lives in Washington with his wife, remember?

No, the Mexican landscapers were not making up excuses to talk to me; I hired them, Ray, or haven't you noticed our lawn is full of weeds and two feet tall because the last time you mowed it was when Madonna was still a Material Girl and a Virgin?

The latter had been an exaggeration, one Ray was quick to point out, but great stretches of truth were often necessary to get my point across, especially since I didn't have access to a gigantic sledgehammer.

I looked up as fluffy nonthreatening clouds began to settle over the San Juan Mountains and walked to the outdoor mini-fridge, from which I retrieved a bottle of Amstel Lite. Across the alley, the pigs began snorting and I could smell their stench because the air in Southwestern Colorado in mid-June was stifling from no rain in weeks. I missed the rain so much, the way it smelled after a long drought, the tapping sound it made as it hit gutters and roofs. That day, I would have paid a high price for a single raindrop on my face.

Not surprisingly, Ray didn't miss the rain.

Chapter Sixty-Two

Ray bragged to his friends back in Washington that it never rained in Montrose, and that the town was a place people dreamt about living in with its clean mountain air, limitless outdoor and recreational activities, rich history, and pronounced seasons. Within miles was the Black Canyon Monument, a place I found as spectacular as the Grand Canyon. Narrow, sheer walls formed from black lava drop straight down. When I finally got the courage to stand at a lookout, the Gunnison River that raged through the gorge below was so far down it looked like gray dental floss.

Once, Ray took me hiking on a section of the Paradox Trail called the Tabegauche Creek Loop. He described the hike as "moderate" in difficulty. I would later discover it was excruciatingly difficult, eight miles over spikes of black rock on trails the width of a bicycle tire, up to an elevation of 6000 feet and overlooking the Uncompahgre Plateau.

It was not a fun hike despite my preparations, including new teal and gray Raichle hiking boots (of Swiss design!) that cost fifty dollars, as well as khaki cargo-pants with a zippered hem from R.E.I. This was because I am a city girl, not a lets-hike-on-treacherous-cliffs-type of person. (Ray would live in the woods with nothing but a backpack and a fishing pole). Sure, the cute teal hiking boots had plenty of arch support, but my feet were still killing me by the time we reached our destination, a river surrounded by a thirsty canyon, and all I was thinking was what kind of snakes inhabited Western Colorado?

Six months after I moved to Montrose, in a sanguine moment, I bought this charming house with the help of a down payment borrowed from my mother so Lily had a place to roam without fear of evicting her owners. The house had two covered porches, a pole barn, and a huge flower garden dominated by pink peonies. The prior homeowners were clearly obsessed with the color pink: The carpet was mauve and the wallpaper in every room was printed with some variant of dainty pink roses. Even the vinyl siding was pale pink, so it was no surprise the peonies in the garden were pink.

To irrigate the gardens, I lifted a board to the "dam" separating our yard from our neighbors' to allow the irrigation water to rush through small ditches that meandered through the soil. This is a chore I did during my lunch break, walking to the backyard from my home office in the spare bedroom, where I did transcription for a company in Denver. I accomplished this with the help of an ISDN line that connected me to the internet, using Ray's new Gateway personal computer. It was convenient but also isolating, especially since Ray was gone so much. Maybe that's why the pigs fascinated me so.

I stood and stretched, while the pigs nearby never stopped snorting or moving. "Oink oink!" I yelled, and the pigs oinked back.

How hard it was to believe that just one year prior, when I wouldn't be caught dead wearing baggy overall and no makeup, I was watching baseball, not pigs.

Chapter Sixty-Three

Patty's knowledge of the game of baseball seemed to come out of left field (pun intended) and was quite extraordinary, especially her play-by-play analyses. They made absolutely no sense to me, but her son, Robbie, confirmed they were mostly accurate. And the way Patty said "bullpen" cracked me up!

In 1995, the year I moved to Montrose, the Seattle Mariners were a red-hot team on a major winning streak, and Patty and I rarely missed a game. In the span of one season, we had gone from sports idiots to baseball fools, enthralled by a sport in which men in polyester pants engaged in what looked more like an experiment in human sputum production. When they weren't practicing the art of self-induced dehydration, they were playing "Where in the World are My Undescended Testicles?" a game of little skill, high intrigue, and mounting suspense, especially if you were a leather mitt.

When it was down to Cleveland and Seattle in the final divisional playoffs, I should have been watching the game with my sister (holding my good-luck blue-haired Joey Cora troll doll) but instead was on the road heading towards Montrose to be with Ray.

Big Moving Day had arrived on September 24, 1995, and it was amazingly not raining. It usually rained when I moved, which is what it had been doing the night before with great vigor, and was the reason I had not slept well. Of course, this might also have been due to the bizarre dream I had involving Barbara Walter's 20/20 investigative team showing up on my doorstep for their segment on compulsive shoppers, and I had nothing to wear!

The dream had a direct correlation to the boxes stacked throughout my apartment, each one carefully labeled: Dress Sweaters, Casual Sweaters, Blouses, Fall Jackets, Winter Coats, Jeans, Shorts, Intimate Apparel. In the kitchen were boxes with labels like Special Wine Glasses, Champagne Goblets, Sunflower Dishes, and Everyday Wine Glasses.

Nervously awaiting the professional movers, I plopped on a box called "Hardback Books." Minutes later, I heard them before I saw them: A high-pitched shriek followed by the unmistakable sound of compression or air brakes. I ran to the window and watched as a huge truck began backing into my apartment's parking lot. It stopped, blocking most of Building C's tenants' cars, and I ran to the door expecting two burly Samoans. What I got were two skinny white guys, both smoking, one walking slightly doubled over. He held out a dirty hand.

"I'm Craig, this here's Hank." He looked at a clipboard. "Okay, let's see, you're going to California."

Nervously, I said, "Colorado, not California."

Craig looked again. "My mistake, but I still need to go through California on my way to Denver." Craig suddenly grimaced. "Got this funny pain in my side, and a bulge."

I was not sure whether to fire them or call 9-1-1. "The destination is *Montrose*, Colorado, not Denver."

Craig grunted. "Montrose? Hmmm, have to look that one up on a map. Hank, did you bring the map?"

Hank wheezed what sounded like "nope."

"Oh well, we can get one on the way to buy cigarettes. Sign here and we'll get started."

The job was supposed to take "a couple of hours" but it took eight. After the truck drove off (but not before flattening some landscaping and denuding a large portion of lawn), I got into my car with Lily in her crate, and off we headed to Plain for one last visit with Mom before my move.

Two hours later and pulling down Mom's long dirt drive, I was filled with memories about Bob and was crying before I even parked. Nineteen months prior, my stepfather had died suddenly at age sixty-nine from an undetected heart arrhythmia. No one was over his devastating death. In fact, Bob's death had prompted me to make the decision to make the move to Colorado despite the problems Ray and I were having because I believed that life was too damn short not to go on adventures when the opportunity arose. I collected my emotions, parked near Bob's studio, retrieved Lily, and went inside. There, over a home cooked meal, Mom asked me, "Why are you moving, honey? Everything you love is here."

"Because it's an adventure, Mom, and it's not forever, just till Ray's job is done."

With each sequential question, I could hear my mother's true unspoken answer:

"An adventure?" *More like a mistake.*

"Are you sure you want to live with Ray?" *He's no better than Tim.*

"Montrose is so far away. And what about Lily and your job?" *Nancy, please don't make this terrible mistake. Ray is so wrong for you, and poor Lily needs stability. Dump that selfish man and get on with your life!*

Despite reading between the lines, I reassured Mom everything was fine but inside my stomach churned with a strong mix of uncertainty and acid reflux. Ray was allegedly allergic to cats and his rented duplex didn't allow pets, so he told me I couldn't bring my precious feline.

On the phone, I told him, "Sure, Ray, no problem. I'll find Lily a good home." *You're nuts if you think I'm getting rid of my cat, and what kind of man asks that of a person?* "See you in a few days."

One week in Montrose, and I had quickly learned several valuable lessons: 1) Montrose was a rural Western town with a single dress code: Jeans and cowboy boots, period. 2) Ringing the customer service bell at the grocery store and inquiring about whether they have Artisan Rosemary Sourdough Loaf like they bake fresh at Larry's Markets in Kirkland gets you pointed to the Wonder Bread aisle. 3) Double tall nonfat vanilla latte is a foreign phrase. 4) Most if not all vehicles are equipped with four-wheel drive and deer deflectors. 5) Number 4 does little to help the deer as evidenced by the number of deer corpses lying mangled alongside the road. 6) Multiple landmarks in Western Colorado are named Uncompahgre, including a river, a school, numerous streets, a mountain range, and I was pretty sure one of the neighbor boys.

I also learned that Ray had been quite serious about not bringing Lily, delegating my Pookie to the heated garage, where she slept in my car at night but was on my lap during the day while he was at work, which was sometimes twelve hours.

Two weeks later, my belongings finally arrived, three days later than expected. I walked up to the moving truck's cabin. "Oh, you aren't Craig. Where's Craig?"

The driver, a Hispanic male, replied, "He no feel good. Have beeg hernia. He een hospeetal."

"Oh." I looked across the driver to the other man on the passenger side, also Mexican. "And Hank?"

The driver's face fell as he glanced at his partner with dark, calloused hands palm up. "Bad lungs. He dead."

"Dead?"

"Si." The driver and his partner crawled down from the moving truck and while I supervised, they unpacked the contents into a heated storage unit. They were more efficient than Craig and Hank, and when they were done I put a few belongings in my car, locked the unit, and drove down an unfamiliar street to Ray's duplex. Once there, I closed the drapes and put Lily on my lap. Then I picked up the phone. I had never been one for gabbing on the telephone, but that was about to change.

I called my Mother, followed by my sister Patty, Moira, Brenda, and finally Trish, from whom I was hoping to solicit some good advice from across the miles.

Chapter Sixty-Four

Mel and Ray allowed their oldest daughter Alison to yo-yo between households following their divorce, seemingly at her teenaged whim. When Ray moved to Montrose, Alison was living with him, but she ended up hating Montrose even more than she had hated her junior high school (and sometimes her mother) in Mesa. Within just a few months, Alison was heading south again, and I was relieved. It was going to be a big enough adjustment for me and Ray to be living together without a teenager around, especially a teenager who would be required to report to her mother every miscalculated move and stupid thing "your father's hussy" did or said. In case you forgot, that would be me.

I, of all people, understood the psychological complexities of divorce when they involved children, especially children as young as Mark and Reba, both four years old when their parents split. For her part, Reba was somehow able to compensate for the fractured household by developing a gregarious, optimistic personality that belied her age. On the downside, the youngster's moods oscillated and it was impossible to predict which Reba would show up.

The summer she was eight, Reba spent it with her father and me in Montrose, and things went well for exactly three hours. We picked her up from the Grand Junction Regional Airport, chatted amicably during the

306

hour-long trip to Montrose, walked into Ray's duplex, and the reality of me *living* there hit her like a ton of bricks. Making matters worse was that Reba was already deep in a pout phase because the static electricity from the high altitude had caused her fine blond hair to stand up on end. She was used to bad-hair days but this day of electric hair put her over the edge, especially after she started unpacking and discovered that stuff she had personally packed was missing from her suitcase. Among those missing items were a blue two-piece bathing suit and a pair of plastic orange flip-flops, which Reba would sleep in if given a choice. What items Reba did have in her suitcase were quickly strewn across the floor of the spare bedroom.

I offered to help her clean her room and put things away, and Reba responded by locking herself in the bathroom. An hour later, she let me help her with her hair and we were back to being friends. Just as I had been with Angie, the need to nurture was overwhelming and I soon "adopted" Reba and put her welfare ahead of everything. That summer, I taught her how to pamper herself and still be a domestic diva (the very things her own mother balked at), and filled in as surrogate daddy for workaholic Ray.

Together, Reba and I baked banana bread and shopped for shoes. We styled each other's hair and we organized the pantry and closets. We swam in the river and we picnicked on the lawn listening to her favorite music. We giggled and giggled and giggled. Reba was the only friend I had that summer in Montrose and I was not looking forward to her returning home. The day before she was to go back home to Mesa, we went shopping for fresh produce at an outdoor market and the saleslady told me I had a beautiful daughter, and that she looked just like me. I was about the correct the mistake when Reba, whose hair had just been cut and styled (my treat), grinned in her trademark shrewd manner. She quipped, "Why, thank you, mam! I do agree!"

The next year, I turned forty. Forty wasn't a particularly traumatic milestone in terms of age because I'd already been prepped by becoming a "step-grandmother" after Angie gave birth to her son, Sean, in January of the same year. I worried that Angie wasn't married to Sean's father,

Duane, who was divorced with two boys already, but she assured me in a letter things were fine, and that her son Sean was healthy and she was happy. Really, I was in no position to judge.

For my birthday, I had intended to spend it with my sister and mother in Salt Lake City, without Ray. Unfortunately, to have left him at home for the weekend would have caused a huge fight between us, likely bigger than the fight he and I had the week *before* my birthday about how much I hated living in Montrose and how much I missed my family. Ray claimed the real reason I hated Montrose was just to piss him off. Sometimes I wondered if he was right, though I kept that to myself.

After the six-hour mostly silent drive from Montrose to Salt Lake City, Ray pulled into the parking lot of the Travel Inn in downtown Salt Lake City, where my mother and sister were eagerly waiting. I hadn't expected such balmy weather in October and was wearing a long-sleeved purple corduroy granny-style dress and Western-style boots. I stepped out of Ray's Subaru and both of them gasped. I thought maybe I had a bug on my teeth.

Licking my teeth, I asked, "What's wrong?"

Mom hugged me and fingered the fabric of my dress. "Your dress. It's, well…it's different."

Different to my mother meant repugnant. I said, "Granny dresses are really in. Plus it is *so* comfortable."

"Well, it looks a bit like a tent."

"I like loose clothes. They hide my hips."

Ray rolled his eyes and snapped impatiently, "What hips? You don't have hips. You can't when you wear a size four dress."

Mom said, "Don't worry, honey. We'll go shopping after lunch."

Meanwhile, Patty was staring at my boots. "Wow, cowboy boots. I didn't think I'd ever see the day you would wear cowboy boots *with* a corduroy dress."

I held up a pointy-toed stitched-leather boot for a better look. "I won these boots in a raffle at the Corn Festival in Olathe. I wear them when we go line-dancing."

"Corn festival?"

"Line-dancing?"

Ray shook his head. "We've been *trying* to take country-western dance lessons on Fridays in Ridgway, but Nancy has two left feet. The instructor said she'd do okay with more practice but she gets too frustrated. Last week, we ended up playing pool instead."

"So, pool's more fun." I turned to Mom and said, "Hey, don't let me forget to give you my tomato-pie recipe. I just kind of made it up but it's really tasty."

Ray agreed. "Nancy has a real knack with tomatoes."

Patty looked unsure as Mom touched my hair. "What happened to your long hair, honey?"

"And why is it sort of...greenish?" Patty asked. She was wearing a flattering khaki skort and white linen blouse tied at her waist. Her hair was the same strawberry blond but longer and layered. She looked fabulous, and I self-consciously patted my head.

"I think it's the water in Montrose, and I had to get it cut off because of an unsuccessful home-coloring job over a bad perm."

I watched them exchange fretful glances and I said, "Don't worry, it'll grow back. Besides, I think the haircut makes me look like Joan Lunden. Come on, let's get unpacked and go to the pool to catch up."

At the pool, I didn't mention to my mother and sister that things were so miserable in Montrose that I was on Prozac. Instead, I told them all about our adventures, starting with the branding and steer castrating party we had attended on a ranch in Ridgway. There, I cringed while others clapped at the young bulls getting their balls chopped off and their backsides burned with a branding stick. I could not believe how many people lined up afterwards to eat those same testicles, called Rocky Mountain oysters, which had been drenched in flour and grilled. Ray called the cooked testicles "cowboy caviar" and doused his with hot sauce. Sounds yummy but I stuck with the baked beans.

Then there was our trip to the outdoor hot springs in nearby Ouray, a tiny town referred to as the "Little Switzerland of North America," where clothing was optional so everyone was naked, including the children. I told them about lunching in the exclusive resort of Telluride, home to Tom Cruise and Nicole Kidman, and ice-skating at an outdoor rink in Gunnison.

I shared with them that my strangest adventure so far had been walking along the banks of the frozen Blue Mesa Reservoir the prior January and suddenly hearing an unearthly, eerie sound that echoed off the surrounding mountains and caused the hair on my neck to stand up. Ray said the noise was caused by huge layers of ice deep below the surface sheering before shifting and sinking. If that was the case, the people ice-fishing inside ice huts scattered across the frozen lake were very courageous, and how strange to see an ice hut with a smoking chimney sticking through its top.

We talked about our Sunday drives to ghost towns and gulches, going to rodeos, and watching outdoor western melodramas being recreated at the River Ranch in Ridgway, performed by a group of local thespians called "Legends of the West."

"The guy who plays Doc Holliday is really good and his wife plays one of the prostitutes, and they always do their shows close to dusk, when the mountains turn purple. They call it alpenglow and it is mesmerizing. You've never seen a sunset till you've seen one in Colorado."

Patty smiled. "Wow, Sis, you guys are certainly staying busy."

I smiled back. "There's a lot to do in Montrose." *Too bad I'm doing it with someone I'm beginning to hate.*

Mom reached across the poolside table to pat my hand. "I'm glad things are working out, dear," her voice hitched, "Bob would be so relieved."

I struggled to keep the tears from coming because if they did, they would never stop. My late stepfather wasn't relieved because he was in heaven watching everything.

Bob had been gone for a year-and-a-half, and it still seemed like yesterday.

Chapter Sixty-Five

There are two types of people when it comes to dealing with grief: There are the bowls, who with quiet dignity contain their grief until it evaporates with the grace of acceptance; and then there are the sponges, those who thirstily soak up their grief because heart-ripping sorrow is the only way they can cope with the loss while showing respect for the dead.

I am the latter, a super-absorbent tampon who mourns not just for the dead but those left behind: The brothers, sisters, sons, daughters, mothers, fathers, aunts and uncles, even the cousins, whose anguish settles in my heart and merges with my soul. Such was the case on Friday, April 28, 1994, when God snatched from earth Robert Francis Adamson.

In a fateful twist, it was also Ray Dickerson's forty-second birthday, a cloudless Friday when I was going to make him a steak and crab dinner, and Bob and Mom were preparing to go on an archeological dig for Indian artifacts as part of a volunteer group through their church. First, however, Bob went on his morning jog and when he came into the house, Mom recalled him looking through the garden window drinking his decaf coffee when he collapsed backwards. Like that, Bob was gone and our lives were changed forever.

We later learned his death was instant and painless, due to ventricular fibrillation. That might have been true, but our pain was unbearable, made worse by being robbed of the chance to say goodbye.

The pastor called me first, while I was at work. I next called Patty, crying so hard I could hardly speak, which is why Patty thought I said "Mom's dead" instead of "Bob's dead." For an hour, Patty and Tom mourned Mom's passing until I arrived at their house. Patty ran up to me, her face twisted with pain, her eyes swollen. Tom was by her side. He asked solemnly, "How's my Dad taking it?"

I momentarily stopped crying. "Your Dad? Bob's dead!"

Tom went pale. "My Dad is dead?"

"Mom is alive?" Patty struggled to understand. Beside her was Brianna, who was also crying.

"Yes, Mom is alive." The misunderstanding was indescribable in the misery it added to our grief. "Omigod, I am so sorry! It was Bob who died. He just collapsed!"

And then we all collapsed in a joined circle on our knees, one tragedy on top of another.

That simple mistake would haunt me, and I would not handle my stepfather's death well. This was a loss that was abysmal and unmanageable, at the heart of which was my mother, who had suffered more losses in her lifetime than any human should endure. Now God had taken the true love of her life. All I could think about were his children left behind—my stepbrothers and stepsister—who were now without a mother and a father. How does a child assimilate such a great loss?

In my weakest hours following my stepfather's passing (and there were many), I began to question God's ways. Why had He taken Bob Adamson and not Bill Nash? My father drank scotch for breakfast, smoked like a chimney, and shunned exercise in favor of watching old John Wayne movies. I would never have wished my father dead as I loved him and cared for him deeply, but it would have made more *sense.*

Alone at night, I was awash in memories of how happy my mother and Bob had been. Who knew old people could giggle so much? The sentiment of the little things my mother would no longer cherish crushed me, and I could not help but wonder *what if?*

What if Bob had known he had a heart arrhythmia? Could he have taken medication to control it?

What if Bob hadn't gone jogging? Was it the strain of exertion that caused his heartbeat to go awry?

What if they had lived in the city rather than the country, where the fire department relied on volunteers? *What if* they had arrived in ten minutes rather than twenty?

What if what if what if?

I would kneel at my bedside hands folded in prayer, and beg through a river of tears for God to help me understand that my stepfather's untimely passing *did* make sense. Mom said heaven needed another artist, and that's what I wanted to believe until I walked through Bob's log cabin studio and came upon the latest canvas he had been working on, propped on an easel in the center of the room. It was a painting of a sunlit mesa with a lone saguaro cactus in the foreground. The sky was partly finished and painted a startling turquoise that conveyed heat, but the lower part of the canvas was a nebulous blend of greens and gold. On a table nearby, brushes of various sizes, their ends brightly colored, were sitting in jars waiting for familiar hands.

"Bob still had work to do on earth," I told Mom as I fingered the painting.

"Yes." She picked up a photograph Bob was using as a reference and held it up next to the painting. "We took this in March in Apache Junction. That was one of the best vacations we ever had, except for the flat tire on the fifth-wheeler while we were visiting the Casa Grande Ruins. It was so hot I thought poor Bobby was going to have a heatstroke."

I glanced at the photo and back at the canvas. "Bob captured the shadows and sunlight perfectly." I blew my nose and choked on my words. "He...was...so...talented."

Mom set the photograph down and pointed skyward. "Just think what he's painting now." She then reached out with that same hand and touched the painting gently. "Maybe one day I'll finish you." She was smiling while I was gulping tears, my eyes drawn to the wedding band on my mother's left hand.

"What makes you so strong, Mom?" I asked, wringing a tissue paper that had disintegrated into nothing but mucus.

She looked up, and I realized for the first time my sixty-seven-year-old mother was now shorter than me. "Faith," she replied, "you won't get through anything in life unless you have faith."

Chapter Sixty-Six

Two months after Bob's passing, lightning caused one of the worst fires in Washington history, named the Tyee Complex Wildfire, which started near Chelan and Entiat. By August, the fire had come so close to the Adamson's property in Plain that the Forest Service forced the evacuation of many of Mom's neighbors. She refused to go, even as the hills burned crimson just miles away and smoke blackened the air so she could not see the river a few yards below; even as she listened to the constant whirl of news-station helicopters above, and the crackling of forest being decimated.

She was not crazy, but was resigned to let God's will design her fate. With Pepper, the stray dog Bob had found wandering near the river, at her side, she went about business, part of which included sorting through Bob's personal belongings and filling out stacks of insurance and other legal paperwork, much of it for the government. Bob had been a veteran of World War II and the American flag that had been presented to his widow at his memorial service was still in its glass case on the floor next to what was now an empty bed.

While no damn forest fire was going to force her from the home she had shared with her dear husband of nearly fifteen years, I begged her to reconsider. I couldn't bear the thought of losing Mom so soon after Bob.

I watched the news in horror and enlisted Aunt Linda's powers of persuasion. She was battling breast cancer but I knew we could count on her support. In the end, Mom remained steadfast, and soon the rains came and the winds shifted. It was clear God had other plans for her.

Nevertheless, I remained an emotional wreck, crying at the drop of a hat. While sitting on the outdoor patio of Anthony's Homeport with Ray, I spotted an elderly couple holding hands and walking down the pier. The old man bent to say something and the old woman giggled. Watching the couple, tears streamed down my face. My mother would never again walk a pier with Bob, would never giggle at something funny he had whispered in her ear. That day, like so many others, my broken heart felt like it would never be one again.

The great depression that followed Bob's death was welcomed because it gave me an excuse to withdraw from the world in general and Ray in particular. Luckily, we only saw each other on weekends due to Ray's self-imposed grueling construction superintendent schedule combined with his duties as a single father. When we did get together, it was his job not my grief that was the prime topic of conversation.

The days and months were a blur as I went through the motions. Birthdays came and went, including Bob's in early December. He would have been seventy.

For her first Christmas without Bob, I spoiled Mom by buying Elizabeth Taylor's "White Diamonds" fragrance kit, which included perfume and body lotion, as well as a picture frame shaped like an artist's canvas. Shopping turned into therapy and I stayed at the mall a long time. When I finally got home and walked into my apartment, the phone was ringing. I set my bags down and answered blandly, "Hello?"

"Where have you been? I've been calling for two hours." Ray's tone hid nothing and implied he thought I was out doing something wrong, like performing fellatio on the paperboy.

I answered, "Christmas shopping. I took my time. Why? What's wrong?" Last time he called he thought he had cancer but it turned out to be hyperlipidemia.

"Nothing's wrong." Ray's perturbed tone was now gone and replaced with excitement. "I called to tell you some good news. My buddy George got me an interview on his job site. It's a superintendent's position and I would be overseeing the construction of a 45,000-square-foot lodge. The problem is, it's in Ridgway, Colorado."

"Colorado?" I rubbed a temple and plopped on my sofa. Outside it was a typical Pacific Northwest wet and gray December afternoon. I knew from Mom that Plain had three feet of snow on the ground, plenty for snowmobiling, but there was little chance Mom would be snowmobiling that year.

Ray was saying, "It's a once-in-a-lifetime opportunity! The pay is way more than I'd ever make here in Seattle and there are all kinds of bonuses. I'd have to fly down for an interview, but George said I'm an ace in. It would start in January but I just need to know if you'd be okay with me moving so far. The job could take three years. That's a long time. We'd have to make some major adjustments."

Major adjustments? How many more major adjustments could I possibly make? Our tenuous relationship took more effort to make work than the entire legal team for O. J. Simpson, but with less positive results. I had never known someone so fragile, insecure, and demanding when it came to love, but because I completely lacked good insight into poor judgment, I didn't see the need to break up with him. Those who loved me I loved back. Plus the sex was really good. If it weren't for the sex, I'd be gone.

Ray said, "You might have to move to Montrose."

I thought he was joking. Besides, the chances of him getting the job were probably slim. "Well, if you get offered the job, I think you should take it. It will be very exciting." My internal compass, one at the mercy of a very blue angel, was directing me to choose a path that pleased those around me.

He replied, "That's great! I'll let you know what happens with the interview. I'm not worried. George has filled them in on my superintendent experience." He paused and said, "So, is that all you did was go shopping? Nothing else?"

Actually, Ray, after shopping I had a ménage à trois with a store Santa and his contortionist elf in the restroom off the Food Court. Biting my tongue, I replied, "Yes, Ray, that's all I did was shop. I bought my mother some perfume, a picture frame, stuff like that. I'm spoiling her for obvious reasons." I quickly steered the conversation, too tired for another fight. "So, this job could take three years?"

"From what George said, this lodge is going to be unbelievable. Everything is imported and top-of-the-line. All the ceiling beams are Burmese teak and there are five fireplaces, which are going to be made of river rock from some famous river and each one is about three stories tall! The plans show *two* kitchens, one a commercial kitchen with stainless steel appliances. The entire lodge will have heated floors and there are going to be six bathrooms with custom fixtures, along with a wine cellar, shooting gallery, and servants' quarters. This is a resume-building job for me."

Wine cellar is all I heard. "That's nice." Lily jumped on my lap and head butted my knee. I scratched her neck under her pink collar and she began purring. It sounded like a motorboat. Yawning, I replied, "Sounds like a great opportunity for you."

"Nance, you sound tired."

"I am, *from shopping*, nothing else." Jesus, I hated to account for every little move. Tim was never this suspicious. We disconnected and I went straight to bed, Lily at my heels.

A week later, Ray flew down for the interview. He got the job.

Chapter Sixty-Seven

"You *got* the job?" I was seated at the edge of what had once been Melanie and Ray's waterbed, a California King style that dominated the room and provided no lumbar support. I felt like I was in the ocean on a raft.

Ray looked confused and readjusted his glasses. "Yes, they offered it and I accepted it. We discussed this, remember? You said I should take the job if I could. Now you seem mad. Are you?"

"Well, not exactly."

Ray interpreted. "So when you said yes, you meant no."

"No. I just didn't think...how's Alison going to take it?"

Ray plopped next to me and we both fell over onto the springy waterbed. He rolled over on top of me. "Alison will love it there." He sat up. "Nancy, it's hard to describe how breathtaking the pristine wilderness is there. I saw a wild elk that had to be eight feet tall just and there are mountains everywhere. The Gunnison River is nearby and George said it's a fly-fisherman's wet dream. When you visit, you'll see what I mean." He paused. "If things work out, I want you to move there with me.

"Oh?"

"Maybe we'll even get married."

I sat up, ignoring the "maybe" part, and repeated, "Married?"

"Sure, why not?"

I wasn't sure how to answer, though "no" crossed my mind. Isn't that what you say when you get a weak, ringless marriage proposal that begins with maybe?

Ray sat up and put one hand up so she felt like a schoolgirl at a crosswalk. "Don't answer yet, just take your time. Besides, let's see how my job goes."

I did a surreptitious eye roll. Ray Dickerson was the emperor of caveats, attaching conditions to everything:

I would have reached my financial goals by now if only...

I feel like I'm turning the corner towards success but need...

My daughters would be fine if only their mother would...

Our relationship will work, but you must...

Ray beamed, full of himself. "If the job works out, maybe we can get married in the mountains of Colorado?"

By then, a normal person would be asking questions, pressing for a commitment; at the very least, expecting a ring. And getting married in the mountains was never my dream. I probably should have told Ray the truth but instead I answered with an empty smile, "Sure, whatever you want."

Chapter Sixty-Eight

After completing several long months of chemotherapy and radiation treatment for stage III breast cancer, "Aunt" Linda developed a lingering cough and was scheduled for a chest x-ray. I met her in the Radiology Department of Evergreen Hospital Medical Center, where she was a volunteer and I worked as a transcriptionist.

In the waiting room, Linda patted her chest. "It's probably just bronchitis." She held my hand and smiled, wearing a silk scarf over her sparse red curls. Her flawless milky complexion hadn't changed much through the ordeal of a chemo, and her spirit was hopeful. Helping her through it all was a very caring husband, Aaron.

"Yes. It's going around." It was a lame response, and not what I was feeling in my gut. "You probably just need some good antibiotics."

"That's what Aaron thinks. So, how's the job going?"

I groaned. "Stressful. I'm lead transcriptionist by choice, but I didn't realize this would mean doing more troubleshooting than typing. Honestly, if I wasn't constantly interrupted by phone calls all day long from nurses or the emergency room looking for lost or stat reports, I'd get a lot more done."

"Oh, I know, they run us volunteers ragged but I don't mind since I come here for all my treatments. Aaron jokes I should just rent a room."

She cleared her throat and said hoarsely, "Your mother said you may be moving to Colorado? Is that true?"

"Maybe, but it's not carved in stone."

"She's not too happy about that. She doesn't think Ray is right for you. She said she has a bad feeling." Linda put a hankie to her mouth and coughed into it. "You know how mothers are about these things."

"I know, Linda, but Mom is worried about nothing."

Linda reached an arm around me and hugged me close. "She only wants what's best for you. It's what all mothers want for their daughters." Linda was seized by another coughing spasm just as her name was called. We both stood and I watched the nurse escort Linda away.

Back sitting at my computer in Medical Records, I knew I could access the radiology dictation system and listen to Linda Kelso's chest x-ray report when it was completed, but I would never violate the rules of protecting a patient's privacy, even if that patient was a dear friend. Like everyone else, I waited for the news from Linda herself, and it was not good: The breast cancer had spread to both lungs.

Linda would be too sick to accompany our family to Plain to honor the one-year anniversary of Bob's passing. We all had gathered at the "Haven of Rest," a private cemetery on Burgess Hill outside Plain, where we had a private ceremony and placed fresh flowers on Bob's gravesite. Later, we went back to the house and built a campfire along the river Bob had loved so much. The moments were bittersweet, filled with nostalgic stories about Bob, especially his notorious color-blindness. My favorite story involves my stepfather's safety-deposit box, one that was clearly green but Bob was adamant it was blue. *Where's my blue box?* he'd ask Mom, who would tell him they didn't have a blue box but if he was talking about the green one, it was in the closet.

Later, in Mom's house, us girls talked about our Aunt Linda, whose illness had forced her to stop volunteering at the hospital. A couple of weeks later, Linda was admitted to The Gene and Irene Wockner Hospice Center, located on the campus of Evergreen Hospital Medical Center in Kirkland, Washington.

The Hospice Center was designed as a lovely Cape-Cod-style facility that was surrounded by rose and alpine gardens. Each suite was appointed like a cottage with private patios and views of the lush courtyard. There were only fifteen private rooms at the center and the day Linda was admitted to Room 9, in June, only six rooms were occupied. The facility had just opened and elegant fresh flower arrangements adorned the hallways.

I walked into Room 9 and found Linda lying in her hospital bed, wearing her own green silk bathrobe. She pointed to the window. "Look at those beautiful, beautiful roses, Nancy, and they're all shades of pink. That's why I wanted this room, so I could see the roses. I adore pink roses."

I glanced out the window. "Yes, I know." I had walked to the center from the hospital after I got off work, and after I learned of Linda's admission to hospice, which by definition was a facility that provided palliative and supportive care for terminally ill patients and their families. In the case of the Wockner Center, it also provided spiritual support and a prayer room.

I turned back around and patted Linda's hand. I was fascinated by Linda's fifty-two-year-old hands, which were youthful and unblemished, just like a China dolls'. I asked, "Don't you feel like you're in a cottage?"

Linda nodded, "Yes, but I won't be here long and as soon as I get home, I am going to tend to my rose gardens. I haven't been doing much of that." Linda's gaze remained fixed on the roses. "Funny the roses didn't bother me when I was doing chemo but the lilacs sure got to me. I was so nauseated by their sweet scent I made Aaron chop down all the lilac trees in the backyard. The neighbors thought he was crazy."

I nodded. "Mom couldn't stand the smell of bacon when she was going through chemotherapy." As soon as these words were out, I felt guilty. My mother had survived breast cancer but Linda would not; that's why she was in hospice care.

I began pacing the room, looking at the framed prints, keeping my mind off the fact that Linda was dying despite her optimistic attitude. We chatted for an hour, when Linda said she needed to rest. I promised to return the next day, and in my parked car I began crying and cried the entire way to my apartment.

On June 17, 1995, Aaron called me and said it was time to say goodbye to Linda. I called Patty, who was in the middle of inventory for the beer and wine distributing company where she worked, and we agreed to meet at the hospice as soon as we could. An hour later, we walked into Room 9, unsure what to expect, and found Linda was still alive but not coherent. She was tucked under a white bedspread embroidered with pink and purple flowers. Nearby, a morphine drip was supposed to help her breathe better but her respirations still came in ragged bursts. Her eyes were half-closed, and her lovely hands were like wax figurines, perfectly manicured, placed at her sides. Aaron excused himself so we could share a private moment with our "aunt."

At the bedside, Patty looked down. "Linda is so beautiful. I swear she has never aged. She still looks just like she did when we lived with her way back in seventy-three."

I choked on my words, "I know." I walked to the tissue box and picked it up. "I didn't expect this. I thought she would be able to talk. I mean, I just saw her a few days ago and we talked about the pink roses in the courtyard." I blew my nose and asked my sister, "Do you think Linda knows we are here?" I was patting Linda's hand, which felt like satin.

"Yes, she knows."

My crying got worse and through tears, I leaned over and whispered, "I love you, Linda."

Patty did the same, though her words were clearer. "Goodbye, Aunt Linda. Say hi to Bob." Her thin face looked stoic and peaceful, and I knew Patty was the bowl made of steel, the rock I would never be.

Linda was still alive when we left and we drove directly to Mom's house in Plain. Not long after we arrived, Aaron called to say that Linda had gone to a better place. Her funeral was held in the same church where she and Mom got married the second time around, to good, decent men. Mountains and mountains of pink roses filled the church and a friend read a poem she had written in Linda's memory titled, "The Pink Rose."

Bob and Linda's deaths had left an enormous void in my life, and would reinforce my belief that life was too damn short not to take chances and make mistakes, like moving to the high desert to be with a man who hated cats.

Chapter Sixty-Nine

My second Christmas in Montrose was one of my worst holidays in memory, and that says a lot for a girl who, at the age of seven, watched her father hold a gun to her mother's head on Christmas Eve. The gun was loaded, my dad was drunk, and Patty and I watched from our parents' bedroom doorway, frozen with fear. Nobody died and nobody got arrested. After Mom calmed Dad down, she went to the kitchen and made us spaghetti and meatballs for dinner, and at the dining table we talked about school. It was a story Ray didn't even know about.

In any case, I had been planning since fall to tell Ray I was moving back to Washington from Montrose, with or without him. Fall came and went, and by mid-winter I still hadn't gotten up the courage to tell Ray this, even though it should have been an easy decision since Christmas Day was spent alone in my car behind our pole barn after I knocked over the Christmas tree and Ray locked me out of the house.

The day after Christmas, a six-year-old beauty queen was found murdered in her parents' Boulder, Colorado, home. JonBenet Ramsey looked like a floozy in the photos and footage that ran on T.V., but she was really an innocent little girl, and I couldn't imagine the suffering her parents were going through. It was a heartbreaking, heart-wrenching story and once again reminded me to count my own blessings. Sure, I was miserable in Montrose but I didn't find my own daughter strangled and in my own basement. I decided to try to make things work in Montrose, especially when New Year's Eve promised to be better. That day was spent making gourmet hor d'ourves and getting the house ready for a party we were hosting. The guest list was made up entirely of Ray's friends and coworkers, including his boss, and I really wanted to wear my favorite little black cocktail dress but I wore jeans instead. In the end, it didn't matter because no one showed up. *No one.* This was my clue I was *living* one of those depressing country songs.

When I had enough of the rollercoaster, I was ready to tell Ray my news. Unfortunately, the day started poorly, beginning with Ray being unable to find his pager. This was how many mornings started because Ray would lose a testicle if it were not firmly attached to his groin. Fifteen minutes into the search, the pager was found in his truck under a pile of unopened mail and fast-food bags that were at least as old as the truck though the French fries on the floorboards looked fresh. Whenever Ray misplaced something, I always looked in his truck first, using a broom to sort through the mounds of litter, invoices, and tools. He admitted the Chevy was "cluttered" but that he knew precisely where everything was. Everything except his pager.

Ray was in a hurry after having spent so much time looking for his pager so I decided to tell him my news when he got home from work, over a really good home-cooked meal.

Six o'clock came and went. At seven o'clock, I was famished and opened the lid to our new gas grill but could not bring myself to turn on the gas to ignite the burner. Propane was another thing I feared, or more precisely dying a fiery, grisly death wearing corduroy overalls.

At nine o'clock, when Ray's beat-up Chevy finally did pull into the driveway, it was dark and I was beyond angry. The minute he walked into the house, I exploded. "You could have called, Ray! How much fuckin' trouble would that have been? I was starving and waited for two hours before I got the nerve to start up the gas grill. I could have incinerated the whole town of Montrose!"

Ray walked to the fridge and grabbed a beer. "I got caught up at work. You know how stressful things are. I'm sorry."

I didn't think he looked sorry at all, and it was the third time in a month he had come home late without calling. "Well, you missed a delicious dinner. I don't understand why you didn't call. That's just plain rude, Ray. I deserve better."

Ray turned to walk away, grabbing the newspaper. "I said I'm sorry. Get off my back."

I replied hotly, "You know, Ray, this is crap. You keep saying you're working on making our relationship better, but you do everything possible to ensure that it will not. You avoid talking to me half the time and the other half are gung-ho to dissect our relationship into pieces before you start suturing it back up. That isn't working, Ray." I was working up to the Big News.

"What?" Ray was interested in the conversation now that the state of our union was brought up. "Are you saying we're done? That our relationship is dead?"

"It's suffering, Ray. We might as well put it out of its misery."

Ray jabbed the air with a dirty finger. "That's so typical! You always want to give up when things go bad. Tim was right: You're always running rather than trying to work things out." Ray tossed the newspaper across the room. "I'm falling apart and you want out. That's just fuckin' great!" Ray hissed mockingly before he stormed out of the house, slamming the old kitchen door.

I was never one to swear, but in Montrose, on top of everything else, I had developed Tourette's syndrome and cursed more times than I peed, which was a lot. I yelled through the door, "Go to hell you cocksucking pompous asshole bastard! And don't bring Tim into this!" In the kitchen, I took a break from swearing to kick the bag of that morning's tomatoes. The bag tore and ripened tomatoes skidded across the pink linoleum like sluggish pool balls. "I'm not picking these goddam fuckin' tomatoes up, you know!" I was cussing at pink wallpapered walls. "They can rot here on the stinking floor for all I care, Ray, because I am sick of you and all these fuckin' tomatoes!"

Ray's truck screeched as it backed out of the driveway. Five minutes passed and I finally began picking up the tomatoes to throw them into the trash. I could not stand clutter, even for five minutes. After that, I swept the kitchen floor and then scrubbed it on hands and knees. I emptied every wastebasket in the house (Mom called this purging) and cleaned both bathrooms, taking special care to wipe the hair and lint from around the toilet base.

Feeling as maudlin as I had ever felt, I retrieved the vacuum when Ray's truck pulled into the driveway. I left the vacuum standing and slumped into a kitchen chair awaiting a boyfriend who was always falling apart and expecting somebody else to put him back together. He had picked his partner well, at least the second time around, though the task had grown old.

The rickety kitchen door flew open, banged against the wall, and glass rattled. It was a bespectacled Humpty Dumpty who, of course, was in pieces.

"You always think everything is so fuckin' easy, don't you, Nancy? Well, it isn't!" Ray's saliva sprayed across the room. "Everybody wants a piece of me: My kids, my job, Melanie, you. It's bad enough the job is turning into a nightmare but then I come home and listen to your nonstop bitching. I can't handle this shit!" He pointed menacingly, "Would it really hurt to *try* to be supportive and less selfish once in a while?"

"Selfish?" I shouted back, "that's a crock of shit, and how dare you say I think everything is easy! What a fuckin' joke! Everything is far from easy and because of you it's ten times more complicated than it has to be. I moved here to be with you and what do I get for it? I'll tell you what I get: A workaholic, jealousy-crazed boyfriend who thinks I'm sleeping with the entire town behind his back, and day after boring day spent alone in this hick town where there isn't even a decent shopping center!"

Ray shook his head in disgust. "That's all that matters to you, spending money."

I ignored the comment and asked sarcastically, "Do you know what the highlight of my day is, Ray? It's picking fuckin' tomatoes. And the highlight of my *week?* That's even more fascinating: It's watching you play pool—though I lose the term loosely because *play* is not what you do—in a smoky tavern filled with ex-cons where the wine comes in a box." I plopped in to a chair with my head down, all energy drained. "I have no friends, no social life. Trust me; you're not the only one falling apart."

Ray didn't respond so I lifted my head. "I can't stand living like this any longer. Do you not remember Christmas?"

"Of course, I remember. You knocked over the tree."

I didn't bother reminding him *why* I knocked over the tree, which was because I was angry over yet another round of groundless accusations that I was flirting with (fill in the blank). I kicked the stupid tree and it toppled. I told Ray, "It doesn't matter. I'm moving back to Washington, with or without you." I was praying for the latter.

Ray remained sullenly silent and I was tempted to throw a tomato at his dense blond head. I asked louder, "Did you hear me?"

"Yes, I heard you." Ray slumped at a table he rarely ate at and began rubbing his temples. He muttered, "I know you aren't sleeping with the entire town." He ventured a sheepish look my direction. "Maybe just half?"

I narrowed my eyes and groaned, "Very funny. The accusations are not only untrue but they're getting old. You have a huge problem with trust that is destroying—"

Ray's hands shoot up, palm flat and facing me. "I know, okay? I fuckin' know."

He may know, I thought, but he refused to do anything about it.

An uncomfortable silence ensued, during which I stood and went to the sink. With my back turned, I said quietly, "You were supposed to *save* me."

He asked, "Save you?"

"Yes." I turned. "I thought it would be different with us, you know? You were supposed to be better than Tim, the one who loved me for who I am, but most of the time you seem to hate me."

"I don't hate you."

"You don't trust me. What's the difference?" I fought back tears. Trust was not our only issue. I knew deep down Ray was not the "one" and that I was staying with him for all the wrong reasons. At first it was the great sex but even that was flailing, and then there was the guilt. I couldn't get past that Ray had left his family for me, and for this I *owed* him. I would not or could not admit it had been a mistake and lives were shattered because of it.

Of course, Ray knew all of this. It was why he was so insecure.

Ray hunched further with his head between his hands. Any minute he'd probably start crying and then I would be forced to feel sorry for him. I closed my eyes praying for the strength to actually do what I said I was going to do no matter how much Ray cried. I repeated, "I *am* moving, whether you like it or not."

Ray muttered something I had to strain to hear. "I'm ready to go back to Washington, too."

"What?"

"You heard me."

I had, just barely. "What about your job? You can't just walk away from the job, can you?" All he had talked about was how important it was to stay on the job until its completion, whenever that would be.

Ray removed his glasses and rubbed beady eyes. "Things have gotten out of control and I can't handle the political bullshit or backstabbing at the job site. There's zero organization in upper management, which is why the job is at least two years—probably three—behind schedule, but no one listens to me. I'm just a fuckin' superintendent." He began cleaning his glasses with the hem of his flannel shirt and put them back on. "Morons do everything backw—"

Ray's pager beeped and he reached for his hip and was instantly in "I'm-in-Charge" mode, gritting his jaw, shouting rudely into the phone, "I know! I'm the one who put the fuckin' work order in, remember? And I've already scheduled a meeting with the subcontractor and Paul tomorrow. The load of teak got delayed and the rock façade was full of defects…"

Ray went on and on and I shut him out. I walked to the fridge and poured myself a glass of Riesling. When he hung up, I took a big sip and said, "I'll call the real-estate company tomorrow." I was suddenly giddy with relief, though the giddiness was mixed with apprehension and I would need more wine. "So, are you hungry?"

Ray drained his beer and pushed the chair back. "No."

I asked again, "You sure you don't want me to reheat dinner? I made teriyaki flank steak and tomato salad with feta and basil." Even in the grips of a major depression, my culinary talents thrived, probably because cooking was therapy and the only thing I excelled at, other than typing. Unfortunately, a typist who could cook didn't make much of an impression on the folks in Montrose, not unless it was done on a horse. I told Ray, "For dessert, I made crème brulee with strawb—"

"Forget about food." Ray pushed himself from the table. "I'm not real fuckin' hungry. Everything I've worked for is going down the fuckin' drain so the last fuckin' thing I want to do is eat. Got it?" He launched his beer can into the sink. "I'm going to bed. I don't care what you do."

I watched him slump down the hallway, where seconds later the bedroom door slammed but I already had my hands on my ears. Ray Dickerson was a slammer, another thing that annoyed me. Women had the exclusive right to be slammers, a right I exercised often.

That night it was me who slept on the sofa, and when my pink house sold for exactly what I paid for it, I tossed my Prozac, along with the scale that showed I had gained another pound because how does one gain weight on a diet of mostly tomatoes and wine?

Chapter Seventy

Everyone has story they tell no one but their therapist, at least not until they write a book and then everyone who reads it knows. *My* story typifies the destructive relationship I had with Ray and could have been made into a taping of the "Jerry Springer Show." I call my story "The Pete and Elizabeth Story."

Pete Finnigan was a journeyman bricklayer from Fort Collins, Colorado, whose company had been contracted to do the masonry work on all five fireplaces on the lodge where Ray was worked, a job that would take months, maybe a year. The contract was too lucrative to turn down so Pete and his wife Elizabeth relocated from Fort Collins to Montrose. Unfortunately, though not surprisingly, Elizabeth became disillusioned with living in Montrose and moved back to Fort Collins, during which time Ray and Pete had become good buddies and teammates on a pool league. Before I actually moved to Montrose and was visiting Ray at his duplex, we had Pete over for home cooked dinner that I prepared, consisting of Salmon Wellington, fettuccini, and an endive walnut salad.

One weekend in late January, Ray, Pete, and me drove to Gunnison to go ice-skating on an open rink. On the way, I told Pete ice-skating was something you never forgot how to do, like riding a bicycle, and even though it had been years and years since I had ice-skated, I predicted I would still be pretty good. Pete bet me a large hot chocolate that I was wrong.

Boy, was I wrong! The skates were rented, the wrong size, and cut into my ankles, and I skidded more than skated, landing numerous times on my back. None the worse for wear, afterwards I held up my end of the deal and bought an extra hot chocolate for Pete *and* Ray. I smart enough not to let a simple bet get me in trouble.

On the way home, we all laughed about how absurd us almost-forty-year-olds looked ice-skating around all those little kids, and about how lucky we were none of broke any bones. Ray dropped Pete off at his apartment and on the way back to his duplex he shocked me when he accused me of having a crush on Pete, which he surmised began after Pete accepted a second helping of my Salmon Wellington.

Let me tell you right now, I didn't have a crush on Pete, and I was pretty sure he didn't have a crush on me, but no man in his right mind would turn down a second helping of my Salmon Wellington, a recipe using fresh spinach (and frozen salmon) in a garlic cream stuffed in puff pastry. Sure, Pete was a nice guy and good-looking, but I was in not interested in having an illicit affair with another married man in a town where I already had no friends.

Ray and me patched things up, and a few weeks later, his pool team had another tournament and I vacillated for hours on whether to go since I couldn't predict what sorts of misbehaviors on my part Ray would invent. In the end, I decided to go and promised myself I wouldn't even smile in Pete's direction, or laugh at one of his witty jokes. I dressed in a baggy jumper-style dress paired with brown ankle boots and put my hair in a ponytail. At the tavern, I was aloof and kept my distance from every man in the bar, not daring make eye contact and willing them all to believe I was a lesbian in my dowdy getup, which was blue plaid and completely camouflaged my best feature, which was my ass.

Then I got to thinking. How stupid was this? Only *guilty* people acted this way because it was supposed to throw everyone off. Anytime you see someone's wife going out of her way to avoid a friend's husband at the same party, you know those two are definitely having an affair. Trust me.

In this case, I was innocent, and was going to start acting like it. I walked up to the bar and ordered a drink, chatting politely with Pete, who in turn paid for my drink. He asked me whose grandmother I robbed to get the dress, and I chortled loudly. Pete was *very* funny. Together we chinked glasses in a toast to their team's win, and I didn't care one bit that Ray was glaring and pouting in the corner. When the tournament ended, I knew what was coming and walked out to my car with Ray on my heels. There in the parking lot, he accused me of having an affair with Pete. It was no longer a crush, but a full-blown affair, and Ray had proof, because he said I smelled like sex. Yep, after spending three boring hours in a bar filled with smokers and pool sharks, I smelled like sex. I actually thought I smelled like a B-52, a sumptuous layered drink of Bailey's, Kahlua, and Grand Marnier that probably cost Pete six bucks.

I got into my car, power locked the doors, and did one of those spinouts where gravel spits up and there's a loud screech and people run out to see what the ruckus is. *My* ruckus was in my rearview mirror screaming like a banshee, and I watched Ray launch his bottle of Bud Light towards my car, just had Tim had done all those years ago.

I *really* did intend to end it with Ray that very day. I was going to go home, put the house up for sale, and start packing. Like all my plans during this dark period of my life, it fell apart just as soon as Ray begged me to forgive him, and to *please, please, please!* go to couples' counseling with him. He wanted to work on his insecurities and jealousies (and hinted maybe I should work on what I did that made him so jealous and suspecting). He sobbed for a week and when I believed he was suicidal, I agreed to counseling.

Counseling did not end the Pete and Elizabeth Story. In fact, the Pete and Elizabeth Story thickened, even though by this time, Pete had tired of the friction-riddled job at the lodge/ranch and moved back to Fort Collins to be with his wife, never knowing that his friend Ray suspected him of sleeping with his girlfriend because Ray didn't bother confronting him. I should have, but that would have made things worse, so I forgot all about Pete, not that I spent any amount of time remembering him, until the week before Easter. That's when Ray came home from work and told me we were going to Fort Collins to spend the weekend with Pete and Elizabeth, at their invitation. I was busy making Easter baskets (actually, Easter purses) for Alison and Reba and looked up in disbelief.

"What are you talking about?"

"Well, Pete and Liz invited us for the weekend. They are really excited about it and want to take us to this bar and grill near Mile High Stadium. And before you answer, let me tell you I want to do this to prove to you counseling worked, and that I don't suspect you and Pete anymore. We can forget all about what happened and get back to being *us*. Come on, Nance, don't say no."

I was speechless but in my mind I was paging every shrink in America to come to my rescue as I came to the realization I was living with perhaps the most twisted man on earth. Clearly this was a trap. A big-time setup, and he had probably hooked Elizabeth. I tried to concentrate on the task at hand, which was filling novelty totes with candy and chocolate bunnies. To make Melanie mad, I also threw in mini tubes of lipstick, perfume samples, and hair accessories. I carefully stuffed the handbags (white vinyl for Alison, green & orange straw for Reba) with pastel confetti, praying that Ray was joking, or the whole conversation was a bad dream.

Ray cocked his head again. "Well?"

I held each bag in a hand. "Aren't these cute? The girls will love them, but maybe I should add more candy?" I set the "baskets" on the table. "Yes, more candy. I'm think white chocolate. Your girls like white chocolate, don't they?"

"Nance, were you listening?"

No, no, no. "Of course."

"Well?"

I warily made eye contact with Ray. I *wanted* to be nice and agreeable since it took less effort, but at the moment, for me to be nice required much more than what was being offered. Being nice would have required George Clooney and Brad Pitt both stark naked and licking my neck. I answered not so nicely, "Well, Ray. I think going to Fort Collins to visit Pete and Elizabeth is the stupidest idea you've ever had, even for a Pollock." Calling Ray a Pollock was a no-no but he deserved to be called much worse.

Ray laughed, "Very funny, Nancy."

I did a double take and was instantly suspicious. Ray usually did not react with humor when I was slinging racial slurs his direction. I asked, "That was funny? Really?"

He grinned and patted his chest like a chimpanzee. "See? You can't even make me mad with the Pollock jokes. I told you therapy was working. Come on, it'll be fun going to see Pete and Elizabeth."

After pleading for hours, I gave in because I didn't have the energy emotionally to fight what was happening, which was the demise of my mental health. Anytime I was given an option, no matter what it was, I decided it was better than what I had. I UPS'd the Easter purse-baskets to Ray's daughters in Mesa, and off we went to Fort Collins. It turned out that Pete and Elizabeth's turn-of-the-century home was lovely, filled with antiques and old world charm, and I had about as good a time as one can have while constantly on guard, waiting to be trapped. I was relieved when Sunday came and we were going home, and was only mildly concerned that Ray hadn't muttered a single word for two hours. I fell asleep and woke up near Vail on Interstate 70 to Ray's cracking voice.

"I wanted to be wrong, but I *know* there's something between you and Pete. You can deny it all you want, but my gut feelings don't lie. Even Elizabeth picked up on the vibes between you and Pete."

I sat up. "What?"

"You heard me. Stop pretending."

I hissed, "I *knew* it was a trap. I *knew* it yet I crawled right in! You should be proud, Ray, real proud."

"I'm not proud, I'm hurt."

"You're crazy, that's what you are. I knew I shouldn't have let you talk me into this. And for your information, there are no vibes between Pete and me except in your stupid blond head." I kept my voice level though I wanted to scream. Actually, I wanted to reach over with my foot and hit the gas pedal so we would go careening off the mountainside interstate but that would endanger others. I decided there was no point in arguing with a person who was delusional and hallucinating, so I didn't try. I focused on the resort of Vail as we passed by, where the white aspen trees jutted from the mountainside like toothpicks. I wished I were somewhere up in the snowcapped Rocky Mountains, far away from Ray.

"All you had to do was be honest with me, Nancy, and admit the truth about you and Pete. I could handle that. What I *can't* handle are all the lies and being made a fool."

He had that right. He was the biggest fool in the world, and was now in tears and shouting, but I couldn't care less. There was only one appropriate response in such a situation. I leaned back and closed my eyes. "Ray, I think you should ask for a full refund from your therapist."

Chapter Seventy-One

Historic Fort Gibson sits like a jewel in the crown of blue lakes, sparkling rivers, and green hillsides. The oldest community in the State of Oklahoma, Fort Gibson offers the quality of small town life with a solid pioneer spirit.

That's how the brochure described Fort Gibson, Oklahoma, my father's newest "home," and I was looking forward to visiting him and Kay before I moved back to Washington. *Why* they had moved from serene Stone Lake, Wisconsin, where they owned an authentic style-style rambler with a dock on the lake, back to Eastern Oklahoma, aka the "Tornado Belt," was a mystery. The prevailing theory was that Dad started drinking scotch and then asked his dog Bucky to shit on a map of the United States. Where his crap landed is where Bucky's owners landed. It wasn't that farfetched; since they got married, Dad and Kay had moved a dozen times, from Michigan to New Mexico and numerous places between. Grass didn't even *try* to grow under my father's feet.

Ray had met my father once years before and they immediately hit it off, probably because both were hardheaded ex-Marines, and he wanted to come with me to see Dad. I didn't care if he came or not. I was just going through the motions, numbed with heavy doses of indifference, hoping somehow, somewhere, I'd be put out of my misery.

The nearly 800-mile trip to Fort Gibson, Oklahoma, was uneventful only if you discount my Ford Tempo's harrowing run-in with a guardrail. The incident occurred because Ray was sightseeing and speeding when a surprise spring storm that began in Northeast New Mexico as hail turned into a full-blown snowstorm by the time we reached Amarillo, Texas. The guardrail was the only thing that prevented our car from careening off the highway, and the impact caused us to spin 180 degrees. When we finally got turned around and headed the right direction on the icy highway, we stopped a few miles up the road at the first saloon. There, I called my sister.

"Omigod, Patty! It was awful! We're in a freakin' blizzard and the car hit ice and we spinned and hit the guardrail. Ray was speeding, as usual." My hands were shaking and I nearly dropped the pay phone. "Ray should not be licensed to drive. He's a maniac on the road."

Patty asked, "A snowstorm? Are you sure you're in Texas?"

"Yes." I was standing in a knotty-pine phone booth next to a wall with a gigantic map of Texas. There was a mechanical bull in the corner of the bar, and an Alan Jackson song was playing on the jukebox. The name of the place was Lone Star Saloon, and I was the only person not wearing a cowboy hat. I repeated, "Yes, Patty, we're in the Texas panhandle, I'm sure."

My Tempo was okay, other than a sizeable dent to the front end, and we made it to Fort Gibson without stopping, and I was so exhausted I barely remember day one of our visit, other than Kay's freshly baked cherry-almond cheesecake. The next morning, while Ray slept, I crept downstairs of the farmstyle house with a wraparound porch to find Dad, now sixty-three years old, sitting in a worn recliner on the north porch. He was testing his blood sugar with a Glucometer.

Upon my approach, he looked up and drawled, "Good mornin', darlin'. Did ya'll sleep okay?" His southern accent never went away, no matter where he lived.

I perched myself on the porch swing. "Sure did. What's your reading?"

My father held the meter up. "One-hundred twelve. Pretty good." He tucked the meter away. "I hope ya'll are hungry. Kay's cookin' us up a big breakfast." He pointed.

I turned and could see Kay on the other side of the screen, standing in her country kitchen. She was every inch the Southern Belle and was perfectly made up. She cooed in her own smooth, southern drawl that betrayed a lifelong smoking habit, "Breakfast will be ready in a short while, sugar. Ah've got sausage and eggs cookin' on the griddle and taters in the oven. Would you like some coffee, punkin?" Kay was smoking as she stirred the skillet, her only vice, she claimed, other than my father.

"Yes, please."

"Cream or sugar?"

"Just black, Kay. Thank you." Moments later, I accepted a cup of steaming coffee from my stepmother. "Thanks. Ray will be down later."

Kay nodded and went back to her kitchen. I turned back and studied my father, whom I had not seen since he and Kay lived in Stone Lake. He looked a bit older and grayer, and was heavier, but personality-wise, he was the same. He still hated public places, idiots, and rules. He especially hated mosquitoes, which is why he was not happy in Fort Gibson.

"So, Dad, why *did* you move here then?"

He pushed himself back in the old recliner and grimaced. I knew a few months earlier he had had shoulder surgery and it hadn't gone well. "It was Kay's fault. She caused so much trouble in Stone Lake, we were forced to move."

Undoubtedly, it was the other way around but I went along with the ruse. "Really?"

Dad nodded. "Yep, we couldn't go into the liquor store, the grocery store, or the tackle store. They'd see mean Kay Nash coming and turn the sign to say 'Closed.' Finally I say, 'Mother, how 'bout we leave this beautiful lake with the loons and cranberry farms and move to the Tornado Belt with all them mosquitoes? Maybe you'll mellow out down there.'"

I mocked, "I don't know how you put up with her, Dad." I took in the view of their acreage and noticed an unusual rockery at the edge of the property. My father followed my gaze yonder, his hands cupping pennant-shaped eyes.

"Are you looking at the rockery?"

"Yes. Did you build it?"

"Hell, no. That's a snakepit. Was here when we bought but we didn't know what was in it till Bucky began explorin'. Poor stupid dog was lucky."

"Snakepit?" My legs instinctively shot up under my butt. Snakepit implied multiple *deadly* snakes. "Seriously?"

"Yep, so ya'll stay clear from that part of the yard. The copperheads around these parts are real cranky, probably 'cause of all them skeeters."

"Dad, don't kid around. You know how I feel about snakes."

Dad slapped at his neck and a mosquito dropped. "Would I fib to you, sweetheart?"

"Yes."

His eyes went wide but he was smiling. He mocked, "Why, I'm offended!" He was enjoying the banter. "You know everything I say is God's truth." He raised one white eyebrow and boasted, "I'm the most honest man you'll ever meet."

From the kitchen, Kay emitted a honey-bathed *huh*. "Honey, your daddy is so full of B.S. I'm surprised he hasn't exploded by now!" She said this good-naturedly and it was clear Kay knew how to handle the likes of Bill Nash.

I told my father, "Kay's right. You cannot fathom telling a story that is unembellished and not steaming with freshly concocted crap."

Feigning offense, he drawled, "Ya'll are ganging up on an old diabetic. That's terrible!" He dumped his coffee over the railing and I changed the subject.

With my legs tucked under my butt and a keen eye on the rockery, I asked Dad, "How's Gramma Nash? Is she doing any better?"

He glanced over and his gray-blue eyes flickered with great sadness. Quickly, he stood and leaned over the railing, where there was a magnificent view of the lush valley below. With his back to me, he murmured, "Mama don't even know who I am. Her mind is completely gone, eaten by Alzheimer's. I can hardly stand to visit."

He mispronounced Alzheimer's as "Altimers" as many do but I didn't correct him. I said softly, "I'm so sorry. Gramma Nash is such a dear lady."

"Thanks, honey. I thought it would be the sugar diabetes that killed her but mama doesn't even know she has diabetes. Damn disease. You know Ronald Reagan has the dementia? It took great courage for him to go public. People need to know how much suffering there is."

"Is Gramma still in Columbus?"

"Yep, she's in a nursing home and my sisters keep an eye on her. They say she's wasting away to nothing." Dad was struggling for composure and it was uncomfortable to watch. He continued, "I wouldn't wish Alzheimer's on my worst enemy."

"Not even a Democrat?" I couldn't help but lighten the moment. It was in my genes and, of course, my father one-upped me.

He turned and grinned. "Nope, not even a queer *colored* Democrat." He sat back down, clearly in pain, and began another spin. "Hey, did I tell you about the time me and Kay was fishin' in the Muskogee River? We both had our lines out and I'm catching catfish left and right, when all of a sudden, we see this snake as long as a broom. Kay jumped up and I lost my pole, catfish and all. Had to go to the Tastee Freeze for dinner."

Kay moaned from the kitchen. "Don't believe anything your father says, Nancy. He couldn't tell the truth to save his own life."

Dad reached down to pet Bucky, his Cocker Spaniel, who hadn't moved all morning, but that could be because the dog was thirty pounds overweight and at that moment being fed molasses cookies that had appeared from nowhere. "Well, I'd tell the truth to save Bucky's life. Isn't that true, Buckaroo?"

Buckaroo was upside down and his eyes blinked and his tail twitched, but that's all that moved. Whenever I looked at the dog, I thought of the map/crap theory. If the dog ever got diarrhea, my dad will end up living in an ocean.

Another fib-filled story followed (punctuated by Kay's interjections from the kitchen) and I accepted that I would never have a truly serious conversation with my father, would probably never get to know things beyond that he loved catfish, was a staunch Republican who admired Ronald Reagan but worshipped Johnny Cash, had found God, loved anything fried but especially okra, adored his dog Bucky, and would do anything to be rid of the diabetes that ran in his family.

Maybe that was enough, and I would have to be content for moments like this. I got up and sat so close to dad we were touching. I patted his hand and asked, "So, Dad, what do ya'll do in Historic Fort Gibson besides fish and fight off the skeeters?"

Chapter Seventy-Two

The riverside property in Plain held precious memories so it was with great reluctance that Mom decided to sell it, but at seventy it was becoming far too difficult for her to keep up. After a long, thoughtful search, she fell in love with a builder's custom rambler in Wenatchee that was blocks away from the senior center. She moved into her new home in the winter of 1996, when I was still in Montrose, and just days before a surprise ice storm paralyzed Puget Sound and sent insurance claims soaring.

Once I was back home in Washington, I was eager to see Mom's new house and accompanying me on the trip to Wenatchee were Patty and Bree. In the car heading east, I filled them in on Montrose.

"Montrose was a hick town full of taverns and Mexican restaurants. They had a Wal-Mart but the nearest mall was sixty miles away and across the most uninteresting land on earth. Occasionally you'd see antelope sprinting about, and tumbleweeds, but mostly the view was of shacks and high desert. Right outside Grand Junction was an ostrich farm. I never saw any ostriches but I hear they taste just like chicken."

Brianna moaned. "Ick. That's why I'm a vegetarian."

Patty turned to her daughter in the backseat and replied dryly, "I thought you were a vegetarian because Rachel is a vegetarian?"

"No, that's not why." Brianna rolled her eyes. "And Rachel says she's a vegetarian but I saw her eat Buffalo wings once. Anyway, I seriously don't believe in eating innocent animals." She muttered, "Ostrich? That's totally disgusting."

I said, "Yes, but Ostrich farm was a good sign. That meant I was close to Grand Junction, and some good shopping. They didn't have a Nordstrom at the mall, but they had a Dillard's." I looked over at my sister, "So, just how pink is Mom's new house?"

"Extremely pink," my sister answered. "Pink with a capitol P."

I laughed. "I'll bet it wasn't as pink as my house in Montrose."

Brianna said, "Gramma's kitchen floor is pink, the countertops are pink, the carpet is pink, the wallpaper is pink, and the toilet is even pink, I think."

Patty giggled. "But it's gorgeous. Wait till you see her backyard, Nance. It's like a park it's landscaped so beautifully." She was leaned back in the front passenger seat with her long, thin legs stretched out on the dash. The scars on her left ankle were still visible, twenty-five years after her trampoline accident. In cold weather, my sister limped from the arthritis that had developed there, but but that didn't stop her and Tom from buying a trampoline for Bree's sixteenth birthday.

"I'm done with yard work. That's why this condo will be perfect."

Patty bit into another Hot Tamales candy, a staple of her diet. "I am *so* glad you decided to look for your own place. I've been worried about you and Ray. He's so jealous, and you don't seem all that happy. Sometimes, I wonder if you are with him because you feel sorry for him."

As soon as the conversation turned to Ray, I tightened my grip on the wheel. Patty's comments reminded me of another theory: That our mother mixed up the birth order of her two oldest daughters. The clues supporting this were hardly cryptic: The oldest was supposed to be more responsible and levelheaded, but these attributes didn't fit me, they fit happily married, supposedly second child Patty with her adoring husband and mostly well-behaved children. Patty would never end up in *two* messed-up relationships. Even sister Sue, the prone-to-misfortune middle child, hadn't fared so poorly in love as I had, though there were hints she and Steve were having trouble.

I looked over and answered, "Our relationship is complicated."

"Well, it shouldn't be. Love should be simple and trusting."

The comment made me think about a "Dear Abby" column I had read in which Abby told her reader, "Faithful in Fort Worth" (whose fiancé was constantly accusing her of having affairs because he had a "gut feeling") that she had described a man who was a potential abuser, whose actions were obsessive and controlling and would only get worse. She advised Faithful to get out of the relationship *fast*. I clipped the article but at the time did little else. Now, however, I was shopping for an affordable condo, a safe haven where I could retreat when things got rough. More importantly, it would be a place where my shit would never be thrown out the front door unless I did it myself.

I said to Patty, "I keep thinking Ray will change."

"Hair styles change. Men don't."

I shared my birth-order theory. "I think Mom got us mixed up. *You're* the oldest who's got her act together. It could easily have happened: We were born in the same hospital in the same city in the same state."

Patty closed the jumbo-sized box of Hot Tamales and grabbed her box of Milk Duds. "Yeah, *fourteen* months apart."

"To Mom, that probably seemed like fourteen minutes in all the chaos. In any case, you definitely popped out first and Mom got confused." I paused. "Patty? How on earth do you stay so skinny on a diet of junk food? I have to constantly diet just to maintain, little good it's doing me."

"Aunt Nancy," Brianna said as she leaned between her mother and me, "you are not fat, but if you want to lose some weight, maybe you can channel your inner anorexic like my friend Rachel?"

Patty and I were still laughing when we hit Wenatchee, where I turned up Maple Street, onto Elmwood Lane, and into the driveway of a beautiful rambler with a wide porch and brick accents. From that porch, Mom was waving and next to her was an elderly woman. We got out of the car and I gave my Mother a long, tight hug. I had missed her the most of all.

"Welcome home, honey." She stepped back and acknowledged the tiny woman next to her. "Girls, this is Jamaica. She was going to come shopping with us but has to go."

Jamaica nodded and despite it being summer pulled a blue sweater across her frail bosom. "I have a doctor's appointment in twenty minutes and still haven't picked up Henry's prescriptions, or my grandson's birthday gift." She reached into a navy clutch and retrieved a carefully folded piece of stationery as well as a pair of glasses. She put the glasses on and unfolded the paper. Peering down, she read, "Nathan asked for a CD, something called Third Eye Blind or Backstreet Boys. Goodness, what ever happened to decent band names?"

Brianna said, "Those are awesome groups. Your grandson has good taste in music."

"Good taste but deplorable grades. It's his 16ᵗʰ birthday and since he's my only grandson, I spoil him. The problem is every store I've been to is sold out of—" Jamaica glanced down at her list, "—Blind Boys. You know, in *my* day a child asked for normal things like books and bikes, but no, Nathan has to ask for the one thing Wenatchee doesn't have."

Brianna asked, "Have you tried Camelot Records? They carry all the number one CDs with great prices."

"Oh?" Jamaica's eyes widened as she removed her reading glasses. "I know where that is, by the Sears. You know, I was just at Sears. Got a great deal on a girdle. Anyway, thank you, young lady!" She turned to Mom, "Lois, have fun shopping and I'll see you Monday."

They watched Jamaica, whose skin was paler than beach sand, totter to the sidewalk with a pronounced limp wearing what looked like orthopedic shoes. Brianna asked, "Did Jamaica hurt her leg?"

Mom replied, "She had knee replacement surgery last fall. Poor Jamaica has more plastic parts then Barbie. She had her hip done last year *and* she has a pacemaker. But she gets around. She only lives a few blocks away and walks everywhere since she doesn't drive."

"Enough about Jamaica, Mom. I want a tour of the inside of your pink house."

"For heavensakes, it's not that pink."

Well, the interior of Mom's house wasn't *that* pink, it was more muted mauve with splashes of white zinfandel. Later over lunch, Mom told us she had a dream about Jamaica.

"Your friend or the resort?" Bree asked.

"My friend. We were at the thrift shop trying to price this god awful blue-and-yellow polka-dot dress when all of a sudden things started shaking and rattling and then a shelf holding appliances broke and fell right on top of me. The next thing I know, I'm falling backwards and land in a canoe in the river."

I asked, "Where's Jamaica?"

Brianna joked, "It's in the Caribbean. Duh."

Patty tilted her head towards her only daughter. "You know where Jamaica is but you can never seem to find the washing machine though it's been in the same spot for six years?"

"Very funny, mother."

I asked again, "Did Jamaica fall with you?" Dream details fascinated me. My own "dream-mares" were worthy of neuropsychiatric scrutiny and like Mom's dream, always involved a body of water of some kind.

"No, it was just me and Bob in the canoe."

"Bob?" We all asked simultaneously. "Bob was there?"

Mom nodded, "Yes, and he was wearing that old red belt. Then the canoe flipped and before I could save him, I woke up."

We all grimaced. One spring while canoeing, they flipped and Bob had become lodged under a submerged log. Luckily, with Mom's help, he was able to set himself free. Surprisingly, the experience didn't hamper further canoe trips.

Patty asked, "Does the red belt still fall on its own?"

"It hasn't in a while, not since Christmas, but I know he's still around."

"Gramma, did Grampa really want to come back as a hawk?"

"Yes, Breezy." Mom reached for her glass of iced tea. "The day he died, a red-tailed hawk flew right over my head and landed on the barn and just sat there watching. I know it was Bob."

I smiled and reached for my mother's hand. My family was fixated on reincarnation, beginning with my maternal grandparents, Georgia and Thomas Taylor, who both claimed they would come back as spiders. This was the reason none of us ever, ever stepped on spiders. I *liked* spiders, especially after I heard there was a Ukrainian legend that if a spider builds a web in your Christmas tree, good luck will follow all year long. Too bad I hadn't known about that legend years ago; I would have collected spiders by the bucket and let them loose around my Christmas trees.

Patty said, "Well, it's Bob's red belt falling for no reason that gives me goose bumps."

"I know." Mom's eyes watered. "Bobby does other things, too. Sometimes I will hear a cupboard open and close, but when the red belt falls, I know Bobby is here."

I nodded sadly. "Bobby" had been wearing a red belt with a blue suit at our last Christmas together. The red belt was his favorite but it didn't match the suit. In fact, the belt was old and frayed and should have been given to the Salvation Army, but Bob loved that old belt. Now, the red belt hangs on a hook next to our mother's maple dresser and every once in a while it drops to the floor for no reason whatsoever. Just drops, like Bob is trying to let Mom know that even in heaven he still likes that red belt, so of course she'll never part with it.

Like Patty, the story gave me goose bumps, but it also gave me hope. I hoped I would be reincarnated as Ray's therapist.

Chapter Seventy-Three

After numerous setbacks, I finally signed the closing papers on my new top-floor, end-unit luxury condo near Boeing in South Everett (that I bought for $105,000) on August 29, 1997. The next day, with Ray, Patty, and Tom's help, I moved my belongings into the unit in the late afternoon, which wasn't the plan but there was a truck rental snafu. In any case, things worked out, and after Ray and Tom left to attend to more important matters, Patty and I unpacked every box. Three hours later, it looked like I had lived there for years. My bed was neatly made, and there were pictures on the walls and towels in the cupboards. This may seem a bit fanatical and definitely Martha Stewartish, but that's what moving every other year of your life does to a person: It makes you extremely organized. My mother had refused to live out of boxes even with five kids, and now so did those same children. The only things I was missing were a working phone and cable hookup to my T.V.

At 10:00 that evening, After Patty went home, I poured a glass of wine and sat in my living room and admired my new, freshly paint-scented surroundings. There was a view of the mountains from an alcove window above my fireplace, as well as the balcony, which I knew Lily would love, if she ever came out from under my bed, and a greenbelt below. In addition to two full bathrooms, the kitchen had Pergo floors, white cabinets with brass fixtures, and tile countertops. Everything was white and crisp. Best of all, it was *mine.*

Ray, a talented carpenter himself, hadn't been that impressed with the carpentry finish work, or the builder's specs, but I suspected his criticisms and nitpicking were more a show of annoyance that I had chosen to get my own place rather than live with him in his house in Duvall, which had been rented out while he was in Montrose. He wondered if it meant we were breaking up, and I assured him that wasn't the case, that I still loved him but I needed my space. It was a mixed message but I meant what I said, keeping in mind "love" to me meant many things, including misery, until Patty pointed out that if you're happily in love, you *share* your space.

Patty was not a big Ray fan and had been trying to convince me to get out of the relationship. She reminded me of the ugly fight we had at her house a few weeks before I found my condo, when Ray discovered that I had donated his skis to the Salvation Army in Montrose, which I had thought were junk. I said I was sorry, repeatedly, and pointed out to Ray that he did tell me—and this is a quote—get rid of all that junk in the garage so we don't have to move it. So I piled all the junk up from the garage, including the aforementioned skis (K2 Four's with Marker bindings that cost a thousand dollars, or so Ray said), which in my defense were covered with dust and grime and standing amidst a pile of torn tents, rusted tools, and a Simpsons backpack of questionable color. Something plopped in a garage corner and being used to hang greasy work jackets, in my book, met the criteria for junk, and who in their right mind would pay a thousand dollars for two skinny slabs of fiberglass?

Ray later apologized, especially after I offered to submit a bogus homeowner's claim to my insurance company for the brazen theft of a pair of very expensive blue and white alpine skis with top-of-the-line binders.

After my insurance company paid the claim—and promptly dropped me—I started shopping for condos.

Chapter Seventy-Four

Seated in the darkness of the Duvall Tavern, I was thinking the bar hadn't changed that much over the years, and neither had its owner, Bricks. The good thing was that Bricks—whose eyesight was poor on account of diabetes—didn't recognize me. Nevertheless, Ray and I were seated far from the pool table at a booth near the front door, and I wondered if I was going to pull off acting like a biker babe. Probably not, I concluded after a quick survey of the tavern, which had become a biker's hangout and was filled with tattooed, tough-looking men *and* women in denim and leather. I needed some biker tips from Patty, who in her heyday had been Tom's bodacious blond biker babe, but my sister didn't even know about the Harley, or the fact Ray and I were back together after a six-month breakup. Mom didn't know either, and I hoped to keep it that way.

Ray immediately began smoking while I tried to relax. I felt completely out of place in a fitted black lambskin leather jacket worn over slim-fit Calvin Klein jeans with a magenta sweater. I was also wearing black leather boots, full makeup, and my freshly foiled blond highlights were pulled back in a silver clip. You'd never know I had done a farm girl spell in Colorado two years prior.

I looked up as the waitress approached and smiled sweetly. "Hi."

She shrugged. "What can I get you folks?" The woman asking was probably in her late twenties but looked forty and wore a bandana on her head. She was built like a box and her midriff spilled over Levis four sizes too tight. Her teeth were the color of a beige crayon.

"Bud Light in a bottle, no glass," Ray ordered before he excused himself to use the restroom.

The waitress used her tongue to pick at a brown front tooth and asked wearily, "And you?"

I continued to smile nervously at bandana girl. Every ounce of me knew I should order a beer because that's what biker babes drank, but the words came from habit, "Chardonnay, please."

The server brought penciled eyebrows together, "Chardonnay?"

"Yes, your house Chardonnay will be fine." It would probably taste like it was fermented in rusted tin cans, but beer tended to bloat me up and my jeans were already tight. White wine was what I drank.

The woman glanced back at the bar and back at me. "Is that wine?"

Nervously, I answered, "Yes."

"White or red?"

"Never mind, I'll have beer." Do you have Amstel Lite?"

"No." She pointed to the bar, behind which Bricks was pouring a draught beer. "That's what we have."

I didn't bother looking at the bar's selection and ordered, "Bud Light *with* a glass." After she walked away, I glanced over at Ray's motorcycle. It was a Harley Heritage Softail Classic parked in the street and in full view from where we were seated. The bike was the color of a glazed pumpkin, and had been purchased brand-new during our breakup earlier in the summer. Now, we were barely two weeks into our newest reconciliation and things were going well, but bubbling below the surface and too close for comfort were years of umbrage, and our relationship had entered a desperate stage. That's why I had agreed to ride on the back of his Harley, just for the fun of it. Naturally, we ended up in bed. Unbelievably satisfying makeup sex was all we had going for us. Really, if Ray invested as much time and energy into improving other aspects of his life—including his interpersonal and work relationships—as he did with sex, he would be eveyone's best friend.

Ray returned just as our drinks were delivered. I poured the Bud into a glass and commented, "This biker thing is going to take some getting used to." I fingered the tube of Lancome lipstick in my pocket, feeling pretty sure biker babes did not worry about whether their lips were chapped and pale.

Ray shrugged. "Riding will be more comfortable when the chrome backrest gets in. I also ordered a better windshield package and a leather knapsack. Those should be here next week."

There was a glow to Ray now that he owned a Harley. Or was it sticker-shock? I joked, "So, now that you have a Harley, are you going to get a bunch of tattoos and join the Burritos?"

Ray dipped his balding head so he was peering over his glasses. "I think you mean the Banditos."

"I guess," I sipped my Bud, "but it doesn't matter because I have a feeling I wouldn't fit in." I looked at Ray, who had taken up smoking in Montrose and had yet to quit, and thought he seemed different somehow. We'd only been apart for six months but I had a feeling he had done things in that time I wouldn't want to know about.

Ray shrugged. "You might need to take Bikers 101. Hey, I saw Dylan and Corinne the other day at Bellevue Square. Corinne is still tan and thin as a rail."

"Really? So they're still together. That's nice."

"They said Tim calls drunk on his ass every once in a while from Las Vegas. That's where he lives now."

I nodded. "I know, Angie told me." I was nervous talking about this part of our past with Ray, and stood to use the restroom when the tavern's front door swung open. With it came a sweep of cold October air and a trail of golden-red leaves. I tightened my leather jacket (the fringeless kind) around my shoulders and watched a friend of Ray's named Nick saunter in, holding a black and gold helmet.

Nick acknowledged me with a dip of his head and placed a quarter on the table. He asked Ray, "Game of pool?"

"Sure, Nick." Ray removed his own leather jacket and set it on the back of his chair before rolling up the sleeves of his flannel shirt. Pool was business and Ray aimed to win. I hoped he did or else the night was ruined.

On the toilet, I pulled out the tube of lipstick and quickly applied a layer without benefit of a mirror. Back at our table, I was studying the tavern's interior, when my eyes caught a large glass jar on the bar. "Pickled Pigs Feet," the sign said, "Fifty Cents Each." Being in the tavern reminded me of Tim, who was someone else's problem now, that person being his fourth wife, Maryanne. From what I heard, Tim hadn't changed much and was still intefering in business that wasn't his, just to stir things up. Sadly, but not surprisingly, he was estranged from his son, Mark, who was rumored to be living in Loganville, Georgia, with his wife.

The memories were making me melancholy and I turned away from the pigs' feet and watched Ray and Nick play pool instead. When I saw that Ray was losing, my heart sank.

Chapter Seventy-Five

Working the 3:00 to 11:00 p.m. shift at the Northgate Office of University of Washington Medical Center's Patient Data Services put me in a constantly foul mood, and seeking revenge against Trixi Greene was frequently on my mind. I had no plan, other than hope that Trixi got a nasty fungal infection under her acrylic nails that morphed into flesh-eating bacteria, which quickly attacked her lower extremities making shoes a non-necessity. Trixi shoeless brought a rare smile to my face.

The transcription at U.W.M.C. was technically and technologically challenging, made even worse by a majority of dictators who spoke English as a second language. On top of that, I felt demoted because as a recent hiree I was at the bottom of the totem pole, even as qualified as I was. When I had been with the University for ninety days, full benefits kicked in and I sought professional help to deal with what I termed job-related depression. It was September of 1999, and the day of my first therapy appointment was gray, cold, and rainy. Because of the inclement weather, I wore a khaki London Fog raincoat over trousers and a cashmere-blend sweater. Walking into the clinic, I was full of confidence that a few sessions would "cure" my depression. I filled out the insurance paperwork, wrote a check for the co-pay, and five minutes later, was called through a door.

Dr. Patricia Warrick, licensed psychologist with a special interest in women's issues, pointed me to a burgundy leather sofa. She pointed, "Please get comfortable."

I sat demurely, hands folded. There were numerous framed prints of cats decorating the walls of her office, which was lit by a lone banker's-style lamp with a green-glass shade on a table in the corner, creating a calming mood. I said, "You have a lovely office. You must like cats."

"Yes. So what brings you here, Nancy?"

I sat back, fully relaxed, and said, "Well, it's not a big problem. It's just that I guess I'm depressed, mostly about my job. You see, I'm unhappy working for the University. I thought it would be challenging, and it is. Unfortunately, the pay is ten percent below what I was making at my last job. The only good thing is I get to work from home. I love working at home because my cat can sit on my lap."

"Oh, that's nice."

"I know! Her name is Lily. She's black and was white, and I adopted her from P.A.W.S. as a kitten. She was my divorce gift to myself. Once she hid in my refrigerator, but I found her right away. She is *so* cute."

Dr. Warrick nodded. She was tall, thin, and clear-skinned and looked more like a ballerina than a psychologist. Her expression didn't change and she didn't look all that interested in my cat. I watched as she jotted something down and glanced back up. "Why don't you change jobs?"

So much for a breezy discussion about cats. "Well, I just started it after losing my prior job at a hospital because they outsourced. I've had four jobs in as many years because I just can't find my niche, ever since I lost the best job of my career thanks to a woman named Trixi. Because of her, the company went under." The anger over that situation lingered and I felt my stomach tighten.

Dr. Warrick replied, "That's too bad." A brief silence followed before she asked point-blankly, "Is your job situation all that's bothering you?"

I replied, "Yes." Despite the office's calming atmosphere, inside I was panicking. *How can she know that there is so much more bothering me? That I feel like a tornado in a hurricane, or that I'm sinking in quicksand?*

"Are you sure? I get the sense there is something else you want to talk about."

I inhaled, realizing I had underestimated Dr. Warrick. I really didn't want to open up a can of worms, but then again, therapy wasn't cheap. I began, "Well, since you asked, it's my boyfriend. We fight constantly but I can't seem to get out of the relationship. Every time I break up with him or try to leave, Ray's a mess."

"Oh?"

"Yeah. He starts crying and begging, the whole nine yards. The problem is Ray is extremely insecure and insanely jealous. When we were living in Montrose, Colorado, he accused me of having an affair with a buddy on his pool team, who was married. It wasn't true but Ray wouldn't believe me. We even went to couples' counseling, and eventually individual counseling, but it didn't help."

"Why not?"

The squirming worms were out, and my heart began pounding as another source of unresolved anger burst open with vigor. "Because I didn't see the damn point! I wasn't the one who had issues with insecurity so I wasn't eager to spend hard-earned money on counseling. The last straw was when Ray came home from one of his private sessions and told me that Dr. Ballinger told him that I admitted to her that I really *was* having an affair with Pete! Of course no therapist would ever breech confidentiality by revealing what she and another client discussed, and besides that, it wasn't true! I immediately called Dr. Ballinger, who confirmed she didn't tell Ray anything such thing. When I told Ray this, he accused us of conspiring against him! Ray is seriously messed up when it comes to trusting women."

"But you are still with him."

I stammered, "Well, yeah. That's another problem. I have a hard time letting go. Actually, I have a problem saying no."

"Can you elaborate?"

"Well, even when I know I should say no, I don't. I just dig myself deeper into bad situations. With Ray, the problem is our past. It's kind of a long story but he saved my life after I had an affair with my husband's best friend." I took a breath. "So, you see, it's not all Ray's fault. I'm not a saint. Just ask my ex-husband." I shook my head sadly. "I don't have much luck with men; they're either alcoholics or control freaks, or married. Sometimes all three."

Dr. Warrick dug through a file and handed over a form. "I'm not a label person. I think applying labels like 'alcoholic' and 'control freak' actually perpetuates a behavior and gives people excuses to behave they way they do. In other words, labels distract from the healing process and are counterproductive."

I managed, "Oh, I see." I looked down at the form. "What's this?"

"That's a self-esteem questionnaire. Let's start there."

"Okay, but I'm sure I'll flunk it," I was half-joking but my therapist didn't even grin. I finished the questionnaire and handed it over, where of twenty questions I answered "yes" to eighteen. Dr. Warrick didn't flunk me, at least not out loud, but did suggest we might want to meet *weekly* rather than every other week.

At our second session, I inadvertently admitted to my therapist that I was obsessed with my weight (or more accurately being thin). That day I hit the scale at a whopping 116 pounds. It had ruined my morning and driven me to tears. "I haven't weighed this much since my college pudding-and-grinder days."

"Do you think you're fat?"

"Well, not fat, but plump." I was convinced "thin white female in no acute distress" no longer applied. I was definitely in acute distress and headed for obesity, something that was not allowed in my family. Fat was the enemy! I pulled my sweater over a perceived pouch and said, "I am always on a diet, but it gets harder and harder to maintain my weight." Keeping in mind my therapist disliked labels, I did not describe my earlier eating patterns as anorexic, nor did I reveal that I wished I *still* was anorexic and could live on Diet Coke and saltines alone. Instead I danced around the issue. "I used to be really thin." *Not eating does that.*

Dr. Warrick tilted her head and replied, "Looking at you, you appear to be within the range of ideal weight for a woman your age and height."

I don't want to be within the range of ideal. I want to be far below it. I want to be runway model/ drug-addict skinny! "I know, but I feel better about myself when I'm really skinny. It's an image thing. I used to be called a waif and liked that role."

"It's hard to accept our changing bodies as we age, but many times to do that we need to work on building self-esteem first. I believe your body image issues, as well as your inability to say no and let go, are both related to this issue, so I suggest we work on that. To start, I am going to give you some assignments to help."

I shrugged. "Sure, you're the doctor."

That night, I went home and per doctor's orders began to practice saying no. After a few "no's" to my cat, which Lily faithfully ignored, the doorbell rang. It was a fifth grader selling cookie dough to raise money for her school. She was quite a little salesgirl and had clearly rehearsed her pitch, apologizing right off the bat that the cookie dough was nine dollars but emphasizing the product was frozen and came in a bucket.

Brown hair pulled back in a headband, the little girl explained, "This way you can make cookies at your convenience, plus the proceeds go to a really good cause: Our field-trip to the Olympic Peninsula to see the rain forest!" She paused as she consulted a list. "I have these popular flavors available: Macadamia White Chocolate Chip, Peanut Butter, Toffee, Sugar, and Regular Chocolate Chip."

It took every ounce of strength and willpower, but I sent the child away without a sale and closed my front door. It was a baby step, and maybe tomorrow I'd be able to say no to a telemarketer selling circus tickets to benefit underprivileged children, or no to Ray.

Chapter Seventy-Six

One week after my forty-third birthday, I was on my way to my therapist's office and the last things on my mind were my weight or my job. What *was* on my mind was that I was a pathetic, ugly mess who, if seen in my current condition by Tim or Melanie, had gotten exactly what I deserved. I checked the rear-view mirror again but nothing had changed since I left my condo: My face still looked like a prizefighter's after the ninth round, and I was drooling. Fifteen minutes later, seated behind the cherry doors of Dr. Warrick' office, I began bawling. I had intended to lie, but that's not what happened.

Dr. Warrick gasped, "Oh dear! What happened to your face?" Her own angular face was filled with concern. "Were you in an accident?"

"No. Ray…he punched…me." It was painful to move my jaw and difficult to talk through such swollen lips. Inside my mouth, the tissue was ragged and bruised. I hadn't lost any teeth, thank God. I reached for a tissue and blew my nose.

Dr. Warrick handed me the whole box of Kleenex. "Tell me what happened, Nancy."

"We had another fight, but this is the first time…Ray has ever…" my words came in hiccups, "…hit me…last Saturday night. We started arguing about Nick, one of Ray's biker friends…and things got out of hand. He said I was flirting...with Nick and wouldn't shut up...so I slapped him. Then he...punched me." I allowed minutes to pass, long enough to gather my thoughts and continue without babbling. "That night I was being a wiseass, I admit, because I was still mad about my birthday. That day, Ray walked out of the restaurant and left me alone for almost an hour because of something I said."

"That's very rude."

"He's not the first one to leave me at restaurant. Tim did that more than once. I probably hold the record for the number of times I've been abandoned by my date at a restaurant."

If she was surprised I could joke at such a time, Dr. Warrick didn't acknowledge it. I said, "Ray is *so* sorry about hitting me. He hasn't stopped crying since it happened. I feel so bad about the whole thing." I bent my head into the tissues, ashamed to look up. At that moment, all I wanted to do was crawl into a hole and never see the light of day.

She asked in disbelief, "Do you think it's *your* fault that Ray hit you?"

"Well, sort of." I massaged my bruised cheek with one hand and fondled the neck of my black turtleneck with the other. It was an outfit chosen to cover the yellow-green fingerprint marks on my throat. I don't remember Ray choking me; all I remember was waking on top of his bed laying the wrong way with a baggie of ice near my face. When I later looked into the mirror, the face that appeared was unrecognizable and had chipmunk cheeks. Looking up, I explained, "I *did* break Ray's glasses when I slapped him. They were new glasses."

My therapist's eyes widened and she wrote something down. She asked, "Did you report this to the police?"

Now my eyes widened. It never occurred to me to call the police, especially since we had both been drinking. By then, I knew the drinking was a problem, a huge problem, because no matter how much I drank, it wasn't enough to fill the emptiness or numb the pain. Maybe if I'd been a pill popper and a vodka drinker, things would have been different. I managed quietly, "No. I did not call the police."

"Did you at least seek medical attention?"

"Oh, of course. I saw my primary care doctor and had a CT scan. Nothing's broken, although I have a concussion and a hematoma inside my gum." Not to mention an eye that was swollen shut and choke marks down my neck.

"So you told your doctor what happened?"

I choked, "Not exactly." Actually, I told my doctor I was in a car accident when my boyfriend swerved to avoid hitting a puppy and my face hit the stick shift. I was proud of the make-believe story and of the sympathy it would evoke. Nevertheless, I told my mother a different story: That I had food poisoning from bad Mexican food, and couldn't make it over for the senior center's annual bazaar. It was a complex web of lies I was spinning and pretty soon I'd need a palm pilot to keep the stories straight.

"You lied to your own doctor?"

"Well, yes. I didn't think it mattered." My tongue played with the hematoma in my left cheek, already hardening from calcification. "What difference does it make? Ray said he's sorry. He even called in sick to work for two days because he's so upset."

"So you've told no one the truth?"

"Just you, and I hadn't plan on doing that. In fact, I was going to cancel my appointment, but at the last minute changed my mind. The whole way here I was trying to think of a good fib to tell you about what happened." The admission was pathetic, and ironically the truth.

Dr. Warrick held her pen at the ready, no doubt mentally planning to schedule me on the books for *years* of weekly sessions. "I think it's significant that you *did* show up and that you are being honest. It's a call for help." She paused and added with trained frankness, "Have you always had such difficulty telling the truth?"

I flinched. "Well, yes, but I don't lie to hurt people. I lie to protect them." Judging by her expression, I could tell Dr. Warrick wanted to smother me with a Get-Real Blanket, or call Dr. Phil for an emergency intervention. It wasn't the first time I had gotten that look. Sheepishly, I added, "That's just the way I am."

"Do you realize that's highly self-destructive behavior?"

I bristled in confusion. "How is protecting other people's feelings self-destructive?"

The doctor evaded the question and asked, "Are you familiar with the term 'de-selfing'?"

"No, but I've heard of detaching. I read that in an Al-Anon book."

"De-selfing is actually much different than detaching. De-selfing is forsaking one's own worth for another person, basically giving up one's identity as an individual. It most often occurs in people who lack self-esteem."

In other words, Blue Angel Syndrome. "Well, I can't help but put other people ahead of me. I'm just not a selfish person."

Dr. Warrick replied, "Not being honest could be considered selfish, don't you think? It undermines trust."

I answered uneasily, "I guess."

"In fact, not being honest in relationships leads to a great deal of resentment and anger, especially in intimate relationships." The therapist reached for her briefcase. "I'd like to give you an assignment: You must confide in one person about what happened. Someone you trust, like your sister. You speak highly of her."

"Patty? Why would I tell her this?" I was shocked by such a thought; I could never, ever do that in a million years! "No, I just can't tell my sister. It's over and done what happened. No one needs to hear the ugly details now. Besides, Patty would tell her husband Tom and then it will get back my mother." Upsetting Mom was something I avoided at all costs; she'd been through enough.

"How about a close friend? You've mentioned a coworker named Trish several times."

"No." My mind was made up. "I just can't."

"Well, please think about it. By the way, are you now safe?"

"Safe?"

"Yes, in light of what has happened, I would suggest you take measures to protect yourself from becoming a further victim of domestic violence."

Hearing the term "domestic violence" applied to me was like being kicked in the gut. How humiliating! I straightened. "Of course I feel safe. My brother Bill lives with me and I know Ray won't ever lay a hand on me again. If you could see how sorry he was, you'd know." The statistics suggested otherwise, especially since Ray's issues with anger were deep-seated and longstanding, and destined to emerge. Once again I thought about Melanie. Ray had hit her, I was sure.

Dr. Warrick glanced at her watch. "Our time is up today, but please think about my assignment. You will be surprised how liberating the truth is."

I drove home, locked my bedroom door, and crawled into bed. When Bill came home from work, he knocked softly on my door to check on me, since being in bed at 7:00 p.m. was unusual, even for me. I muttered from under my comforter that I had the flu. One more lie would hardly matter.

What I did next epitomized the kind of logic only a Blue Angel would use, but it was the only thing I felt I could do: I left my brother a note that I was spending the nights at Ray's house to baby-sit Reba all week long, so not to worry if he didn't see me. It made sense to me because Ray was the one person I didn't need to hide my face from. I also felt completely safe. He was paralyzed by remorse, and I expected, and got, the royal treatment.

I had planned to stay at Ray's until the bruises along my jaw had faded to a greenish-yellow that could be concealed with good makeup. Every night, Reba—a Blue Angel herself—sat behind me on Ray's bed and massaged my neck or played with my hair, all the while talking about boys. Whenever we chatted, it was usually about boys, and Ray had reason to be worried about his youngest daughter's growing interest in the opposite sex. Reba had grown into a far-too-shapely and becoming 13-year-old girl who had no idea of the impact she had on men. More than once, I had caught a man my age doing a double take as Reba passed in a flirty outfit.

One night, as we passed the mirror in Ray's bedroom, both of us stopped and turned. In the mirror were two sets of blue eyes filled with secrets. Reba's gaze dropped to my puffed, yellow-green cheek before she turned to the real me.

"Nancy, I have something that will cover those bruises really good." Her tone was matter-of-fact. This was a child accustomed to high drama and dysfunction.

I asked, "Really?"

Reba nodded vigorously. "Oh yeah. This stuff covers my zits, even when they're the size of raisins. Come on to my room and I'll let you borrow it. I can also show you a picture of Brandon. He is so hot!"

I giggled but when I caught another glimpse of my reflection, I had to catch my breath. Looking at my disfigured face in the mirror, it was like déjà vu as I was hit with the sick realization that I was with another abusive man for the sake of his daughter. As it had been with Angie, who needed who more was uncertain.

The following week, at my next session with Dr. Warrick, I announced I had completed my assignment. "I know I said I could never do it, but I was watching *Dharma and Greg* and then all of a sudden, I picked up the phone and called Trish. We had coffee the next day and I spilled the beans."

Dr. Warrick said, "That took great courage. I'm very proud."

I added, "Trish said she wasn't surprised, which floored me. I feel like an idiot."

"Why?"

"Because Ray and I weren't fooling anyone. My mom tried to warn me about him, and even Trish tried to get me talk about Ray and what was going on, but I just couldn't open up. I was living with her after my divorce and we talked all the time, but never about me and Ray. I am very good at steering the conversation so it isn't about me."

"You're talking now, and that's important. You've broken the ice."

I agreed. "I also told my brother, Bill, who thought Ray was an ass *before* this happened. Bill walked over and hugged me." The poignancy of that moment combined with the ugliness of what happened with Ray had finally sunk in, and I began to sob. "I hate this whole ordeal and I hate that every time I fall in love it hurts! I especially hate hating the person I love!" I put my face into my hands, ashamed.

"If it hurts to love, it isn't love."

I looked up and asked through tears, "Then what is it? Insanity?" I wasn't kidding.

My therapist said, "It is easy to mistake love for other feelings: Insecurity, fear of the unknown, desire to change or control the other person, guilt, false sense of responsibility, even feeling sorry for someone. There is a wide range of motivators that keep someone in relationships that aren't always healthy."

All could apply to me, especially guilt. "If that's true, I want to change. I want to love for the right reasons, without it hurting me or them." I reached for my handbag and pulled out a folded piece of paper.

"Dr. Warrick? Do you think I'm a Blue Angel?"

"A blue angel?"

"Yes." I unfolded the paper and read the definition:

Blue Angel Syndrome: A pathological infatuation in which one partner in a relationship sacrifices themselves and their own best interests for the sake of the relationship.

"Oh, that kind of Blue Angel. I have read some articles about the subject, but as you know, I'm not a label person. Even if you are, there's hope." She paused and asked, "Does Ray know you told someone about what happened?"

"Yes, I told him. He's okay with it, sort of." Okay, not. Ray *claimed* he wasn't angry that I had told our dirty little secret to Trish Elliott, but I could tell that he was very mad, and that he sensed this was a turning point in our relationship. He admitted he was afraid the stronger I became through therapy, the weaker our relationship would get. He found his own therapist and asked me to once again go into couples' counseling, which he would pay for. I declined and he asked me an odd question: *Are you working on "us" in therapy or just "you"? You know I'm working on us.* I could tell he expected brownie points but it was an egocentric question, one rooted in self-preservation. I gave Ray my answer: *I'm working on my self-esteem and how to love without it hurting.*

Ray was flummoxed. His eyes watered and he once again asked for forgiveness. I knew what he was really asking for was exoneration and believed his repentant beseeching was just an act. I was right because almost immediately, our relationship fell back into its usual pattern of crisis-triggered collapse.

Chapter Seventy-Seven

Telling Trish turned out to be a pivotal point in psychotherapy. It was like the act of opening up had literally turned me upside down so all the crazy poison that was inside me was able to slowly drain out. Telling Trish somehow gave me permission to acknowledge that I was unhappy, and forced me to ask myself, why? And can I change that?

My therapist pointed out that a good place to begin was my childhood, and soon after my confession to Trish, I began exploring, and analyzing, the effects of my upbringing on my adulthood. It had been one of dysfunction, chaos, and constant change. My mother raised five kids mostly on her own as my father was always working at the air-control towers. When he was around, we walked on eggshells, and while there was abuse, it was never sexual. Mostly it was abuse in the form of fear, and if it hadn't been for my strong-willed mother, I dread to think how we would have ended up. Her intelligence and optimism, along with a keen sense of humor, made things tolerable even as we were uprooted nearly every year by Dad's so-called "transfers." I was born in Moline, Illinois, and by the time I got into therapy with Dr. Warrick, I had moved twenty-eight times over seven states. During that time, my family and I survived tornadoes and tarantulas, Hurricane Donna, hepatitis, a ghost sighting, a near-fatal trampoline accident, two near drownings, multiple fractures, and countless beatings. Last but not least, we survived Christmas, the biggest feat of all!

Given all this, it was not surprising in adulthood I would seek the same familiar chaos in my relationships with men, alternating between coddling and enabling the very behaviors I loathed. In essence, I was gravitating towards men just like Dad, and the pattern started with Stevie. The only normal man I had ever loved was Bill Vann, and I not only let him go but cheated on him with perverted Carl Callahan, a married man whose last act with me had derailed my life. It hadn't been rape, or *had* it? If nothing else, Carl had taken advantage of me and I probably wasn't his only young victim.

I was suddenly viewing past events in a different light, peeling away the obscure layers of my life until there was the raw, ugly truth.

Dr. Warrick explained, "The father/daughter relationship is one of the most complex and important. Its' dynamics shape us quite profoundly." She poised with pen at the ready. "You've told me your father was not a good father when you were growing up. Could you elaborate?"

I cringed. I felt like I would be betraying Dad by talking about him, and had to resist the urge to measure my words, keeping in mind sugarcoating the truth had never done me any good.

"Dad was physically and emotionally abusive. He ruled like a general and terrorized my family, especially my Mother." I paused. "He burned Mom's box of college memorabilia for no good reason and when I was seven, he held a gun to her head right before Christmas. I wet my pants because I thought he was going to shoot her." I was now sobbing.

Dr. Warrick allowed a great deal of time to pass so I could collect myself. She handed over the box of tissue paper and said softly, "That had to extremely traumatic for you."

I closed my eyes, reliving that horrible night that no one talked about. Through haggard breaths, I told her, "My mother was so calm and strong when it happened. She pushed Dad away and went to the kitchen to make dinner. We were having spaghetti. She told him if he shot her, who would make dinner?"

"Wow."

My heart was pounding as I told this story. I could feel the fear all over. "Dad went to get another drink and my sister Patty and I helped Mom with dinner. No one dared cry. We all pretended it didn't happen, even when Dad threw Patty's keepsake lamb against the Christmas tree and broke it." I paused to blow my nose once more. "It wasn't the only bad Christmas we had. Mostly they were all terrible. One Christmas Eve, when we lived in California, Dad walked out to see his mistress and didn't come home until the next night. Another time, he knocked over the Christmas tree and tossed some of the presents that were under it off the balcony."

As these words were spoken, I realized for the first time why I hated Christmas. That alone was worth therapy.

I continued, "You know the funny thing, Dr. Warrick? My family could easily have fractured and gone separate ways to forget the pain, yet we've all felt this strong need to remain close. None of us wallow is self-pity about our dysfunctional childhood. In fact, I don't consider it dysfunctional but more an adventure. Most of the time we look back and laugh. It's like all the bad things have made us all stronger."

She replied, "The past is what shapes us but it is the way we handle it that strengthens us."

"Then my family, especially my mother, is a made of steel." I looked up and said, "It may be surprising after what I've told you about my dad, but we have a good relationship now. He tells me he loves me and that he's sorry. I have no doubt my father wakes up filled with remorse every day. It's why he prays now. He's a changed man, or at least I think he is."

"That's amazing."

My eyes moistened. "You know, I love my mother and my father both, but there was a time when I thought I had to choose."

"Many children of divorced parents feel that way."

"I know, but I'm an adult. It seems silly to feel this way." I wiped my lumpy cheek. "There's something else I've realized. I keep hooking up with men who already have kids and are fixed so they can't have more. What do you make of that?"

Dr. Warrick tilted her head. "Well, what do *you* make of that?"

"I don't know. Maybe I want kids but don't want to go through the trouble of pregnancy and giving birth, or getting fatter. I know that is selfish. Anyway, it's probably too late." I paused. "See, I had an elective termination when I was twenty-one and now my uterus is lumpy. They think I have a condition called endometriosis. On top of that, I'm forty-three, so my ovaries aren't exactly spring chickens."

"Have you thought about adoption?"

I looked up. "Me adopt? I don't know. Besides, I think it's a phase anyway. Sometimes I think the only reason I want a baby is to dress her in really cute baby clothes. Every time I pass Baby Gap, I want to go in and buy a pair of infant booties to hang on my rear-view mirror. There is nothing cuter than pink baby shoes that can fit in your palm."

For the first time I could recall, Dr. Warrick, a mother herself, smiled. "I agree."

My last assignment, at a point where I was well on my way to recovery, was to read the series of "Dance" books by Harriet Lerner, Ph.D.: *The Dance of Anger, The Dance of Deception,* and *The Dance of Intimacy.* I picked them up at Half-Price Books and while poring over their contents, highlighted and underlined entire paragraphs. These books were all about me! Damn, Dr. Warrick was good!

The dreaded holidays arrived and, by choice, I spent them alone. Bill had met someone special named Colleen and was spending a lot of time with her, so I had the place to myself and used the solitude to focus on my personal journal, which I titled "The Emergence of Me." I started my journal, "Without self-esteem or a sense of worth, people settle, and I have definitely settled. It's time to put myself ahead of others."

In January, my Blue Angel was not buried but her days were numbered and that's when I permanently ended things with Ray Dickerson. (Drumroll please!) When he asked why I was breaking up with him, I told him I thought I could do better.

In April, that's exactly what I did.

Chapter Seventy-Eight

From my stool in the bar of the Red Robin Restaurant, I watched the downpour. It had been raining nonstop for twelve hours and the parking lot was a small lake. It was not surprising the bar was packed with patrons trying to keep dry. Some were watching the Sonics' basketball game on the various T.V.s scattered on high shelves throughout the bar, while others were socializing over drinks and appetizers. The place smelled heavenly and I quickly placed my order for a Banzai burger, along with a glass of chardonnay. I then pulled a notebook and mini-calculator from my briefcase to crunch some mortgage re-fi numbers.

Next to me, a young man stretched out his right hand and began shaking his wrist. I wasn't flirting but the "doctor" in me couldn't resist. I asked, "Carpal tunnel syndrome?"

The man turned and smiled. He looked in his late twenties and had beautiful blue eyes that twinkled. He replied, "I doubt it. I don't type and have never touched a computer in my life."

My jaw dropped in surprise. "Really? I live in front of my computer. In fact, I just got tested for carpal tunnel. The nerve conduction studies were negative, thankfully."

"Oh? I guess that's good." He lifted his mug of beer and took a sip. He was wearing a uniform, including navy pants and a short-sleeved gray shirt with the logo, "Miller Genuine." A few minutes passed and the Miller man excused himself to use the restroom and I absentmindedly turned my attention back to my notebook. The primary reason I couldn't refinance was the fact I had started a new job and their underwriters required at least two years at one job.

Damn! Double damn Trixi Greene and now-defunct PD! *That's* where the real trouble began, when Trixi the President forced hard-working employees out of good-paying jobs. True, that debacle was years ago but the resentment lingered. Since the company's demise, I had worked at various hospitals, including one that outsourced its entire transcription department to a company in Atlanta and gave their employees a choice: Come aboard "*a truly innovative company in meeting all your transcription needs*" called Transcend Services, Inc., or find other jobs. Transcend turned out to be a technical nightmare lacking consistent management, whose payroll system was complicated and unreliable.

The only positive experience was meeting another Transcend trainee who lived nearby and was as disenchanted with our field as me. Diane Stengler had worked for Overlake Hospital, which had also outsourced (or offshored, as it is sometimes called) and we both believed Transcend treated us like parts of an assembly line rather than human beings. My chosen career was losing its attractiveness and there was no question in my mind that eventually—perhaps in another decade or so—the job of medical transcriptionist would be replaced by voice-recognition technology. Occasionally I wondered what else I was good at, besides gourmet cooking, if I needed to find another job. The only thing that came to mind was hiding the truth and protecting the guilty. With such resume-building skills, I probably could have landed a job at Enron.

After working for Transcend for two months, I was behind in bills and borrowed money from my mother to pay my mortgage, but I knew my relationship with Transcend couldn't work because the company's constant changes in management and workflow had too big of an impact on my paycheck (and thus my lifestyle), so I applied for a job with the University of Washington Medical Center. Trish was working there and I accepted a third-shift position, eager to refinance my condo and get back on track. The saving grace in all of this was that my brother Bill was going to move in with me to help with expenses. He was going through a contentious divorce from Debi and was having his own work-related problems. *From adversity comes character*, we told each other. It also brings heartache and headache that does a good job of masking any character, but therapy was helping.

Mr. Miller man returned and began chatting amicably with the bartender, a pretty blond whom he seemed to know well. Eventually he turned my way again. "So, you said you type for a living?"

I closed my notebook and took a sip of Kendall-Johnson chardonnay. It tasted as smooth and creamy as butter but at seven dollars a glass, it would be my only one. "Yes, I'm a medical transcriptionist. I type medical reports. Plus, I'm writing a book." I left out the part that writing the book had come about through therapy.

He introduced himself as Dave and for the next two hours we chatted, mostly about his roommate's upcoming wedding, a lavish and expensive affair that was to occur that November. He told me there was a guest list of five hundred people.

"Five hundred? I could never go through such a production and would hate all that attention. I've been married once, but it was on a small boat and our guest list was even smaller." I paused and added, "He wasn't my family's favorite person of the year, but we're long divorced."

Dave shrugged. "I've never been married. I'm waiting for it to clobber me on the head."

I burst out laughing. Dave's sense of humor was so sweet and innocent, lacking any trace of sarcasm or cynicism. If therapy had taught me anything, it was to appreciate such qualities. At nine-thirty p.m., after Dave bought me another glass of wine, I glanced at the clock. "Oh my, it's way past my bedtime. I really need to go." I stood, handbag over my shoulder. "It was very nice talking to you, Dave." I turned to leave.

"Hey, Nancy?"

I was headed for the door and stopped and turned. "Yes?"

"What's the name of your book?"

I answered, "*Never, Ever Step on a Spider*. It's about my childhood but I changed the names. My family threatened to sue." I was joking, and Dave somehow knew that. He laughed politely and set his mug on the counter.

"Well, I was wondering? If you aren't seeing anyone, would you like to go out? Maybe we could drive over to Leavenworth for the day. You could tell me more about yourself."

I was completely caught off guard and blushed. The last thing on my mind was getting involved in a relationship, especially after what happened with Ray the night we were at the Duvall Tavern. Dave was also much younger, not necessarily a bad thing. I paused briefly and answered, "Sure, but do you know how old I am?"

Dave hesitated politely, "No but I don't—"

"Forty-three." Another lesson in therapy was to be upfront. There would be no more skeletons in my closet. Maybe be a glut of cute but impractical shoes and novelty handbags there, but no skeletons.

Dave smiled the kindest, most genuine smile I had ever seen. He said, "That don't matter to me if it don't matter to you."

How could I not give Dave my phone number? On the way home, I was so flustered about being asked out on a date by a thirty-year-old man, I locked my keys inside my car at the gas station and had to call AAA.

Chapter Seventy-Nine

Dave and I had our first date at Ivar's Restaurant in Mukilteo. Our seafood dinner at a table overlooking Puget Sound lasted three hours; the actual date lasted twelve.

After our third date, I was anxious to share with my family that I had met a normal guy. Bill was first on my list but I had to wait for him to return from Herriman, Utah, where he was visiting Mark and Darla. When he did, he walked into the condo wearing his baseball uniform and it was smudged with dirt. He explained that after the plane landed, he went directly to Kasch Field, where his softball team was playing in a tournament. Since his team had won, he was full of nervous energy, so my news would have to wait.

Bill showed a toothy grin and asked, "Guess what, sis?" He didn't wait for an answer. "You won't believe this story! Me and Mark are golfing, right? And we're on this eighteen-hole golf course outside West Jordan and we get paired up with these two older guys. It's really windy and they act like pros, but we know we're gonna kick some ass, and after we introduce ourselves, one of the guys asks, 'So, your name is Bill Nash? You don't have a father named Bill Nash do you by any chance?' and I look at Mark and then I say, 'Yeah, why?' and the guys both look at each other funny. One of them says, 'Was he chief air traffic controller at

O'Hare?' and we say 'yeah' and then you won't fuckin' believe this! These two guys are traffic controllers and say they used to work under a Bill Nash at O'Hare in the late eighties and said he was the meanest sonofabitch they ever met! I mean, here we are out in the middle of nowhere on a public fuckin' golf course and run into two guys who *know* Dad. All afternoon, we talked about some of the crazy shit Dad used to do. They thought he was six feet under by now."

"Wow, that's unbelievable. Are you going to tell Dad?"

Bill chuckled, "I already called him from my cell phone. Told him their names but Dad didn't remember them guys. 'Course, Dad don't remember much but he said it was probably all true, whatever they said." He grabbed a Pepsi from the fridge and said, "Why are you grinning so much? You look guilty."

Glad he finally noticed, I blurted girlishly, "No, *happy*. I met someone and he's really, really nice. We've been on three dates and are going out again tonight."

Bill's eyes got wide. "Nice?" He was skeptical, for good reason. "I thought you said after you and Ray broke up that you were never dating again?

"I know." Actually what I had said, to my entire family at an April Fool's BBQ at Patty and Tom's, was that I was never, ever dating again and was perfectly content living alone with my cat, Lily. Besides, who needed men when the Love Pantry sold battery-operated special buddies for under twenty bucks? The prospect of spinsterhood had not looked all that bad in the harsh light of my reality.

I smiled at my brother. "I did say that and believe me, I wasn't looking. Anyway, you'll meet Dave tonight. He's only thirty, and when I told him I was forty-three, he didn't bat and eye and said, 'That don't matter to me if it don't matter to you!' Is that not the cutest thing?"

"Sure, sis, if you say so."

I gushed, "Bill, this is the best part: Dave has no baggage! He's never been married, has no kids or ex-wives, and has been at the same job for twelve years. His parents are still married and live right up the street from my condo. And you won't believe this! Lily jumped on his lap. Lily, my neurotic cat who's afraid of ladybugs and falling paper, sauntered in and didn't bother sniffing him out. She just jumped on his lap!" I didn't mention I did the same thing.

Bill's jaw dropped. "No way!"

"Way! Bill, I think he's my lobster!" *Sorry, Phoebe. I know that's your line.*

Bill put down his Pepsi and gave me a bear hug. "Wow, that's unbelievable! Lily hid under the bed a full eight hours after the cable guy was here, and she hissed at Ray."

"I know. You're the only male on earth she's ever liked, but now she's given her stamp of approval to Dave. I should send my therapist a thank-you card!"

Bill nodded, "I'm so happy for you. You deserve it."

"Thanks." I leaned against the counter, facing my sweet brother. He may have looked like our father but he had the heart and soul of our mother, and was not only a brother and roommate, but my friend. The arrangement had brought us closer when others warned it would do the opposite. I sighed, "And here it is April."

"April?"

"Yes, *April.*" Big, *big* things had happened to me in the month of April: My nose got fixed, I met Tim in April and our divorce was final in April. Angie, Reba, Bill Vann and Ray Dickerson all had birthdays in April.

April was the month my stepfather died. It was an anniversary that would never go unacknowledged.

Last but not least, this very April, I had "graduated" from nearly nine months of therapy working on building self-esteem and trying to piece together a ragged but not shattered spirit. It was expensive, emotionally wrenching, and the best investment I had ever made because it literally saved my life. Therapy wasn't making me normal, but it was teaching me to make better choices.

Falling in love with Dave was definitely one of those.

Epilogue

I guess you could say I clobbered Dave over the head, metaphorically speaking. A year after we met, we got engaged after a proposal that was the real deal. On July 10, 2001, we were married in a sunset beachside ceremony on the Island of Maui. It was just the two of us (if you don't count the minister and the photographer) and there was no drama surrounding our simple but romantic wedding. I wore a lilac one-piece swimsuit with a matching sarong, and it was the kind of wedding I had longed for but never realized, to a nice, normal man I would have never given myself a chance to love had I not been in therapy. While Dave may never know how difficult it was for me to get to this place of self-acceptance, what's important is that I *am* in this place, and no longer live by the self-defeating rules of a Blue Angel.

Unfortunately, I had to let go of some people during my journey, among them Ray's daughter, Reba (not her real name). To try to maintain an ongoing relationship with her would have been emotional suicide for me because it kept Ray and I connected, and my therapist and I both agreed that was not in my best interests. I regret this, and hope, Reba, if you ever read this, you are doing well.

In the years since my husband and I met, there has been a lot of national tragedy, including the terrorist attacks on 9/11 and the Iraq War.

I could not have asked for a stronger, more grounded and supportive partner than Dave to help me deal with the wide range of emotions these events have caused. Not a day goes by that I do not think of the victims, or the heroes.

On the positive side, I no longer dread Christmas. (This is *huge*!) Last Christmas, I met my step-grandsons for the first time, and learned nine-year-old Aaron looks exactly like Tim did at that age, with freckles and unruly red hair, and Sean is quiet and reserved like his mother, Angie. Sadly, she is raising her sons alone following the tragic death of their father, Duane, who drowned in the Sagavanirktok River in Northern Alaska while on a caribou hunting trip.

This Christmas, we are going to flock our tree, which was a tradition in Dave's family when he was growing up. He told me his dad would get out the flocker machine (after traipsing through the cut-your-own X-Mas tree farm for hours before his mom found the perfect Noble Fir tree, which was always too tall) and set the machine up on a tarp on their back patio, hoping and praying the air would be *just* right—not too moist and not too dry. Otherwise, the flocking clumped together and upset his mother, who would supervise from inside the warmth of the house.

Dave and his siblings had another name for Flock Night, mostly because flocking is finicky, and the matter of how much flock is enough is not easily resolved, but to me, Flock Night sounds like the kind of tradition I'd like to adopt.

It sure beats fight night.

THE END

Printed in the United States
63689LVS00003B/68